The Metropolitan Library

The MIT Press   Cambridge, Massachusetts, and London, England

The Metropolitan Library

edited by Ralph W. Conant and Kathleen Molz

Copyright © 1972 by
The Massachusetts Institute of Technology

This book was set in IBM Composer Press Roman
by Jay's Publishers Services, Inc.,
printed on Finch Paperback Offset
and bound in Columbia Millbank Vellum MBV-4275
by Halliday Lithograph Corp.
in the United States of America.

Library of Congress Cataloging in Publication Data
Main entry under title:

The Metropolitan library.

Bibliography: p.
1. Libraries and metropolitan areas. I. Conant, Ralph Wendell, 1926–
ed. II. Molz, Kathleen, 1928–   ed.
Z716.2.M46   027.4   72-4338
ISBN 0-262-03041-1

Preface

In 1963 the Symposium on Library Functions in the Changing Metropolis was sponsored by the National Book Committee with funds from the Council on Library Resources and the Joint Center for Urban Studies of the Massachusetts Institute of Technology and Harvard University. Attended by a number of social scientists especially interested in the conduct of urban affairs and librarians of several major American cities, the conference was an effort to initiate a dialogue between the theorists of urban life and change and the administrators of an urban tax-supported institution—the public library. Some of the papers presented at that meeting were subsequently prepared for publication in a volume entitled *The Public Library and the City*. The success of that book, one of the few specifically addressed to the concerns of metropolitan public librarians, has prompted this sequel, which, like the original volume, combines the viewpoints of specialists from the disciplines of both social and library science. The need for this dual perspective actually prompted the choice of the editors—the first, an observer of urban public libraries, and the second, a practitioner in their service. Certainly, it is our hope that the exchanges begun here will result in a fruitful partnership between the social scientist and the librarian, both of whom share concerns for the future of the nation's cities and the informational needs of their citizens.

Ralph W. Conant
Kathleen Molz

Notes on Contributors

The Editors

Ralph W. Conant is President of the Southwest Center for Urban Research and Director of the Institute for Urban Studies in Houston. He is a member of the faculties of Rice University, the University of Houston, and the Baylor College of Medicine. He was formerly with the Joint Center for Urban Studies at the Massachusetts Institute of Technology and Harvard University, and the Lemberg Center for the Study of Violence at Brandeis University.

Kathleen Molz is Chief of Planning in the Bureau of Libraries and Educational Technology, U.S. Office of Education. She was formerly editor of the *Wilson Library Bulletin.* She has worked in three major metropolitan library systems, those of Baltimore, Denver, and Philadelphia.

The Contributors

Edward C. Banfield is Professor of Urban Government at Harvard University.

John E. Bebout is with the Institute for Urban Studies. He is Professor of Political Science at the University of Houston and consultant to the Southwest Center for Urban Research in Houston.

John W. Bystrom is Professor in the Department of Speech-Communication at the University of Hawaii.

Norman Elkin is Director of New Programs, The Planning Group, Urban Investment and Development Company, Chicago.

Philip H. Ennis is Professor of Sociology at Wesleyan University.

D. J. Foskett is Librarian of the Institute of Education at the University of London.

Leonard Grundt is Director of the Library and Professor at Nassau Community College.

William F. Hellmuth is Vice-President of Arts at McMaster University.

Dan Lacy is Senior Vice-President of the McGraw-Hill Book Company.

Claire K. Lipsman is with the Office of Planning, Evaluation, and Research, Manpower Administration, U.S. Department of Labor.

Lowell A. Martin is Professor in the School of Library Service at Columbia University.

David Popenoe is Associate Professor of Sociology at Rutgers University.

Robert H. Salisbury is Professor of Political Science at Washington University.

Jesse H. Shera is Professor in the School of Library Science at Case Western Reserve University.

Lester L. Stoffel is Executive Director of the Suburban Library System in Hinsdale, Illinois.

John Tebbel is Professor of Journalism at New York University. He is a regular contributor to the *Saturday Review*.

The Metropolitan Library

I Introduction

1 The Urban Public Library: A Perspective

Kathleen Molz

Central to an understanding of this book is a sense of historical perspective about the formation of urban public libraries. The best single source remains the 1852 *Report of the Trustees of the Public Library of the City of Boston*. The report acknowledges the book as the "principal instrument of instruction in places of education" and extols the library as the vehicle by which "the means of general information should be so diffused that the largest possible number of persons should be induced to read and understand questions going down to the very foundations of social order. . . ."

While recognizing the fiscal and political independence of the free city library, the trustees totally identified the purpose of their new agency with that of the public schools. Indeed, the public library was expected to "supply an existing defect in our otherwise admirable system of public education" and to become "as far as possible, the crowning glory of our system of City Schools; or in other words . . . an institution, fitted to continue and increase the best effects of that system, by opening to all the means of self culture through books, for which these schools have been specially qualifying them."[1] The public library, then, was viewed as the last and most independent stage in a hierarchical system of public education that began with the enrollment of the nation's children in the public schools.

Since that time, many factors have contributed to the truncation of the public library's mission. Within the context of their times, the founders of the movement could scarcely have anticipated the impact of the Morrill Federal Land-Grant Act of 1862, passed only a decade after the establishment of the Boston Public Library, which ultimately made possible postsecondary education for the benefit of those machinists, engineers, and instrument makers originally identified as the clients of public libraries. Nor could the founders have predicted the print-glutted market that followed World War II. Yet, as important as the development of tax-supported higher education and the profusion of inexpensive reading materials are to an understanding of the subsequent inefficacies of the public library, neither factor is as crucial as the impact of John Dewey on twentieth-century educational thought. As Lawrence A. Cremin has cogently pointed out, American education was initially marked by diversity: the public libraries and lyceums, the mechanics' institutes and agricultural societies, the penny newspapers and dime novels. Although cognizant of this variety, Dewey nonetheless made the complaint that industrialism was destroying the educational functions carried on by home, shop, neighborhood, and church. In what Cremin terms *"the grand jeté* of twentieth-century educational theory," Dewey identified the public school as "society's great instrument for shaping its own destiny."[2]

The centricity of the public school in public education has now become so well established that the schools have added to their traditional tuitional concerns for children an entire gamut of societal responsibilities ranging from health and nutritional care to driver instruction and sex education. Faced with this obtrusive agency, the public library inevitably lost all pretensions to serving as the "crowning glory" of the public school system. Envisioned once as an independent utility, through its provision of materials to persons outside the traditional school system, the public library found itself increasingly drawn toward the vortex of formal education, its resources deployed for homework, college term papers, civil service examinations, and correspondence lessons. Though it lacks the rhetorical grandeur originally invested in the formation of the public library, such a function might have proved ultimately useful to the American public.

The problem of public libraries is compounded, however, by the increasing trend of educational institutions to establish libraries of their own. The advent of a formidably supported elementary and secondary school library movement, the tendency of postsecondary technical institutes as well as community colleges to assemble new collections of materials for the use of their students, and the emphasis placed on a well-stocked library by accrediting agencies of institutions of higher learning all contribute to a reconsideration of the public library's purposes and goals. "One cannot deny the fact," writes Jesse Shera, "that the future of the public library is closely linked with the future of our educational system." And a number of contributors to this book, nota-

bly Salisbury and Lipsman, urge close coordination of public library–
public school efforts, especially in inner-city communities where both
schools and libraries suffer from insufficient fiscal support. Others,
however, identify clienteles whose requirements transcend the present
school and academic library apparatus: Banfield speaks of the "serious
reader"; Martin notes the needs of the commuting student and "the
unaffiliated amateur scholar"; and Shera denies the stereotype of the
"general reader" in commenting rightly that "every reader is unique,
special, or atypical." Yet, the fact remains that school enrollment is
mandated, a mandate that necessitates financial commitment and public
interest.

"Education," Peter Schrag has observed, "has now become the most
effective way for an advantaged family to endow its children, to provide
them with the privilege that birth, wealth, and family standing no longer
supply."[3] If education is so valued by advantaged parents, then less-
advantaged families will place even greater emphasis on the education of
their children, since educational achievement is inextricably linked with
career choice, job fulfillment, and higher income.

The public library, then, has open to it a variety of options: It could
proceed on an elitist course, affording its resources primarily to the
cognoscente and permitting its present community services to be absorbed by the libraries of the public school and the community college;
it could conceivably coalesce its functions with those of the educational
establishment serving, as it now does, as a backstop for students who
cannot or do not use school-based libraries; or it could through the
provision of the entire range of multimedia educational devices stake
out a claim to providing an educational alternative for an array of non-
school-based clients, such as school dropouts, returning veterans, preschool children, or out-of-school adults.

The first of these courses seems too harshly elitist and would place the
library in the same financial predicament now plaguing community art
museums, symphonies, and repertory theaters, none of which has ever
enjoyed the same level of tax support accorded public libraries. The
second alternative puts public libraries well within the educational
mainstream and could do much (if programs and services were jointly
planned with the public schools) to allay the criticisms of government

administrators that the commonwealth is supporting two distinct and, therefore assumed, competing library systems for young people.

The third of these options has several points in its favor: First, it would provide a multimedia community facility permitting both adults and children the chance to watch educational television, listen to a phonograph recording or tape, or read a book or magazine; second, it would identify for public libraries a discrete clientele who could profit from the learning resources without the direct intervention of professional educators ("Sesame Street" for preschoolers and "Civilization" for adults are cases in point here); and third, it could represent an exemplar of educational diversity, combining the resources of both print and nonprint media within a learning environment that lies outside the direction and standards of the public schools.

At present, municipal librarians are uneasily operating in all those camps. They provide reference searches for the professional community, they struggle to eradicate the academic Maginot lines that separate their resources from those of the schools, and they experiment with neighborhood outreach programs that incorporate some of the characteristics of the multimedia learning center. Coping with so disparate a constituency continues to be one of the major management problems of public libraries. Aware "that the library is and has long been a multipurpose institution, serving diverse publics and clienteles with quite distinct services," Robert Salisbury asks an important question: "Is there any eternal virtue in providing neighborhood reading centers for book distribution, scholarly research facilities, and business reference services within the same organizational framework?"

Plainly, the answer is *no*. But the library, as an institution, may continue to serve the needs of scholarship, whether such scholarship is of a professional or amateur nature. By contrast, the library, as a facility, situated in rented quarters or temporary buildings, can exert a responsiveness toward the community in both collection content and programming, enjoying a flexibility denied the central library with its long-held tradition that the book is the "principal instrument of instruction."

The public library need not seek a decrease of its clients or a diminution of its goals, but rather a relinquishment of its own bureaucratic rigidities, which insist that the book selection policies of branch librar-

ies accord with those of the main library, demand citywide adoption of
fines and charges, and require that all forms of community programming and publicity conform to administrative policies set by those who
work only within the central agency.

More significant than the administrative redirection of public libraries
is the need for librarians to regard their services as a functional part of
the educational enterprise of the country. "Students are not a public
that the community library expressly sought," comments Lowell Martin,
"and when students flocked to public libraries in large numbers after
World War II, some librarians considered them a problem." Yet, with
60 million students enrolled in formal education from kindergarten
through college and another estimated 60 million persons engaged in
informal educational activities, over half the population of the country
is participating in the pursuit of education. At a time when educational
expenditures represent at least 6 or 7 percent of the American economy,
the "fiscally insignificant" expenditures for libraries, cited by William
Hellmuth, remain a mute but persuasive argument for the partnership
between education and the public library, whether the public library
fulfills its role as auxiliary resource or energizes its mission as an agency
of self-learning.

In the same way that the conceptualization of the library's single role
as the "crowning glory" of the city school system suffered a gradual
diminution, the view that the book is the "principal instrument of
instruction" has been subjected to repeated challenges. Foolish conten-
tions that the book is becoming obsolete only obfuscate the complex
issues inherent in a multimedia society, but an ostrich stance, which
refuses to admit that learning is much influenced by media other than
print, is equally awkward. There are valid reasons for the librarian's
dependency on print: the medium still embraces all but a token percentage of the world's records; it is conveyed in an eminently portable
and inexpensive format; and unlike the media of films, radio, and television, which began as vehicles for popular entertainment, print origi-
nated as the agent of scholarship, when publishing was confined to the
"University towns where academic authorities kept an eye on the supply
of reading matter to their students."[4]

In spite of these precedent-setting factors, however, the monopoly of books as the instruments of education has been, in Claire Lipsman's phrase, "seriously eroded." As she and others have pointed out, inexpensive paperbacks can be bought for less than the cost of cataloging and processing books in the library. It is now the hardware, the audiovisual equipment, and live experiential stimuli that are scarce resources. Yet, "these are the resources that are valued by the educational professionals and also the media that serve as the principal channels of communication for community residents."

Unlike innovative school media centers, which have respected their roles as purveyors of these scarce resources (even to the deletion in their names of the historic title of library), public libraries continue to regard most nonprint media as unwelcome guests to the bibliothecal wedding feast. Thus, with the exception of a few central-library film centers or an occasional service of circulating phonograph recordings, the purchasing power of public libraries is largely concentrated on books.

Compounding the situation is the increasing responsibility of the major municipal public library to serve as the hub of a statewide or regional public library network. Like the discipline-oriented networks begun for medical practitioners or research scientists (for whom a control of the periodical literature is practically mandatory), public library networks are almost exclusively directed toward the printed record. Yet, to posit public library networking almost entirely within the context of the bibliographic control of books may prove futile. In this era of television-reared children, ubiquitous long-playing records, and self-taught film makers, the networking activities of public libraries that serve the community at large, not the discrete needs of the specialist, must ultimately take cognizance of the future demand for art films or recordings, items that remain expensive and elusive of easy bibliographic identification.

John Bystrom is optimistic that the "availability of network capabilities . . . will encourage expanded nonprint services," but he also observes, somewhat cautiously, that "beyond interlibrary loans, centralized reference, and copy transmission, all on a relatively small scale, there are few uses for state telecommunications networks that would not be disputed by working librarians on practical grounds." His recommendation of "a carefully programmed effort . . . to encourage conceptualization and testing in libraries of new practical methods for distributing information to the public by means of telecommunications" is a sound one, which, unfortunately, will probably go unheeded in pragmatic operations.

Another facet of the public library remains to be discussed, one that was not emphasized or perhaps even perceived by the founders of Boston's public library; and that is the inherent link between the library and the city. Academic libraries are, of course, situated within the university community, and such communities, whether England's Oxford or Cambridge or America's Princeton or New Haven, often lie outside the city. Public libraries, on the other hand, are peculiarly urban institutions. Their origins may indeed have been a part of small-town development, yet, as Jesse Shera has pointed out:

The greatest single contribution to the development of the public library movement made by the founders of the Boston Public Library is to be understood largely in terms of the size and importance of the Bay State capital. After all, Salisbury, Lexington, and Peterborough were only small, isolated New England towns, and though they had established a pattern that later generations were to follow, what the public library movement most needed in the fifth decade of the nineteenth century was the stimulus to be derived from the acceptance of its principles by a major metropolitan community. Such recognition and prestige were exactly what Boston could, and did, give.[5]

However revered the antecedents of social, circulating, and subscription libraries in isolated New England towns, it was the public library of Boston that catapulted civic library development into Baltimore, Philadelphia, Cleveland, and New York. And it was the child of another city, the mill hand Andrew Carnegie, whose remembrance of a book-starved youth led him to support the development of municipal public libraries.

Ironically, the very soil that gave life to the furtherance of the public library now threatens it. The declining circulation figures of our major urban public libraries are but one small barometer of the changing atmosphere of the city. The influx of an undereducated populace, the crime rate, which occasions a fear of city streets, the deterioration of municipal facilities, such as parks and schools—these are a mere handful of the problems harassing city government, problems of such magnitude that they inevitably overshadow the concerns of the municipal public library system. Hence, the shortened hours of opening, the curtailment of programs and services, and even the cancellation of such modest staples as the subscriptions to popular journals.

In light of the fiscal instability of the present-day public library, some contributors to this book suggest a larger role for the national government. "It is inevitable that the greatest portion of public library funds in the years ahead will . . . come from the federal government," writes Conant. Both Martin and Bebout underscore this point, though more tentatively; Martin writes, "Potentially, federal resources could solve the big-city library financial dilemma, for while both local and state governments are tied to protective, housekeeping, and transport obligations that make a prior claim on the public purse, the federal government has some freedom in reassigning priorities."

The legislation, however, that inauguarated a federal support role for public libraries was totally rural in its orientation, mandating the use of funds only for those communities having a population of less than 10,000. Subsequent amendments to the Library Services Act provided for the inclusion of municipal libraries, but even with some increases in funding levels, the program was utilized in the states as a "seed-money" operation, providing funds for planning, innovative demonstrations, or services to hard-to-reach clienteles, such as the homebound or the institutionalized. Since its passage in 1956, the program has enjoyed considerable bipartisan support in Congress, but nothing in its legislative history would seem to support the idea that it would inevitably provide a federal subsidy for ongoing local public library operations. It should be noted, also, that the passage of other major educational laws (notably, the Higher Education Act of 1965 and the Elementary and Secondary Education Act of 1965) extended federal benefits to the libraries of elementary, secondary, and higher education. That the public library is no longer the unique recipient of federal funds was indirectly borne out by President Johnson's comments (September 2, 1966) on the occasion of the creation of the National Advisory Commission on Libraries: "Are our federal efforts to assist libraries intelligently administered, or are they too fragmented among separate programs and agencies?"

If increases in federal funding for municipal libraries do occur, they will probably be manifested under other legislative authorities, those directly targeted toward the urban areas, such as the Demonstration Cities and Metropolitan Development Act. Even here, the results may be slight unless libraries address themselves in broadly responsive terms to the problems of community development and renewal.

However crucial the financial plight of the municipal library may seem to be, this particular problem fades before the long-range effects of the changing character of the city itself. The nineteenth-century city, which sheltered the central library, the civic symphony, and the city art museum, is no longer an integer, substantively different in work opportunities, cultural resources, and educational advantages from its rural neighbors. Metropolitanism, so often referred to in these papers, is synonymous with a drastic shift in population, the flight to the suburbs, with their shopping centers, movie houses, bookstores, and public libraries. The climate of nineteenth-century Boston, Philadelphia, or Baltimore was one of centralization; in contrast, the contemporary atmosphere is permeated with concepts of decentralization.

In terms of a major symphony or art museum, decentralization is a myth. The elements of superb talent, characterized by a first-rate orchestra, or the collections of a museum devoted to art forms that can never be replicated are not so easily transported to suburbs. But public libraries, whose holdings are invariably in reprinted formats, are particularly susceptible to new beginnings. Even the coinage of the phrase "opening-day collection" for the nascent offerings of brand-new community college libraries attests to the fact that library resources are not unattainable and certainly not confined to urban outlets.

It is conceivable that the wealth of the great inner-city central libraries is such that only technology, with its facilities for facsimile transmission, can tap these resources for the use of nonurban specialists and scholars. Such a postulate, however, negates the importance of academic libraries and their increasing support of consortium activities that provide active bibliographic interchange among scholars.

So there it is: public libraries, once sheltered by their uniqueness to the urban scene, with their historic mission of aiding the educational enterprise through the confident medium of the book, now find themselves situated at random throughout the urban sprawl, detoured from the concerns of formal education, and dubious as to the future hold of the book on the historic record.

This configuration of phenomena might inevitably lead to a verdict of obsolescence, yet such a verdict runs counter, in Lowell Martin's words, to the "durable, respected, and responsive" attributes of public library development. These attributes may not be innovative or exhilarating, but they evince tremendous staying power. Even though the survival of the institution may not be in question, its effectiveness and utility in contemporary society is a matter of concern. Clearly, there is no one panacean course, a conclusion that almost all of the contributors to this volume, whatever their discipline, reach. Yet these essays are not without suggestion for alternative strategies that would vindicate the purposes of public libraries to the constituents they serve. Such strategies relate to that education that aims, not at facts or information, but at the enhancement of a quality of life. Trite as that phrase may seem, there is a need for education that emphasizes sensibility, not sense. Elkin delineates a role for public libraries as "sanctuaries of privacy"; Martin supports their function in respect to a value-oriented civilization as opposed to one aimed only at productivity and materialism; Foskett suggests that libraries must impart values as well as facts, insight as well as information; and Shera regrets that libraries do not do enough to make men "hospitable to knowledge."

A hospitable learning situation, affording the child or adult a variety of materials from which to choose for his own personal educative purpose —can this be a public library? "All the world's a city now, and there is no escaping urbanization"[6] encapsulates the only certainty of this book; the question remains: Can the public library adjust to servicing this urbanized world, this universe of cities?

Notes

1. The Boston *Report* is reproduced in full as Appendix V in Jesse H. Shera, *Foundations of the American Public Library* (Hamden, Conn.: The Shoe String Press, Inc., 1965), pp. 267–290, *passim.*

2. Lawrence A. Cremin, *The Genius of American Education* (New York: Vintage Books, 1965), pp. 8–9.

3. Peter Schrag, "A New Standard of Accomplishment," *Wilson Library Bulletin* (February 1968): 584.

4. Cyprian Blagden, *The Stationers' Company* (Cambridge, Mass.: Harvard University Press, 1960), p. 22.

5. Shera, *Foundations*, p. 170.

6. Morton and Lucia White, *The Intellectual Versus the City* (New York: Mentor Books, 1964), p. 238.

2 The Metropolitan Library and the Educational Revolution: Some Implications for Research

Ralph W. Conant

The library in all its diverse institutional forms is a permanent and highly valued facility in American intellectual and cultural life. It has long been a symbol of our aspirations for knowledge and for social and technological progress. It is a live depository of the cultural past and sustainer of the intellectual activity that anticipates the future.

Libraries are facilities of increasing importance in a society whose knowledge base provides the vital key to the future of civilization. How well libraries adapt to the conditions and requirements of the next few decades will depend upon the capacity of library leaders to identify and interpret relevant social and technological trends. Library leaders must increasingly turn to policy-oriented social scientists for guidance. To ensure the competence of their successors, they must broaden the scope of library education to include areas of training in the social sciences for planning and institutional management and in the information sciences.

The papers in this volume point up some important elements of change that are likely to have a significant impact on libraries of all kinds in the next few decades. How libraries respond to these changes in the immediate future will, of course, determine what libraries will be a century hence.

Americans have embarked on an era of extraordinary change rooted in new and rapidly developing knowledge about our physical and social environment. We have learned how to curtail many diseases afflicting the human body, and we are on the verge of perpetuating man's life-span far beyond the seventh decade. We know how to control most environmental threats to human life, and we are gradually converting this knowledge into effective political and administrative mechanisms. In a little more than a decade, we have produced the technical capability for exploring other planets.

Parts of this paper have previously appeared in *The Library Bulletin* (May 1967); *The Library Journal* (May 15, 1968); *Wilson Library Bulletin* (May 1969); *Illinois Libraries* (March 1969). Most of the paper was published in *The Changing Environment of Libraries*, ed. John Eastlick (American Library Association, 1971).

Knowledge feeds upon knowledge, and its growth in our age is assured by an educated constituency eager for new discovery. The expansion of knowledge is encouraged by the ready patronage of political leaders who see the products of scientific inquiry as new sources of power. Man's capacity to anticipate and solve physical problems does not necessarily transfer to social and political problems, yet the search for solutions to the problems of war, poverty, and disordered behavior now constitutes a major intellectual and physical effort. The trend among college youth toward the social sciences and the humanities is evidence.

Social innovation is going through a period of trial-and-error inventiveness that characterized technological innovation at a comparable stage. Confronted with enormous costs and spasmodic payoffs, political leaders who must have political profit out of social experimentation must eventually shift random strategies of social problem solving to highly rational methods. What is needed, of course, are new tools of social analysis that will provide policy makers with a systematic understanding of the social problems for which they are seeking solutions.

We have entered an era in which man's intellect—his ideas, aspirations, plans, and problem-solving capacity—holds sway. This control is predominant in problem areas susceptible to the physical sciences, and we are moving toward the intellectual attack in social and political areas. This means that our intellectual institutions—universities, libraries, and research industries—are moving into positions of central influence in determining the course of man's activities.

Those institutions that move with change and maintain a position of relevance to contemporary problems will fulfill themselves. Others will simply wither and be absorbed by the more vigorous and imaginative ones. Libraries will fare according to their individual quality and leadership. Those that are part of a larger institution may have little choice in their destiny except to be technically competent and farsighted in terms of institutional objectives. Individual libraries can keep ahead of fast-moving societal development only if they are in close touch with major trends of the times and can adapt services to them.

The trends that yield the most useful clues to change are: (1) population growth and distribution in urban areas; (2) expanding knowledge and increasing leisure; (3) technological advances; (4) increasing wealth and declining poverty; (5) evolving governmental policies that require intergovernmental cooperation and interinstitutional planning; and (6) the prospects of minority assimilation into the larger society.

Population Trends

The population of the United States may reach 300 million by the year 2000, when, according to some experts, it is likely to reach a plateau of growth. While many demographers are still predicting a doubling of population every 35 years beyond the turn of the century, present trends belie this pessimistic outlook. Whereas birth rates climbed steadily from 1935 to 1957, they have been receding ever since. From an all-time high of 26 live births per thousand in 1957, the rate had fallen below 17 per thousand by 1969—the lowest ever recorded. The availability and widening acceptance of new types of contraceptives plus extensive private and public efforts to promote education and research in population control are paying off. This gradual leveling will be noticeable by 1985.

Population statistics for the United States as a whole are of limited value to librarians whose institutions are located in areas where population trends are out of line with national averages. Birth rates among blacks in central-city ghettos are much higher than among whites in other areas. Migration patterns within and between cities are locally unique and fluctuate over time. The migration patterns of cities, of course, have a much greater impact on individual library markets than simple population growth. It is apparent, for example, that Northern and Western cities whose nonwhite populations were still below 30 percent in 1970 will experience massive shifts within the next two decades of the kind experienced by cities whose nonwhite populations were over 40 percent in 1970. As the blacks and other minorities move into cities, whites disperse. It was evident by 1960 and even more so by 1970 that central-city populations were thinning out and dispersing to suburbs. Thus central cities, especially in the North and West, cannot yet foresee the time when their fluctuating populations will stabilize. A back-to-the-city trend began in the early 1960s among affluent young singles, the older middle class, and the well-to-do who could afford to send their children to private schools. Whether this trend will continue depends upon the success of central cities in solving the worst problems of these areas: air pollution, public education, traffic congestion and transportation, and crime. With sufficient effort, however, conditions in central cities could be so improved that a sizable middle-class population would be lured back.

The Educational Revolution

In spite of significant gaps in opportunities for education, Americans have firmly established the principle of public responsibility for quality education through vocational, graduate, or professional schools. Equality of educational opportunities is still severely restricted in minority and poverty sections of cities and in rural and underdeveloped areas. Only a few states have undertaken a full range of higher-education facilities at nominal direct cost to students. Teacher education is still a long way from the standard of excellence set by a few outstanding graduate schools of education. Yet the states are on the move, and the federal government is likely to allocate increasing resources to education at all levels. Within a decade or so no local school system will lack the support to provide an acceptable education for all youth. One can hope that in a few years no qualified student will be without an opportunity to attend a college or university and that no youth who wants technical skills training or ordinary job training will be denied an appropriate opportunity. The federal Manpower Act of 1962 laid the groundwork for such training programs; the new Manpower Act of 1970 continued and broadened established programs. Thus, by 1985 our public educational system will be fully structured and adequately financed, and the variety of training offered will come close to meeting most of the requirements of a postindustrial society in which more than one-half of the employed population is involved in an occupation other than the production of food, clothing, shelter, and other necessary goods.

Expanding educational opportunities coupled with expanding demand for highly trained workers, both professional and subprofessional, indicate a corresponding demand for sophisticated facilities for continuing education in communities to supplement the intensive educational experiences provided by institutions responsible for formal training. In order to meet this demand, libraries, commercial distributors of educa-

tional materials, cultural organizations, schools, and universities must
keep their capabilities in tune with the rush of new knowledge and new
techniques.

The special role of libraries is to provide the materials of continuing
education that are not available from any other source in the community. If the public library is to assume primary responsibility in this area
(as it should), it must develop methods to identify the needs in the
community and take steps to meet them.

New Technologies

The application of radical new technologies in older cities of the United
States will be slow, especially in housing and mass transportation. We
have too much investment in old techniques, old habits, and old hardware to move quickly to new modes. Yet the demand for improvements
in housing, transportation, communications, waste disposal, water supply, and other key facilities are pressing hard on policy leaders. The
demands to make cities more comfortable, convenient, and economical
will prevail eventually, but only gradually.

Improved urban transportation will create market areas for public and
private institutions of cities that will be several times greater than present ones. Moreover, the coverage, convenience, and economy of new
modes of urban transportation will permit libraries and other cultural
institutions a wide choice of locations within the urban region. In many
cases, it will be feasible to place specialized segments of such institutions
in locations that serve a specialized clientele. New applications of communications coupled with information storage and retrieval techniques
will enhance the feasibility of scattered locations in response to market
demands.

Improved multiple-unit housing design in central cities will be a critical
factor in attracting the affluent middle class back into the city. Large
condominiums with built-in community facilities—and perhaps built-in
schools—might be the answer. Large tracts of "urban renewal" land in
central cities will be available to meet the inevitable upsurge in the
family housing market anticipated around 1973—the year the "war
babies" will begin moving into the housing market in great numbers. By
then the inflation crisis that drove interest rates to high levels and

crimped the housing market in 1969 and 1970 should have subsided.

If imaginative and practically minded designers succeed in bringing to the heart of cities moderately priced, aesthetically pleasing residential units that "feel" more like houses than apartments, a revolution could occur in the preference for suburbs over the central city. The flight from the city was, after all, a flight from the tenement, from life-styles associated with poverty, and from low-status newcomers. At the present time there is still no widely available and acceptable alternative within the central areas of cities for middle-income families. Schools are a problem, but they would not be if there were enough middle-class children in cities to populate them.

The technological revolution will place new kinds of demands on libraries and other institutions in the knowledge industry while at the same time offering opportunities for adapting old institutions to new requirements and new opportunities.

The End of Economic Poverty

Within a decade or so the poor among us will most likely be those who are dependent on society because of physical or psychological incapacity. Even these individuals will probably have minimum resources for the necessities of life, for everyone in the nation whose income falls below a defined poverty line will benefit from a flexible income maintenance program sponsored by the federal government. The beneficiaries of such a program will, by and large, use the subsidy as a basis of family and personal stability and as a foundation on which to build toward economic self-sufficiency. The income supplement program and the purposes to which most beneficiaries will put it will bring into the knowledge industry market a whole new segment of the population whose previous educational level and state of demoralization were so great that many of them could not relate in any effective way to educational and training opportunities ostensibly open to them.

Education will be among the priority demands of families emerging from poverty, as it has been in the past. When the poor emerge from poverty aided by the guaranteed income supplement, they are likely to turn first to public institutions for guidance toward opportunity. In this context one contributor to this volume, Dan Lacy, has urged that libraries assume active responsibility for expressing demand and providing channels of distribution for materials needed by segments of society not effectively literate; that is to say, the public library has an additional responsibility in the adult education field to identify and make available materials that can increase effectiveness of the educationally disadvantaged in the community. Lacy explains that private publishers are effectively confined to the middle- and upper-class segments of society because only their purchasing power is adequate to sustain the publishers' machinery of distribution.

Edward Banfield's pessimistic view of the library's capacity to serve the poor is qualified in the following passage from this volume: "If one believes that lower-class adults can be enticed to read, there is much to be said for making this the primary purpose of the library and for trying any approach that offers the least promise."

Libraries, of course, cannot and should not try to take on an educational task, except in the traditionally passive sense. But once the poor are helped out of destitution and hopelessness, the incentive to move to a self-sustaining economic level will be strengthened among them. Libraries and other public institutions of the inner city, where the poor will continue to live for a long time hence, must be prepared to contribute to the dignity and self-education of the low-income residents.

As Kathleen Molz so aptly put it in an article in the Winter 1964–65 issue of *The American Scholar*,

> If reading for everyone . . . is still relevant to the modern library, then the cultural content of the "good" book collection has to be reassessed, and room made for less sophisticated materials that will lead the patron not upward into literature, but outward into a literate world where jobs are found, bus schedules and street maps understood, and children's report cards read.

Institutional Centralization and Planning

The long-standing trend toward large-scale enterprises, both public and private, is a correlate of population growth, concentration in cities, specialization in the labor force, an expanding economy, and an ever-rising standard of living. These factors add up to bigness in almost all forms of organized human activity. The wealthier a society becomes, the more knowledge its members acquire; the better technologies it produces, the more incentive people have to convert these advantages to profit by means of the scale economies of large organizations. But once the payoffs of centralization are realized and the wealth accumulated, the process of centralization may then be reversed to personalize services through concurrent decentralization while maintaining the beneficial features of large-scale operations.

With respect to libraries, the outpouring of new book titles in nonfiction categories compels new space, larger staffs, an efficient division of labor, and improved intellectual and technical skills within each individual institution. By the year 2000, when present staff members will be directors and department heads, the demand for library services will have risen severalfold. Libraries will not necessarily be larger, for competing institutions may take over some library services; and staffs may not increase greatly, for machines will do many routine operations such as acquisition, cataloging, and repetitive reference. Even individual library buildings may not need to be much larger, for library institutions will probably occupy several locations. Films will in some cases take the place of books. Nevertheless, the services that libraries now monopolize will expand, not on direct educational levels, but as part of the accelerating pace of technological development and the new predominance of scientific problem solving.

If the library profession is to hold its customary place among the major facilities that meet the intellectual demands of the future, library administrators must acquire sophisticated new skills in institutional management and make plans for a new scale and style of institutional development. A matter of immediate priority is the establishment of network libraries in metropolitan areas. These networks in most places must cross municipal boundary lines, which are often hard to breach unless required by some higher authority at the state or federal level. City-county contracts, now fairly common, may lay the basis for regional cooperation in the future. Such contracts do not require new grants of authority in many states.

Perhaps the most serious obstacle to effective networks of libraries will be the need to create hierarchies of libraries and specialized facilities within the networks so that they serve the widest possible range of clientele. The trouble comes when some library units within systems are seen by librarians as more prestigious, more challenging, and more interesting than others. At least one-third of the states have established telecommunication library networks in which the larger unit, often the city, services its smaller brothers.

Nevertheless, centralized regional library institutions and a carefully planned hierarchical network of subregional library facilities could assure a key role for public libraries in the next half century. Studies of present institutions and the tentative linkages among them by systems analysis and cost-benefit analyses already support this conclusion. Actually, library administrators and municipal officials will not have very much choice in the matter. For some years the federal government has been constructing a policy of intergovernmental and metropolitan planning and cooperation. Title II of the 1966 Demonstration Cities and Metropolitan Development Act includes libraries in the requirement of a metropolitan planning review of applications for certain federal loans and grants. The review must be made by a regional planning agency, which also reviews grant applications for most other federally sponsored projects in the urban region. The broadening roles of the state and federal governments have encouraged and supported the multipurpose regional planning agencies. These agencies are now operating in the Standard Metropolitan Statistical Areas throughout the country and form the skeletal structure of a system of future de facto metropolitan governments.

When they are fully developed, these agencies will be the means by which local communities may participate in regional services such as comprehensive public and research libraries, which require a broader geographical and organizational base to administer. These agencies will also be the apparatus through which federal and state governments may decentralize programs that require local and regional direction. This network of metropolitan planning agencies will permit a more equitable distribution of government services and resources from all levels of government than this country has ever had before.

Two Societies
One cannot write about the problems of American cities without including a discussion of the consequences of the ghettoization of blacks, Mexican Americans, Puerto Ricans, and other excluded minorities. One

cannot discuss the political and social aspects of institutional change in the central city without primary reference to the twin phenomena of white dispersion and minority confinement. One cannot discuss serving the unserved in our central cities without focusing on ghetto communities and their complex requirements, because many more central cities in the future will be nonwhite in their voting majority, their politics and political decision-making apparatus, the fabric of neighborhood society, and the clientele of their public institutions.

Central cities have already become isolated, walled-off ghettos of severely restricted opportunity. The physical ghetto has created a psychological ghetto characterized by fear, suspicion, antagonism, frustration, misunderstanding, and mutual ignorance of life-styles and aspirational values. The psychological ghetto is itself a barrier to opportunity and mainstream acculturation. The psychological ghetto is imposed and reinforced by the dominant white community, but its conditions are absorbed and internalized by the minority community; the result is reluctance of blacks to participate in the white community even when opportunities are available. Witness the slowness of middle-class blacks to move into predominantly white neighborhoods that *are* open, the reluctance of black parents to have their children bussed to white schools, and the preference of blacks and other minorities for neighborhood services even when downtown merchants solicit their business. The fear of painful and degrading daily contact with hostile or condescending whites is justified by contact with some whites whose conscious or unconscious attitudes and actions are what minorities call racist. The psychological ghettoization is the consequence of a pervasive (often unintentional) attitude of paternalism on the part of whites. Some examples are oversolicitousness to blacks because they are black (the attitudes of some white welfare workers); suppressed hostility (becoming angry at unappreciative blacks); active resentment toward a black who violates some persisting taboo (dating or marrying a white); price and rent discrimination on some spurious excuse (a high rate of pilferage); and differential police behavior toward white and black communities.

Many of the largest cities in America will eventually be run by blacks and other minorities when their numbers become predominant in those cities. I have estimated that a dozen or so major cities will have black mayors and black bureaucracies by 1985 or sooner. This will occur because the myopic white majority has wished it to be so. Even if whites decided otherwise tomorrow, the trend in central cities is irreversible. Even if our national open-housing policies were immediately invoked as local policy (not likely), it would take at least two generations of suburban-bound blacks to achieve a dispersal comparable to that of whites.

The white institutions of the central city (prominent among which are public libraries) that serve central-city clientele must adopt new organizational behavior patterns and staffing modes. A library must have the staff who know, or learn to appreciate and respect, the values and aspirations of clientele in the community it serves. The typical black urban community is extraordinarily diverse and complex, far more so than the typical white urban or suburban community, because blacks of all economic and social levels live in the black communities of cities. They cannot easily disperse, as whites can, into homogeneous communities throughout the metropolis. Thus, serving the heterogeneous black communities of central cities cannot be achieved according to traditional norms, habits, values, and objectives of white librarians in white communities. Claire Lipsman's essay in this volume points up this fact.

Central-city institutions that come within the purview and influence of local government will eventually be shaped by political leaders as the majority of voters want them to be. The unserved of the present day will be served as they wish to be served within a few years after their voting strength produces officeholders from their own ranks.

As black leaders take over the political apparatus of central cities, they may temporarily insist upon the inward focus of local institutions. Black mayors, black library directors, and black voters will be less interested in the participation of city-supported libraries in a metropolitan library system than are the present white administrators of central-city libraries. Black political leaders are likely to condone a metropolitan orientation only insofar as they cannot prevent it or it serves an inner-city purpose.

Functions of Libraries in the Future
It seems to me that libraries of all types should continue to be what they have traditionally been—facilities for the collection and dissemination of cultural and educational materials within the communities they serve.

But library leaders face the problem of defining what materials fall within the cultural and educational categories in terms of the market of individual library institutions. What may be frivolous for the users of a research library might be appropriate for users of an urban public library in a culturally deprived neighborhood.

Library leaders themselves must define the various markets and hence the function of different kinds of library institutions as an aid in distinguishing appropriate goals from inappropriate ones. Most public libraries know their current clientele, but few know the nature of their potential market in terms of additional services people might want if such were made available. Library leaders face the problem of adapting the organization and management of individual institutions to the changing requirements of shifting markets and to new modes of storing and presenting materials. Finally, library leaders face the problem of striking a balance between centralized and decentralized organization within library institutions and establishing interinstitutional arrangements in a workable hierarchy of specializations that achieve a full range of library services in and among metropolitan communities.

As matters now stand, the public libraries of suburban communities may become a little larger and a little more sophisticated in the decades ahead; but they are not destined to compete in services with research libraries, or to keep up with the bulk of demand in fiction reading, or to meet the specialty reference requirements of modern industry. Nevertheless, the small suburban library is becoming part of a network, for example, in New York, Maryland, and Illinois. Each node of the network contains highly specialized material available to all members of the suburban system.

If school libraries develop their full potential, the public library may be relieved of a very large proportion of its student clientele. What then will be left for the small suburban library? A margin of the fiction market, household and family reference services, circulation of musical records, and preschool reading services. A few suburban libraries will offer facilities for community activities such as reading and discussion groups, lectures, and documentary and special-interest films.

A function of suburban libraries already being carried out in some states will be as a local outlet in a regional system. The role of the suburban library in the metropolitan network will depend on several factors: what other kinds of library facilities are in the system; what kinds of materials are available from the system; how research and special libraries choose to serve their clientele; whether any significant portion of these demands can be met through local distribution points in suburban branches; and, from the standpoint of the consumer, whether local public libraries are logistically the most convenient and efficient pickup point for such materials.

Public libraries in the big central cities have literally grown up with those cities, catering primarily to the needs of the middle class and to the striving lower classes. These libraries have been an oasis of learning for the self-taught, a research resource for students, a sanctuary for loners, and a depository for an endless variety of published and unpublished materials. In recent times the big-city public library has endeavored to be a neighborhood reading room and distribution point by providing branch locations in areas where the demand for services seemed to warrant the effort. A few of the larger, better-endowed libraries have become cultural and research centers of high standing. These institutions harbor collections that are the envy of some of the young giants among the state universities whose own research collections fall far short of the requirements for graduate programs.

What is the future of the big-city libraries? Actually, there is no one developmental trend that is likely to be predominant in the period ahead. Development in the past rode the wave of demand for a diversified but accessible cultural resource in the community on which an expanding and mobile middle class could rely for fiction reading, for intellectual stimulation, and for meeting the knowledge requirements of a changing industrial economy. The scale and compactness of urban populations and the simplicity of industrial technologies before World War II made it possible for public libraries (as well as schools and research institutions) to meet demands placed upon them. The big-city public libraries of the past did not have to have very extensive or especially sophisticated storage systems or staffs. Also, the public library has always existed on a restricted budget amounting to what was left over after other municipal services got their own inadequate allotments. Private endowments have seldom provided much additional leeway in library budgets.

The big-city libraries of the future will be diversified institutions responding to new demands, new opportunities, and new resources, which are just beginning to be evident. A few may close their doors. In cities like Boston, where great private research libraries have flourished for a long time, the public libraries will for the time being concentrate their efforts in community service "outreach" programs in neighborhood centers and mobile units among the underprivileged, free or low-priced nonreturnable paperbacks, greatly expanded preschool reading services, continuous showings of films, and perhaps lecture series shared by branch and suburban units through closed-circuit television. Public libraries in cities like Boston will also be part of a metropolitan system capable of providing instantaneous printouts of specialized, annotated bibliographies showing the location of published and unpublished materials in all library collections in the metropolitan area, as well as in large national collections.

The public libraries in urban areas that lack accessible university research collections will develop a strong research capability. These libraries may even be the locus of the urban data banks, although it is more likely that planning research agencies will serve this function. Generally, the data bank specialists are not even considering public libraries as a potential facility for local and regional information systems.

The public libraries that are important research institutions (for example, the New York Public Library) also have an obligation to serve in the community. If this dimension is treated as a chore rather than as an opportunity, service may be less vigorously pursued than in those libraries where research is of minor importance. The public research libraries will be the keystone institution in the metropolitan systems of which they are a part. The systems led by research libraries are likely to be better integrated and technologically more sophisticated than ones that are not research oriented. It may be that the research-oriented systems will service private industry directly through special contractual arrangements, especially if an urban data bank becomes part of the available service.

What I have described are prototypes of urban libraries and library systems. Actually, urban libraries in the future will fall along a continuum of these prototypes. Most big-city libraries will be part of a metropolitan system, but not all of the systems will operate effectively in serving the diverse and conflicting demands of metropolitan clientele. Some public libraries will cling to a parochial autonomy while going through the motions of cooperation. Some, no doubt, will resist technological innovation—but not many. The power of the federal dollar will win out, and high standards of planning and services will be developed and maintained.

It is inevitable that the greatest portion of public library funds in the years ahead will, and should, come from the federal government. The price of federal funds, even in conservative administrations, will be specialized services to the underprivileged and metropolitan-wide organization of public library services. There is little doubt that most libraries will respond to these requirements (as many already have). The real question is whether librarians are prepared or preparing to respond.

Not many library administrators are now adequately trained to design and manage metropolitan systems. They know very little about the metropolitan demand structure for library and information services, the technological requirements of such services, and the problems of planning and coordination (let alone solutions). They have hardly begun to experience the problems of interjurisdictional politics, which plague every effort in the no-man's-land of metropolitan planning and cooperation. Most white librarians are not yet psychologically or professionally prepared to deal effectively with problems of serving the deprived and excluded minorities. It is clear that adequate leadership of the public libraries of the future will require a drastic overhaul and broadening of the education of librarians coupled with the establishment of permanent library research and evaluation programs within library institutions.

Leaders in the library profession have to some extent recognized the need for changes in formal programs of education for librarians. Whether they have recognized the urgency of the need is hard for the outsider to judge, for changes in the curricula of library graduate schools are steadily taking place. Further steps in broadening these curricula must encompass urban sociology and urban planning, including the politics of planning in the American metropolis. Future library administrators must be experts in information science and in large-scale organizational management. They must also know the mission and capability of other institutions in the knowledge industry and know how to adapt national goals and policies to regional and local needs. The big-city or metropolitan librarian must be a skilled administrator of great executive capacity, a talented politician, an information specialist, and an egghead. The graduate schools of library science have the responsibility for meeting these formidable educational requirements. This objective could be served by encouraging students to take the relevant courses elsewhere in the university (as some now do) or by adding to library school faculties specialists in the urban social sciences and in the management and information sciences.

Problems of market, management, and organization require continuous systematic attention in any public or private organization that aims to provide optimum service at an economical level. Discovering and defining one's market is an ongoing process, as are organization and management review. Problems of functional specialization, centralization versus decentralization, and organizational interrelations are classic in organization planning. Continuous expert attention to these matters is a minimum requisite of organizational growth in response to new demands.

In order to meet these problems, individual libraries or groups of libraries should establish small, highly competent research and management teams to conduct a continuing review of the local market for library services, the appropriateness of internal organizational structure, and the character, quality, and relevance of services provided. These teams should also propose and help implement the development of network library systems, intergovernmental agreements, and other arrangements across jurisdictional lines.

Such teams would be a staff arm of large urban libraries or could serve as research staff to cooperating groups of libraries in metropolitan and rural areas. Their function should include collecting data for state and national library policy planning. Perhaps the local research teams should be components of a national research network, which should be largely supported by federal funds.

In a paper that appeared in *The Public Library and the City*, Ralph Blasingame and I suggested several areas of inquiry that could be helpful to public librarians in their search for ways to adapt library services to change in cities. One such area was an investigation of consumer trends and tastes. Who are the present clients of the library? Who were clients a few years ago who dropped away? Who may be the library users five or ten years hence? How are social and economic trends in urban library market areas likely to affect library use in these areas? Will present customers of the urban public library stay put? Will others replace those who do not stay? What new services and facilities should be developed to meet potential markets among current users? Some of the papers in this volume suggest that public libraries should reshape services for special appeal to the urban poor. Are there, in fact, untapped markets among the urban poor for services and facilities that librarians are peculiarly competent to develop?

These problems cannot be solved by asking limited questions. Both "accessibility" and "relevance" depend on what people find interesting and why, where they feel comfortable, with whom they like to interact and in what ways—in sum, on their entire style of life. Research designed to make libraries accessible and useful to the poor should approach communication in its whole social and cultural context, in the same way that Richard Hoggart's inquiry into *The Uses of Literacy* in England became a classic analysis of British working-class culture as a whole.

Librarians could further benefit by research into the culture of urban poverty that focuses on the uses that the printed word has for the poor —whether of entertainment, information, or self-definition—and into the other sources of ideas, information, and entertainment with which reading competes. Such research should also focus on the sorts of reading experience that may contribute to the learning of skills and the redefinition of the self, which might help people move out of the poverty level. Research on library users might include such questions as these: What are the social and economic characteristics of urban library customers? What are the similarities and differences, if any, between users of the central-city library and those who use branches and suburban libraries? How do the salient characteristics of users compare with those of the general population? What are the implications of the findings for library services? What are the long-range changes in individual libraries in demands for materials and services and in characteristics of clientele? Do such factors as education, social and economic status, and occupation relate to specific demands upon the library as revealed by choice of books or by reference questions asked?

A second research area might be on the order of cost-benefit analyses.

No one knows exactly how librarians spend their workday time or how much library money is spent on specific library functions. Likewise, there is no reliable knowledge about who benefits from specific library services. Intensive time-budget studies would reveal how library staff members spend typical workdays and thus how funds allocated to staff services are spent. These data, added to other specific library costs, could be compared to a detailed analysis of customer use. The objective would be to determine who benefits from library services and at what cost. One might discover that housewives who read best-seller fiction place a weighty cost burden on the public library as compared to the "serious reader" Banfield favors, or that libraries already serve the public purpose for which Banfield argues. In any case such research would produce valuable tools for the library administrator and extremely useful data for officials who shape library policy.

An investigation of users and uses of libraries should also include a close look at the competing intellectual goods the library offers—paperbacks, book clubs, television, newspapers, etc. Philip Ennis's work is suggestive of this line of research.

A third research area might be the political environment of the public library. Researchers might consider questions such as those that Oliver Garceau addressed many years ago, which Salisbury reconsiders in his paper in this volume: Who makes the decisions on the level of financial support for the public library? To what extent do these decisions reflect community opinion? What is the role of the library administrator in determining the main objectives and basic policy of the library—the role of the library trustees? To what extent are library policy makers represented in the "power structure" of the community? What difference does it make either way?

A fourth area of research might focus on the traditions and public image of the public library. What are the stated objectives of libraries and the library profession? How do the stated objectives affect the ability of libraries to adapt to urban change? How do stated objectives compare with actual objectives as revealed in time-budget and unit expenditure studies? If stated and actual objectives differ, what functions does each serve? Do library users impute objectives to libraries of which librarians are unaware? What influence do imputed objectives have on library service?

The library establishment is in many respects an in-group professional system capable of organizational reactions that may selectively encourage or discourage library use. The library institutions may have characteristics that aid innovation or retard innovation, that affect their ability to obtain financial support, and that attract or repel able people. What attitudes, organizational characteristics, or traditional modes of operation constitute real or perceived obstacles to use by the urban poor, youth, the aged, and other specific categories of nonusers? How important have these factors been in determining the present categories of regular users?

A fifth and very critical area of research would focus on the education of librarians. Schools of library service, like law schools and medical schools, should recruit and train candidates, provide intellectual leadership, sponsor innovative research, invent new administrative procedures, and in a variety of ways reinforce professional values and traditions. Their strategic position in the profession should make them extremely influential in shaping new ideas and reshaping old ones. Indeed, the library schools may importantly determine whether new ideas ever come into currency at all and whether old ones ever get reshaped.

An objective analysis of curricula, research programs, and modes of faculty and student selection would reveal a great deal about the real aims and aspirations of the library profession and about its adaptive potential. What are library students expected to learn before, during, and after library school? What are the principal objectives of the formal training? How do the training objectives square with what is expected of the career librarian? What kinds of recruits do the training and career expectations attract? Are library educators satisfied with the caliber of students their programs attract? Are library administrators satisfied with library school products? Do library school research and teaching programs encourage intellectual and technical innovation? To what extent is the emphasis of teaching and research on perpetuating tradition? What are the main standards governing the selection of library school faculty members? What are the main consequences of the faculty selection policies for research and curricula, for prestige of the library school in the profession, for attracting able students, and for creative leadership of library institutions?

There are other possible areas of research on libraries. For example, in the previously mentioned paper we were tempted to suggest a variety of administrative and management studies that might improve current services, but we purposely avoided such questions in favor of categories of research that in our judgment would contribute to an understanding of the fundamental conditions of the urban library and the human and physical environment of which it is a part. Thus we seek to encourage the library administrator and the library scholar to rethink the concepts by which his profession and institutions are bound.

Permanent research teams in libraries would provide a nearly ideal place for some aspects of the training of future library administrators. In the training function, the teams would be the focus of an intellectual liaison between graduate library school faculties and library administrators, thus strengthening both institutions. They would also provide the American Library Association and its affiliates with ready-made local research units.

Several steps should be taken in preparation for meeting the requirements of planning metropolitan public libraries: (1) a prototype evaluation of present library services, programs, and facilities in the context of benefits to users and functions of other related institutions; (2) a prototype analysis of unmet needs of users and nonusers; (3) a prototype formulation of alternative ways of meeting needs through new or expanded programs and services and by developing locational, architectural, and organizational guidelines; and (4) a comprehensive evaluation of library education as administered by the graduate library schools.

How individual libraries respond to broadening opportunities for library services will be determined by the extent to which the present professional leadership adapts traditional modes to new challenges. The influential leadership is in the American Library Association, in the graduate library schools, in the U.S. Office of Education, and, to a lesser degree, in state libraries and large urban libraries. The library profession is tightly organized; traditions are deeply rooted; methods of librarianship are universally accepted and perpetuated. Personalities at senior levels play by the rules of the game, and, even when they are vying for positions of influence, they preserve and reinforce the system.

These observations apply to most professional groups. The closed system is functional in maintaining a disciplined standard of services, in controlling the quality of personnel who enter, and in shaping professional development to the standards of the system. These features are all to the good, provided they do not also function to shut out influences that would encourage vital adaptations to a changing environment. The points of entry of important new influences into the library profession are still extremely limited in spite of recent efforts of its more visionary leaders. Some of the entrenched professionals do not welcome new markets, new techniques, new approaches to traditional services, new patterns of institutional and interinstitutional organization, or even potential new sources of revenue.

A climate of receptivity to new influences will be at best a gradual development. A logical point of change is in the graduate library schools where the capacity to tolerate new influences is bound to be the greatest in the profession. Steps to liberalize the formal education of library professionals and to put faculty into direct contact with other relevant disciplines will, in time, bring helpful influences to bear in changing the profession at large.

Another way to bring new influences into the profession would be to provide extensive mid-career opportunities for library administrators in fields outside traditional library training. There should also be annual programs for career librarians to take intensive courses in urban sociology, business management, planning, and related fields.

The aim of such educational programs would be to broaden the perspective of library professionals and to acquaint them with the intellectual and practical tools of other disciplines. New perspectives and new tools will aid librarians in preparing their institutions for change and make it easier for senior professionals to accept the new product of a liberalized library school curriculum. In the long run, innovation in the education of librarians will be the key to the success of library institutions in meeting the imposing demands of the educational revolution.

II The Functions of the Public Library

3 Who Reads?

Philip H. Ennis

It has been more than twenty years since the Public Library Inquiry was published. Its seven books and five mimeographed studies constituted the most comprehensive review of the public library's work to that date. World War II was over. The new era was about to begin—The Century of the Common Man, the United Nations, the GI bill, the new World of Communication, technological growth, peace. The recasting of the public library's mission, set in this optimistic frame, called for expanded efforts to serve "all the people" in spite of the stubborn fact that only a minority of the people used the library.

What has happened since then? The cold war. Two Asian wars at the periphery of the two largest new states to emerge in the postwar explosion of nationalism that also produced nearly a hundred other new nations. In the United States unprecedented growth and affluence, yet recalcitrant poverty; the civil rights movement, the youth movements, the women's movement—conflict. Hardly the picture envisioned in 1945. One of the few predictions of those days that has matured has been the growth of mass communications. We have worldwide broadcasting via satellite, in the United States near saturation television coverage, the ubiquitous automobile and personal radio, and paperback books in almost every corner store. How is the public library doing now? Where and who are the readers of today? Pending a new Public Library Inquiry the following brief review of some of the social changes that have occurred in the past twenty years may be useful.

We begin with three sets of demographic changes in the American population. Between 1950 and 1960 the total number of people in school (kindergarten through graduate school) grew from 30.3 million to 46.3 million, an increase of 53 percent. Over that same period the number of high school and college graduates in the nation rose from 44.3 to 60.0 million, a growth rate of 34 percent. These two groups

An earlier version of this paper appeared in *The Public Library and the City*, ed. R. W. Conant (Cambridge, Mass.: The MIT Press, 1965).

comprise the broadest approximation of the present and future reading audience. Their combined growth rate during 1950–1960 was 42 percent, far higher than the 18 percent increase of the total population in that decade.

From 1960 to 1968 total population growth slowed to 11 percent. So did the increase in the number of students in the country, down to a growth rate of 24 percent, reaching 57.5 million in 1968. The number of high school and college graduates grew to a total of 83.5 million individuals in 1968, a 40 percent increase from 1960. Together the number of high school and college graduates increased 33 percent from 1960 to 1968.[1]

As impressive as these growth rates are in themselves, they convey only a part of the increased educational activity that has occurred in the United States in recent years. Education generates the desire for more education. In his national inventory of adult education for the Carnegie Corporation, John Johnstone of the National Opinion Research Center reports that at least one out of five adults was engaged sometime in the year 1961–1962 in some kind of organized or independent study. Johnstone reports further that participation in adult education increases steadily with every year of formal schooling achieved.[2]

I do not know how many of these programs develop book readers in the ordinary sense of the word, but it is almost certain that these adult students are reading something. Our culture's deeply institutionalized value of personal achievement has been channeled into educational attainment, which still largely means reading. Therefore the public library has a continuing and deepening responsibility not only to meet these reading needs but also to be able to redefine the underlying quest for education in flexible terms.

Another demographic change of significance for the public library is the growing number of older people. The number of people over sixty-five years old increased from 12.3 million in 1950 to 19.1 million in 1968, a 55 percent increase.[3] While reading declines with age, there are definite pressures on libraries to create special services and programs for the aged. This enlarged group of older people, mainly a potential, rather than an actual, audience for the library, clearly creates a special problem of allocation of library resources.

The third major population change important to the library is the geographical reshuffling of the population. The nation is moving into the West and Southwest where different traditions and different political and social arrangements are creating new challenges to traditional library perspectives. Moreover, the sizes and types of communities in the nation as a whole have experienced a variety of significant changes. Metropolitan areas continue to gather in more of the nation's population; they contained 59 percent of the total U.S. population in 1950 and 65 percent in 1969. Within these great urban agglomerations, however, the movement has been from the core to the suburban periphery. Between 1950 and 1960 the central cities of these metropolitan regions grew at a rate of only 11 percent, while their suburbs grew at a rate of 49 percent. Nonmetropolitan areas of the country during this time period increased their population by only 7 percent. Between 1960 and 1969 the nonmetropolitan areas of the country grew at a comparable rate of 9 percent. During the same period the central cities of the metropolitan areas grew by only 1 percent, while their suburbs increased in population by 28 percent.

Not only was there a greater *rate* of growth in the suburbs, but over the twenty years the absolute numbers of suburban dwellers surpassed those living in the central cities to become the majority: in 1951, 41 percent of the metropolitan dwellers lived in the suburbs; by 1969 they constituted 55 percent of the metropolitan population.[4]

Three major problems for public libraries arise from this high-speed development of the suburban ring. The first is that the librarians will try to follow their patrons by building branches and putting bookmobiles in the areas where the population has moved, because they know that use of the library is closely related to distance from library facilities. However, this effort is expensive in terms of capital outlay, duplicate purchasing, and staffing. Moreover, the quality of a collection at a small branch simply cannot match that of a centralized and specialized collection. The librarian must make a decision. To what extent should he develop his central library's collection and services? To what extent should he try to expand outward to meet the needs of a physically dispersing clientele? Perhaps some day technological innovation will let him do both by greatly facilitating central storage and processing while maximizing dispersion of the collection to where the patrons are. Such developments are likely to be expensive and in any case are not on the immediate horizon.

A second aspect of the decentralization of the metropolitan city is that the outlying suburbs have become fragmented into autonomous localities, each with its own laws and traditions, each jealously guarding its own boundaries. The result is that it is exceedingly difficult to create larger library districts or to consolidate resources in any fashion. Recent efforts at suburban regionalization have far to go. In the meantime the proliferation of small, inadequate libraries around the city forces the demand for books to express itself through channels other than the public library.

Third, because of patterns of residential restrictions and low economic power, ethnic minorities, particularly black and Spanish-speaking groups, have been slowest to move from the center of the city. These groups are hungry for education. Guy Garrison has repeatedly shown that the greatest support for library bond referenda comes from those areas with the highest educational background and from those areas with a large minority population.[5] Here is a tremendous task for the urban library in predominantly black areas: to create collections of materials of all kinds that meet the informational needs of the community, to create the channels of communication that can connect those materials to the programs of education and training that have proliferated in the ghettos, and to create programs that will take those materials out of the library and get them into the hands of families with enough encouragement and guidance to use them effectively. Such programs, while confirming the traditional role of the library as an auxiliary agency to education, will certainly require radical innovations in staff and procedures.

It would be useful to know how these demographic changes have altered reading habits and library policies. There are many gaps and inconsistencies in the available data, and much of the important information has simply not been collected. Nevertheless, these questions can be asked: How much are the American people spending for books and libraries? How are they allocating that money between individually purchased books and support for public libraries? And finally, how have the amount of money and its allocation changed over the past two decades? Table 1 attempts to answer these questions. It shows for 1950, 1960, and 1968 the consumer expenditure for books and the total income for public libraries. The monies expended for the support of special and academic libraries, it should be noted, are not included, since the general public is our concern here.

While the Gross National Product in the United States increased by 39 percent between 1950 and 1960, the amount expended on books and public libraries increased by 108 percent. Between the years 1960 and 1968, while the GNP increased at a rate of 45 percent, book and library expenditures grew by 84 percent.[6] These are impressively high increases. Still, it must be recalled that books and libraries were only a tiny fraction of the GNP, so gains in this small sliver of the economy are unduly

Table 1 Distribution of National Resources for Books and Public Libraries (in millions of dollars)*

	1950	1960	1968
Consumer Expenditures for Books†	723	1,548	2,854
Total Income for Public Libraries‡	209	387	698
Total	932	1,935	3,552
Percentage of Total Book Expenditures Made by Public Libraries	22.4	20.0	19.7
Percentage Increase in Total Book Expenditures		108	84

*In constant 1968 dollars. U.S. Office of Business Economics, *Survey of Current Business* (Washington: U.S. Government Printing Office, July 1961), Table 6, p. 8; July 1969, Table 8.6, p. 49; July 1970, Table 6.5, p. 40; July 1961, Table 52, p. 27; July 1952, Table 26, p. 22; and *The Bowker Annual of Library and Book Trade Information* (New York: R. R. Bowker Co., 1968), p. 5, and *The Bowker Annual*, 1970, pp. 21, 22.
†*Survey of Current Business*, July 1953, Table 30, p. 23; July 1961, Table 15, p. 14; July 1970, Table 2.5, p. 28.
‡*The Bowker Annual*, 1962, p. 7, and *The Bowker Annual*, 1970, pp. 21, 22. (Figure for 1960 averaged from 1959 and 1961 figures.)

magnified when stated in percentage terms. Even if we assume that the reading audience increased, on the average, by 40 percent over the past twenty years, it is clear that books are being bought faster than can be accounted for by a simple increase in the relevant population. This fact is both important and difficult to interpret. It should give pause to Marshall McLuhan and other celebrants of electronic media who claim that television and the film are now the vital conduits of our culture. The world of print is economically alive, if not culturally significant.

It is also clear from the figures in Table 1 that library funds are relatively a very small part of the total expenditure for books. Somewhere around 20 percent of the public's investment in books is made through public libraries. This means that the market is choosing most of the books, not the professional librarian. However, it should be noted that approximately 20 percent of the total consumer expenditures are for elementary and secondary school texts and workbooks.[7] Since this money is spent by school systems, the total amount spent for books by individual consumers is smaller than indicated in Table 1.

Over the period 1950–1968, the proportion of total book dollars that went to public libraries decreased steadily but gradually from 22.4 to 19.7 percent. When measured in uncorrected dollars, however, the public library's share increased from about 15 percent in 1950 to almost 20 percent in 1968. This means that the cost of libraries (mainly salaries) increased faster than the cost of books directly purchased by consumers. The result was an offsetting effect that shifted dollars to individual book purchases and overpowered the "income" effect of more absolute dollars going into books as a whole. Whether this is to be interpreted as the public libraries' failure to spread their services more aggressively, or whether it is to be regarded as a victory for the paperback book and the book club, or whether it should be seen simply as muddling through, I do not know. The point is that for this period the library slightly but steadily declined as a resource for the public's books.

Next we want to know what has happened to the stock of books: how many there are, how fast the number has increased, and in what directions. Then we want to know about the flow of books: what kinds of books are moving more or less rapidly through the various distribution channels.

It is of course impossible to make an inventory of the total stock of
books in the country.[8] Instead, we can assess the annual contribution
to that stock as indicated by publishers' sales receipts. Data from the
years 1947, 1958, and 1967 show the shift in book production over
approximately the same decades discussed earlier. Table 2 shows the
percentage of types of books sold during each of the three years and
the percentage change in sales over each ten-year period. The categories
are those of the book trade, and both paperback and hard-cover books
are included.

The first important, if obvious, observation to be made from Table 2
is that over twenty years the *relative* order of magnitude among the
different categories of books has remained much the same. The next
most striking point in the table is the *overall* regular and rapid growth
rate in book sales, mirroring again the basic facts shown in Table 1. The
growth has been uneven, however. The percentage decline in educational
books from 1947 to 1958 (28.6 percent of the total to 22.8 percent)
was reversed in the next ten years, up to 35.1 percent. Perhaps the
movement away from the single textbook in favor of opening the diverse
contents of libraries and specialized literature was overwhelmed by the
sheer increase in the nation's student body, resulting in continued reliance on traditional textbooks. It is still a challenge to all libraries,
though, to provide that diversity of materials called for by modern
educational practices.

Two categories of books did decline steadily over the twenty years:
religious books, in percentage terms by more than half (8.7 percent in
1947 to 3.5 percent in 1967), and technical, scientific, and professional
books, at a less precipitous rate. Given the enormous expansion of
science, technology, and professionalization, an increase of only 38
percent in sales of technical books over the past decade could very well
represent a decline in the use of books in scientific communication. As
scientific specialization continues to whittle away the numbers of people
prepared to buy increasingly expensive monographs, as the number of
scientific journals increases (for this very reason), and as near-print
research reports (Xeroxes, mimeos, etc.) continue to proliferate, it is no
wonder that the traditional book declines in relative importance for
technical and scientific fields. Thus if public libraries are to be informa-

Table 2 Number of Books Sold by Publishers in 1947, 1958, and 1967 (in millions)

Type of Book	1947		1958		1967		Percent of Change 1958–1967
	Number	Percent	Number	Percent	Number	Percent	
Textbooks and Workbooks	139.1	28.6	204.7	22.8	542.9	35.1	+16.5
Encyclopedias and Reference	14.6	3.0	30.6	3.4	31.3	2.0	+2
Religious	42.5	8.7	70.8	7.9	54.8	3.5	−23
Technical, Scientific, and Professional	17.5	3.6	23.7	2.6	32.6	2.1	+38
General Adult	140.4	28.8	340.9	37.8	507.4	32.7	+49
General Juvenile	53.8	11.0	172.9	19.2	206.4	13.3	+19
Other	79.3	16.3	56.6	6.3	175.1	11.3	+209
Total	487.2	100.0	900.2	100.0	1,550.5	100.0	
Total Change							+72

Source: Fritz Machlup, *The Production and Distribution of Knowledge in the United States* (Princeton: Princeton University Press, 1962), Table 6–3, p. 215; and *The Bowker Annual*, 1970, pp. 51–53.

tion centers for the business, technical, and professional communities, they are going to have to move toward the employment of document specialists and more sophisticated acquisition and retrieval systems.

It is not clear why encyclopedia and reference books show such a sharp percentage decline between 1958 and 1967. In any case, it is an especially significant trend because these books are expensive. When recast in dollars, the 2 percent of book volume comprised 9 percent of total publisher receipts in 1967; in 1958 this category turned in 15 percent of all publishing sales dollars.

General adult and juvenile books both showed a zig-zag trend over the years, with the highest rate of growth between 1947 and 1958. In the next decade both declined to almost the same level they had occupied twenty years previously. What is to be made of such changes? Ad hoc plausible facts abound, but I know of no satisfactory explanation for these trends or for the puzzling fact that general adult books sell from two to three times as frequently as children's books, when public library circulation figures show the situation to be reversed—children's circulation is twice that of adults. It is difficult to estimate from these figures how much children are underrepresented in the consumer market. Whatever that statistic turns out to be, the actual underrepresentation will be even greater, since 80 to 90 percent of all juvenile books priced over $1.00 are bought by public libraries. If adults have maintained their individual option to choose their own books, they have largely relegated the choice of children's books to librarians—or, perhaps more accurately, to book publishers.

A second measure of the nation's book stock is the number of books in its public libraries. This is difficult to estimate at any moment and almost impossible over a period of twenty years. One statistical series of the United States Office of Education shows for the years 1950 and 1959 the holdings of public library systems in large cities. While these comprise only a small percentage of all libraries, they do include most major metropolitan centers. In 1950 these 225 library systems held 58.6 million volumes, and by 1959 the stock had grown to 78.6 million, an increase of 34 percent.[9]

During that period the stock of library books increased at a slower rate than the national stock of books, as inferred from total publishers' sales.

Recall from Table 2 that there was an 84 percent increase in the number of books sold during that same time. Perhaps this is as it should be, given the professional standards of book selection in libraries. Without some estimates of quality and some standards for comparison, the only conclusion that can be drawn from these statistics is that the public library is not increasing its stock of books as rapidly as they are being produced. There are no comparable figures for the years 1960–1970 on library holdings, so judgment must be reserved as to whether the past ten years have witnessed any change in the library's basic acquisition rates.

Although it is difficult to come to any conclusion about the quality of the stock of books in the country, in two ways it seems deficient. Because of its historic commitment to "reach all the people," the public library has, by and large, been unable to create specialized research collections. Main libraries in some cities, such as New York, Cleveland, and Pittsburgh, are among the few exceptions. The compromise necessary to provide service to all the various groups of people comprising the clientele of the library has weakened the depth and scope of the collections of most public libraries. However, this weakness is not inevitable, and shortly I will suggest a way to mitigate the difficulty.

The other deficiency in the quality of the stock of books in the country is the relative absence of nonbook materials, such as original data and finished research reports or memoranda. There are mountains of statistical materials—attitude survey data, market research information, routine accounting statistics from industry, government, the courts, hospitals, the schools, and so forth—that are not collected and stored. To what extent is this task beyond the scope of major metropolitan public libraries? As social scientists and different lay publics increasingly demand such materials, various data bank arrangements will have to be made.

Private collections of books add another component to the national book stock. While it is possible to make an estimate of these books based on sample surveys, the reliability of such an estimate is unknown. Nor is there any way of identifying the contents of these holdings, which must include thousands of old textbooks, piles of paperback mystery stories, and the like. Therefore we must work around that uncertainty for the present.

Now for the problem of the flow of books: What kinds of books are being distributed, and through what channels? The main distribution channels are bookstores, drugstores and newsstand outlets for paperbacks, direct mail from publishers, book clubs, door-to-door salesmen (primarily for encyclopedias), schools, libraries of all types, and finally the secondary flow from individual private collections.

Since there are no comprehensive statistics showing the relative contributions of these channels to the total flow of books, some patchwork with available data is necessary. The data in Table 3 are taken from *The Bowker Annual of Library and Book Trade Information*. They are abstracted and combined to emphasize channels of distribution rather than types of books. The picture is not complete, because some types of books are omitted and for some channels of distribution we have no information. Next to the raw figures for the number of volumes sold in 1959 and 1967 is the percentage of increase between those years.

The interesting points about the relative size of the various book channels are the massiveness of the educational component and the smallness

Table 3 Distribution of Book Sales

Type of Book	Number of Books Sold (in millions)		Percent Change in Sales Volume 1959–1967
	1959*	1967†	
Educational	209	543	160
Adult Trade, Hard-cover	35	48	37
Adult Trade, Paperback	10	144	1,340
Wholesale Paperback	286	201	−30
Book Clubs	74	114	54
Subscription	32	31	−3
Juvenile over $1.00	40	62	55
Juvenile under $1.00	153	144	−6
Total Books	839	1,287	
Average Percent Change			53

*From *The Bowker Annual*, 1962, pp. 47, 48.
†From *The Bowker Annual*, 1970, pp. 51–53.

of the adult trade sold in bookstores. Note that book clubs distribute about twice as many books as do bookstores. In terms of growth, the volume of hard-cover books sold in bookstores is the smallest of all the channels of distribution listed. The sales of high-quality paperbacks have increased the fastest, and a considerable number of successful paperback bookstores have been opened. It is also clear that the so-called "paperback revolution" has lost its rapid growth rate. Indeed, there has been an absolute decline in the sales volume of mass paper-back books. Subscription books and inexpensive children's books have also suffered a loss in sales volume.

The book clubs have grown at a slower rate than the total. It should be noted, however, that although the top three book clubs are respon-sible for about 80 percent of all book club sales, smaller specialized book clubs have proliferated enormously. Thus, there are various ethnic and religious clubs—Irish, Jewish, French, Catholic, and Lutheran. There are occupationally specialized clubs, such as lawyers', business leaders', mechanical engineers', and real-estate brokers' book clubs; and there are special-interest clubs in such areas as art, history, sports, hi-fidelity, horsemanship, science, and science fiction. In 1968 *The Bowker Annual* listed almost 120 adult and 21 juvenile book clubs.[10] The existence of these specialized clubs underscores the fragmentation of the American reading public into a series of subpublics insulated from each other by the boundaries of their tastes and the absence of a general forum bring-ing together all book readers.

The flow of books from libraries is easier to define. The circulation figures of public libraries, at least, are available. However, the growth of other kinds of libraries during the past twenty years has been very important. Neither college, university, research, nor public libraries expanded greatly in number, while special libraries—those in industrial corporations, government agencies, and so forth—grew suddenly and at a tremendous pace. The number of special libraries increased from about 1,400 in 1959 to almost 2,400 in 1960, an increase of 70 percent;[11] but by 1968 there were 2,861 such libraries, a slowing growth rate of only 20 percent. This spurt in the number of special libraries again emphasizes the fragmentation of the American reading public into narrow and relatively isolated units.

To return to the public library and its part in the flow of books: there are several figures that define the trends. In 1950 public libraries in cities of over 50,000 people circulated 174 million books; in 1959 the circulation had increased 50 percent to 261 million. The new index of circulation prepared at the University of Illinois and based on 39 libraries representative of the cities around the country shows the same trend: From 1950 to 1960 their circulation increased by 68 percent.[12] During the years 1960–1968 circulation as measured by this index increased steadily until 1965 and then declined in 1968 to a point only 7 percent above the 1960 level.[13] Before attempting to interpret these statistics, we must consider how the populations served by these libraries have grown.

The population served by libraries in cities of over 50,000 people increased by only 11 percent during 1950–1960. This is almost exactly the rate of growth of the central cities of the Standard Metropolitan Statistical Areas during the years 1950–1960 and 1960–1968, as noted at the beginning of this paper. In other words, city libraries, without reaching beyond their natural constituency, have augmented their circulation by five to six times the simple population increase. In the University of Illinois sample of 39 cities, the population served over the decade 1950–1960 increased 25 percent. For these cities, then, circulation grew almost three times as fast as population. This is a significant achievement.

The question is: What kinds of books are libraries circulating? Two slivers of data provide a partial answer. The first is the old University of Illinois Index of Circulation, which shows the trends in circulation from 1930 to 1960 for a sample of representative libraries. Over the thirty years there was a 50 percent increase in total circulation. During this same period, the circulation of adult nonfiction remained fairly stable, increasing from 21 to only 26 percent of the total circulation.[14] These percentages remained at roughly the same level in 1968. These figures imply simply that the public library is responsive to larger trends. It has followed the publishing industry's expansion of children's literature and the public demand for children's books. It has reflected the rise of low-priced paperback fiction by its diminished circulation of fiction, but it has not developed its nonfiction circulation to any great extent.

The second clue to what kinds of books are circulating comes from matching the Dewey decimal classification of all titles published by the American book industry in 1969 with the Dewey classified circulation of the Chicago Public Library for the same year. Such a comparison, though quite rough, allows us to see to what extent the library is circulating books that are different in kind from those being offered to the public by publishers. Table 4 shows a remarkable parallel between the two sets of figures.

The only important differences are that religious books are undercirculated compared to new titles and that books in the field of fine arts are overcirculated. I do not think that any conclusions about quality can be drawn from this table; basically, it shows that the public library,

Table 4 Dewey Classification of New Nonfiction Titles Published and Nonfiction Books Circulated in Chicago

Dewey Classification		Percent Nonfiction Titles Published, 1969	Percent Nonfiction Circulated from Chicago Public Library, 1969
Generalia	000	3.0	0.8
Philosophy	100	3.8	6.3
Religion	200	7.1	3.0
Social Science	300	23.0	18.4
Languages	400	2.0	1.1
Pure Science	500	9.6	8.7
Applied Science	600	15.5	18.4
Fine Arts	700	8.1	12.4
Literature	800	12.6	11.7
History	900	6.1	9.8
Geography	910	4.7	4.2
Biography	920	4.5	5.2
		100.0	100.0

Source: *The Bowker Annual*, 1970.

at least in Chicago, is again offering simply what the publishing industry presents.

There are, finally, two sets of questions that go to the heart of the book circulation question. The first begins with the query: How many readers are there now in the country after twenty years of expanded educational and library efforts? Berelson, in *The Library's Public*, concluded in 1948 that 25 to 30 percent of the adult population read a book a month, that about 20 to 30 percent of adults used the public library with some regularity, and that if the definition of "book reader" was extended to include everyone who had read one or more books in a year, then almost one-half of the adult population qualified.[15]

There is considerable evidence that the situation today is no different. A 1959 Gallup poll showed 77 percent of the American people seldom read books; an even more recent Gallup study indicated 46 percent of a national sample had read at least one book within the previous year. A study by Hajda in Baltimore showed that in 1962 about 25 percent of a sample of adults were registered borrowers of the public library and that 52 percent had read a book within a year. Johnstone's study of adult education revealed that 60 percent of the sample had read a book within a year. My own studies of adult reading confirm this general order of magnitude.

How do we account for the fact that the reading audience has not increased appreciably over the past twenty years, during which the numbers of high school and college graduates has doubled and the number of books sold has trebled? This is a major puzzle.

A possible explanation is that "regular" book readers are reading more books now than twenty years ago. The "concentration-of-use" curve may have become steeper; that is, a smaller proportion of readers is accounting for a higher percentage of reading. However, this does not appear to be the case. Table 5 compares the number of books read in 1948, as reported by Berelson, and in 1962, according to data from Johnstone's national study of adult education.

These distributions are remarkably similar. At least in this respect there does not appear to have been any basic change in the reading habits of the population. Unfortunately, comparative figures on the amount of money spent on books now and twenty years ago are not available. It

Table 5 Distribution of Number of Books Read (in percentages)

Books Read in Past Year	Berelson 1948 (N = 1,151)	Johnstone 1962 (N = 2,845)
1–4	36	37
5–14	32	36
15–49	18	16
50+	14	11
	100	100

Source: Philip H. Ennis, *Adult Book Reading in the United States* (Chicago: National Opinion Research Center, University of Chicago, September 1965).

might be that some people are buying more books than they are reading. If one considers the general affluence of the country and the publishing industry's development of a line of showpiece and gift books, this explanation seems probable; but since the necessary data are not available, it must remain conjecture. For the present, then, the main paradox remains unexplained—the sales volume of adult trade books has expanded far more rapidly than the growth of the reading public.

It is perhaps time to begin basic research into the nature of the reading public, its composition, its manner of recruitment, and the conditions of its maintenance. One line of attack, begun several years ago, is the search for the social determinants of adult reading, beginning with early experiences in reading. Adults can and do identify themselves as readers or nonreaders in the present. They can also recall if and when they read books (other than textbooks) at various times in the past.[16] The question is: Are current and early reading related? Is reading like home woodcrafting, a hobby almost invariably practiced by people who had early familial experience with woodworking, or is reading more like skiing, an activity that, in the United States at least, draws a high proportion of its adherents from people having no early experience with the sport? Reading, it turns out, is somewhere in between these two extremes. Table 6 compares the presence or absence of early reading with the presence or absence of current reading as shown by their rates of appearance in the general population as of 1965.

Table 6 Types and Distribution of Book Readers (in percentages; N = 1,466)

| | | Early Reading | | Total |
		Yes	No	
Current Reading	Yes	Regular Readers 34	Late Starters 15	49
	No	Deserters 24	Nonreaders 27	51
	Total	58	42	100

Source: Ennis, *Adult Book Reading in the United States*, p. 35.

Table 6 shows the current reading audience to be composed of two groups: regular readers (34 percent), who read at some time in the past and continue to do so now, plus late starters (15 percent), who did not read when young but who began later in life. Their total, 49 percent, is the familiar estimate noted previously. Note, however, that there has been a considerable loss of potential readers. Twenty-four percent of the sample began as readers but deserted books as adults. The last cell is comprised of those 27 percent of the sample who say they do not read now and never have. The question now becomes: How are groups of people with different educational backgrounds distributed with respect to the four types? Table 7 shows this distribution for the same national sample of adults, now divided into those who have had at least a high-school education and those who did not finish high school.

The table substantiates the expected higher rate of current reading among the better-educated (65 percent for those with high school or better compared to 30 percent for those with less than high school). More important is the internal distribution of types. Nearly half (47 percent) of the better-educated are regular readers, and only 15 percent are nonreaders. Among those with less than a high school education the situation is reversed: only 19 percent are regular readers, and more than twice as many (42 percent) are nonreaders. The critical figure is the ratio of deserters to late starters. Among the better-educated there is a near balance—for every deserter there is a late starter. Among the less

Table 7 Educational Differences in Reading Distribution of Table 6 (in percentages)*

High School or Better (N = 779)		Early Reading			Less than High School (N = 686)		Early Reading		
		Yes	No				Yes	No	
Current Reading	Yes	47	18	65	Current Reading	Yes	19	11	30
	No	20	15	35		No	28	42	70
		67	33	100			47	53	100

*From the NORC Amalgam, 1965.
Source: Ennis, *Adult Book Reading in the United States*, p. 35.

well-educated there are nearly three deserters for every late starter. If this group continues its present attrition rate, the share of readers will drop considerably; those with better educations should remain in near equilibrium.

It is likely that different experiences at school, at home, and in society account for these two different patterns of reading. It is also likely that different social policies with respect to books and reading will differentially affect individuals of various educational backgrounds. Similarly, distinctions of age, sex, race, occupation, and so on will also yield specific reading recruitment and maintenance patterns. If ever the ritual phrase "further research is needed" has any meaning, it is here—the elaboration and explanation of these patterns.

The second basic question to be asked about the current reading situation is: How has book availability changed over the past twenty years? Unless the skill and motivation to read acquired in youth is sustained by conditions in adult life, reading will wither. The availability of books is one crucial condition. Research is needed on the question of how book availability should be thought of (and measured) so that this assertion of necessity can be evaluated as to its implication in adult reading. Once this has been done, the next logical question of what accounts for variation in availability can then be tackled. For some purposes it might suffice to know how many bookstores there are in the country now as compared with twenty years ago, or how many branch libraries there are in a city. However, such fragmented information would be misleading if the purpose of the inquiry was to assess the effect of availability on the amount and nature of book reading on the part of the public. A more comprehensive approach is necessary to do that job. There are perhaps ten ways that a person can get a book into his hands:[17]

1. Public libraries
2. Research and special libraries (public and private)
3. College and university libraries
4. Rental libraries
5. Bookstores (for both new and used books)
6. Mass paperback outlets
7. Book clubs
8. Direct mail from publishers
9. Local direct sales (mostly subscription books)
10. Private collections (that is, rereading one's own books and borrowing from friends).

How many and what kinds of books a person gets or whether he gets any at all depend on the patterning of these ten sources.

Research into patterns of availability requires the selection of a spatially delimited unit of analysis. That is, if we attempt to show how availability affects reading, we need a set of communities that vary in their extent of providing books so that we can test for the resultant variation in reading. Such a research enterprise must be of sufficient scope to encompass the undoubtedly large range of availability patterns —some communities may have strong public libraries and weak bookstores; others, vice versa; still others may be strong on both these outlets; and, of course, some communities will be weak on both. When these patterns are expanded by considering all the other sources of books, the number of different community availability patterns is quite large. Similarly, the variations in adult reading patterns are enormous.[18]

The patterns of book availability must then be matched with the patterns of book reading. Given this largeness of scale, it is not surprising that such a study has not yet been funded or executed. However, such a study seems to me to be an obvious must on the research agenda of the library profession and the publishing industry.

Notes

1. Figures from *Statistical Abstract of the U.S.*, 1969, Table 45, p. 103; *Current Population Reports*, Series P. 20, Nos. 91, 182; and *Pocket Data Book*, p. 36.

2. John W. C. Johnstone, *Volunteers for Learning: A Study of the Educational Pursuits of American Adults* (Chicago: National Opinion Research Center, University of Chicago, February 1963), Report No. 89, p. 25.

3. *Statistical Abstract*, 1970, Tables 24, 36.

4. *Statistical Abstract*, 1970, Table 14.

5. Guy G. Garrison, *Seattle Voters and Their Public Library* (Springfield, Ill.: Illinois State Library, September 1961), Research Series No. 2.

6. *Statistical Abstract*, 1969, Table 471, p. 312.

7. Data based on share of these texts among all books in Fritz Machlup, *The Production and Distribution of Knowledge* (Princeton: Princeton University Press, 1962), Table 6–3, p. 215.

8. Bolt Beranek and Newman Inc., *Estimates of the Information Content of the World's "Literature,"* Report No. 983, Job No. 11112, submitted to Council of Library Resources, Inc., March 1963.

9. U.S. Office of Education, *Statistics of Public Libraries in Cities with Populations of 50,000 to 99,999 for 1950*, Circular No. 339 (Washington: U.S. Government Printing Office, April 1952); *Statistics of Public Library Systems in Cities with Populations of 50,000 to 99,999: Fiscal Year 1959*, PE 15015, August 1960; *Statistics of Public Library Systems in Cities with Populations of 100,000 or More: Fiscal Year 1959*, OE-15014A (revised), October 1960.

10. *The Bowker Annual of Library and Book Trade Information* (New York: R. R. Bowker Co., 1970).

11. *The Bowker Annual*, 1970.

12. Data sent to the author personally from the Library Research Center, University of Illinois.

13. *American Library Association Bulletin* **63**: 556.

14. University of Illinois Graduate School of Library Science, "Index of American Public Library Circulation," *ALA Bulletin* **55** (July–August 1961): 646.

15. Bernard Berelson, *The Library's Public: A Report of the Public Library Inquiry* (New York: Columbia University Press, 1949), p. 7.

16. P. H. Ennis, *Adult Book Reading in the United States* (Chicago: National Opinion Research Center, University of Chicago, 1965).

17. Ibid., p. 61.

18. Elizabeth Warner McElroy, "Subject Variation in Adult Reading: I. Factors Related To Variety in Reading," *The Library Quarterly* **38**, no. 2 (Chicago: University of Chicago Press, April 1968): 154–167; "Subject Variety in Adult Reading: II. Characteristics of Readers of Ten Categories of Books," *The Library Quarterly* **38**, no. 3 (July 1968): 261–269.

4 The Dissemination of Print

Dan Lacy

This chapter was written in 1963. It has been left unchanged, as a statement of the situation as it existed at that time. Where they are available, more recent statistics have been added in brackets. In the intervening years, the crisis in urban library funding that was foreseen has arrived and has been even more severe than had been projected. Far from expanding their services, many urban library systems in 1971 were fighting for survival.

In spite of the acute general financial stringency, however, some efforts at improved services to central-city racial minorities, a high proportion of whose members are poor and of limited education, have been made possible through federal funding. The Elementary and Secondary Education Act of 1965 made possible the radical improvement of school libraries in central cities, removing some of the burdens of school service from public libraries. Title III of the act made funds available for central services to all schoolchildren, and some of this money went for projects of public library systems. More specifically affecting urban public libraries was the enlargement, in both scope and funding, of the Library Services and Construction Act, which now offers support for a number of urban public library projects designed to reach library nonusers in disadvantaged groups. As this volume's chapter by Dr. Lipsman indicates, however, even when funds are available, to make the library realistically useful to present nonusers in central cities will require major and imaginative innovations in service and collections and will not be easy to achieve.

D.L.

It is the purpose of this paper to describe the characteristics of the book publishing and distributing industry in the United States, both as the producer of the principal body of materials used by libraries and as a complementary means of disseminating those materials to the residents of large cities. Because of the symbiotic relationship between publishing

An earlier version of this paper appeared in *The Public Library and the City*, ed. R. W. Conant (Cambridge, Mass.: The MIT Press, 1965).

and libraries, the potentialities and limitations of the publishing industry help to define those of the library system, and the reverse is also true.

Book publishing has certain economic and technological characteristics that distinguish it from the other communications industries. I have described these in some detail in an article entitled "The Economics of Publishing" in the Winter 1963 issue of *Daedalus*. Some of these distinctions are:

1. The publishing of books, unlike broadcasting or the publication of newspapers, does not require the ownership of an expensive plant. With rare exceptions, book publishers do not manufacture their own books but rather contract with printing and binding firms for this service. Other services as well can be contracted for, such as warehousing and shipping and even sales and promotion, with the consequence that it is possible for very small firms to enter national publishing.

2. Every book must be advertised and sold on its own. This means that a large publisher does not have the overwhelming competitive advantages of greater advertising resources enjoyed by a large manufacturer of automobiles or cosmetics. The advertising budget available for any book depends on the size of the edition rather than the size of the publisher.

3. In contrast to broadcasting—in which it costs the same amount to televise a given program, whether a thousand sets are tuned in or a million—there is a considerable correspondence between the total cost of publishing a book and the number of copies produced. Hence it is possible to publish books for very small audiences indeed. The sale of five thousand copies, or even fewer of a highly specialized book, may suffice to sustain the national publication of a book, even though those sales may take place over many months or even years, while an instant audience of five million or more may be necessary to justify a nationwide telecast.

4. In contrast to magazines, newspapers, and broadcasting, books are not supported by their advertising content. Hence they are published to satisfy the needs or demands of their purchasers rather than to serve as a means of assembling a potential market for a product or group of products.

5. Books are produced in a physical form that permits them to be used

by individual readers at times and places of their choice without those readers being assembled, as at a theater, or set before a screen or loudspeaker at a predetermined time; to be preserved indefinitely; to be gathered in large collections from which a user can make a choice; and to treat subjects extensively and in detail.

The consequence of these factors is that book publishing can be more responsive than any other communications medium to a wide range of diverse demands from audiences large and small. Publishing enterprises can be started with very little capital—while there are three national television networks, there are many hundreds of book publishers selling to a national market. And the smallest of these as well as the largest has the opportunity to reach that entire market. Moreover, every publisher can expand or contract his list with great flexibility; he is not confined to twelve or fifty-two issues or required to fill a specified number of broadcast hours.

And the demand to which this complex mechanism responds, which indeed it eagerly seeks out, can be a very small one indeed. The thousand people who may become interested in the slender volume of a previously unknown poet, the few hundred concerned with a recondite aspect of Russian research in plasma physics, and the millions who may want an exciting novel are all served.

Hence the book publishing industry is in many ways an ideal instrument to respond to the extraordinary variety of the demands of the metropolis: for complex and specialized information, for a fresh and experimental culture, for mass enjoyments.

But in many ways it is a relatively ineffective instrument. Its ineffectiveness arises, not from its inability to produce books—as we have seen, it can successfully issue them in response to a relatively slight demand—but from its difficulty in distributing them to potential users. In order to understand this problem in general and in its specific urban context, it will be necessary to examine the distribution structure of the book industry in some detail.

In 1962 American publishers sold nearly $1.6 billion worth of books. Something less than 10 percent of this total was exported, leaving a domestic book distribution on the order of $1.45 billion. About $400 million of these were textbooks. Most elementary and high school texts were purchased by local school authorities and provided free of cost to the students. The distribution of these books is hence almost entirely dependent on public authority. In general, the largest urban school systems, hard-pressed for funds as a rule, have made a less adequate provision for textbooks and other teaching materials than the school systems of smaller cities and suburban areas.

The problems of urban textbook distribution have not been entirely quantitative. There are qualitative difficulties as well. The economics of textbook publication makes it highly advantageous to publish for a national market, rather than for a series of geographically or socially differentiated markets. Recently the complaint has been made by a number of large-city educators that most textbooks, aiming at this national market, have addressed themselves to the children of a vaguely defined middle-class, white, suburban or small-city population, without providing materials relevant to the experience of the large city, or, for that matter, the rural child, or for those reared in poverty or belonging to minority ethnic groups. The preparation and distribution of such specialized materials would, of course, be considerably more expensive than producing for a relatively uniform national market, and though some experiments have been undertaken, no one, including the urban school authorities, has yet been willing to meet the costs involved. [Largely as a result of the funding of the Elementary and Secondary Education Act of 1965, however, the production of texts adapted or specially prepared for urban children has increased enormously in recent years.]

Approximately $375 million represents domestic sales of encyclopedias. Perhaps 3 to 5 percent of the sum represents sales to schools and libraries, but the remainder represents sales to individual families by salesmen. Since the price of encyclopedias is necessarily substantial, such sales efforts are directed primarily at middle-class homes.

Of the remainder, about $190 million represents sales of professional works: legal, medical, business, scientific, technical, and university press books. These are published to meet the needs of specialized groups and are nearly all distributed through highly specialized channels. Their ready availability is indispensable to the functioning of the complex activities of any metropolis, but it presents no major problems within the purview of this Symposium on Library Functions in the Changing Metropolis except that of money. The demand for such materials upon college and university libraries and the larger urban libraries usually very considerably exceeds their budgets for purchase.

The real problems of book distribution concern the remaining 850 million to 900 million books published annually, representing sales of about $500 million—of which about one-third are children's books.

[In 1969 American publishers sold $2.75 billion worth of books; domestic distribution represented $2.5 billion. During that same year, the sales of textbooks and standardized educational texts came to about $800 million. More than $600 million represented domestic sales of encyclopedias, and $286 million derived from sales of professional works. Other books numbered about 1.5 billion, representing sales of about $1 billion. Of these, 20 to 25 percent were children's books.]

The traditional method of distributing these other books to their appropriate readers has been to publicize each new book by advertising it as extensively as funds will permit, by sending copies to a large number of magazines and newspapers in the hope that it will be reviewed, and by achieving as much publicity as possible through whatever means are appropriate. Meanwhile, salesmen try to induce bookstores to stock the work so that those who have learned of it in one of these ways may be able to buy it.

Consider the difficulties in this method. There are approximately 20,000 titles published annually in the United States. Perhaps 200,000 backlist titles are in print. [In 1970 more than 36,000 books were published, and perhaps 300,000 were in print.] Save for the specialized professional books that can be promoted to an identifiable professional group, their potential readers are indistinguishably scattered through the tens of thousands of American communities. Every one of these 20,000 books has to have its own advertising campaign, yet except for a few dozen annual best sellers, their advertising budgets can be only one or two thousand dollars, or even less, with which to try for a national impact. The largest reviewing service addressed to the public is the *New York Times* Sunday book section. It reviews about one book in eight and reaches less than one home in one hundred. Most books therefore pass almost entirely unnoticed.

Nor are the actual channels of sale any better. There may be as many as 20,000 establishments in the country that buy books from publishers for resale, but there are probably not more than about 1,500 that seriously attempt to maintain a respectable stock. Few of these have more than two or three thousand out of 200,000 or more books in print. Most of them are in cities of 50,000 or more or in college towns. An informed guess is that as much as 75 percent of bookstore sales of hardcover books takes place in the twenty-five largest metropolitan areas. City folk are hence far better served by bookstores than are residents of smaller communities, but even here the distribution achieved is very limited indeed. Another guess is that the patrons of bookstores in a typical city are fewer than 1 percent of its residents. This corresponds to the fact that probably only about 35 million hard-cover trade books, adult and juvenile, were sold to buyers other than libraries last year. If three-quarters of these were indeed sold in the twenty-five largest metropolitan areas, this is still a sale in those areas of only 27 million books, or less than half a book per capita. For the rest of the country, the situation would be far worse, with sales of about 8 million books to nearly 120 million people, or about one-fifteenth of a book per capita. [Though the numbers have increased in recent years, the ratios have remained about the same.]

Moreover, there were further limitations on the types of books sold through bookstores and the purposes for which they were bought. A high proportion were works of utility: garden books, manuals on bridge, etiquette handbooks, and the like. A very high proportion of the remainder, quite possibly half or more of the total, were bought as gifts. As a general channel for the dissemination of books, therefore, the bookstore in fact served only a very tiny elite within the urban population. This service is of great importance, particularly in the introduction of new writers and literary trends, in which the bookstore serves a role not unlike that of the legitimate stage in its relation to television and the cinema; but it is not a very meaningful contribution to solving the general problems of establishing an adequate flow of needed books to the urban population as a whole.

To escape the limitations of the bookstore as a method of distribution, publishers have developed four other principal channels. One is house-to-house selling, already mentioned in connection with encyclopedias. In the nineteenth and early twentieth centuries, this was a major means of book distribution for a variety of types of books in the United States, but at the present time the high cost of employing salesmen prevents its use for anything except relatively expensive sets of books whose sale guarantees a substantial commission. Another method is selling by direct mail. This, too, imposes high costs and is practical for only two types of books: specialized works likely to be wanted by members of a particular profession for which there are specialized mailing lists and relatively expensive works or series whose purchasers usually have some concrete motive for buying in addition to the pleasure of reading the work.

Another method of distribution, which is applicable to books in general, is derived from the method of distributing magazines. This is the book club, developed in the late 1920s. It is a method of distributing books by mail to a group of persons who have subscribed in advance and who, unless they request otherwise, receive the book automatically, just as do magazine subscribers. Premiums are offered at less than the retail price. Book dividends are also frequently offered to purchasers.

Recent years have seen the growth of many relatively small specialized book clubs in such fields as gardening, psychiatry, history, and religion, as well as a number of children's book clubs. Perhaps one hundred different clubs are now in existence, and a good guess would be that about 60 million books a year are distributed through their channels. [This figure was about 75 million in 1969 and has contined to rise rapidly.] They embrace a joint membership of several million, and possibly 3 to 5 percent of the families in America include a book club member. Book clubs hence reach considerably more deeply into the socioeconomic strata than do bookstores in providing material for general reading. They are not, however, nearly so urban-concentrated. Probably cities enroll no more book club members, perhaps even fewer, than their proportionate share of the population. In any event, the book club, requiring some initiative to enroll, the ability to maintain regular payments and the habit of doing so, and a sustained interest in middlebrow books, appeals primarily to the economic and intellectual middle classes. For these people it is a most convenient and useful service; but with one exception it does little to penetrate any sector of society not already book oriented. That exception is the classroom book club, which is not typical of general book club operation. In the classroom book clubs, a group of paperbound books is offered to each participating class each month, and a collective order is made up from among the children in the class. There is no individual membership in the club, although the children do individually select the books they wish to buy. The stimulus of the teacher's endorsement and the participation of friends probably does lead children from families not previously interested in books to buy through this channel.

The remaining method of distribution is the sale of inexpensive paperbound books, priced at about the level of magazines, through magazine distributors and wholesalers and through typical magazine outlets, such as newsstands, drugstores, and cigar counters. This method of distribution has grown up since World War II. In part it was made possible by the development of high-speed presses and inexpensive binding techniques and materials. But the principal savings that have made possible the exceptionally low prices of books of this sort have come in distribution rather than in manufacture. Of the price of an ordinary five-dollar novel, over two dollars and seventy-five cents represents costs of distribution: retailers' and wholesalers' discounts, salesmen's salaries and commissions, warehousing and shipping, advertising and promotion. This cost is reduced to twenty-five cents or less in the case of a fifty-cent reprint of the same book, an economy made possible by the mass distribution of 100,000 or more copies through more or less automatic channels.

Distribution of mass-market paperbounds reaches farther into the population than distribution of books through any other commercial channel not only because the price is lower but also because paperbounds are ubiquitously available. They do not have to be ordered by mail, subscribed for in book clubs, or sought out in bookstores but lie across almost everyone's daily path—in kiosks on the street, in the bus or railroad or subway station, in the drugstore, at the cigar counter, even in the schools. Even so, the Gallup poll has estimated that 11 percent of the population buys 85 percent of the mass-market paperbounds. These figures may be open to some question, but at the broadest estimate even this method of distributing books can hardly be said to bring books to more than one-fifth of the people.

Like book clubs, and in contrast to bookstore sales, the per capita sales of mass-market paperbounds seem to be fairly evenly distributed among population centers of various sizes. The twenty-five largest metropolitan areas, which account for perhaps 75 percent of bookstore sales, probably account for little more than 40 percent of paperbound sales. This would amount to about 100 million a year, or a little more than two books per capita in those areas.

There are also limitations as to the kind of book that can be successfully distributed through mass-market channels for paperbounds. They must be books that can sell 100,000 or more copies without extensive individual advertising, reviews, or promotion—merely upon exposure. This means generally that they must be books already made well known by the success of their hard-cover editions or books that will have a mass appeal because of their author or subject. Originally it was thought possible to distribute only westerns, mysteries, and light romances in this way. As time has passed, however, a far wider variety of books, covering indeed almost the whole gamut of literature, has been sucessfully sold in inexpensive editions. Now there are more than 20,000 paperbound books in print, of which perhaps half are mass-market editions. [There were in 1971 more than 90,000 paperbounds in print, but the number of mass-market titles in print had increased very little.] Nevertheless, limitations remain. Only a national market can usually sustain a mass edition, and the interest in books adequate to provide a sufficiently large market is really to be found only in reasonably literate "middlebrow" circles. Paradoxically, it is far easier to break out of the "middlebrow" pattern of both paperbound and book club publishing in the direction of the "highbrow" than in that of the "lowbrow." There are a lot more unskilled laborers than Harvard professors, but the latter buy a lot more books, and it is easier to publish even paperbound books aimed at their interests than at those of the laborer.

This means that the mass-market paperbounds are the book industry's best means of reaching the more or less "nonliterate" urban audience. They carry none of the connotations of the traditional bookstore or the traditional library or school that might be intimidating to the nonuser of books, they are cheap, and they are physically available. Yet even these "mass-market" books reach only in limited degree those who are not already active book users. This is because that audience simply does

not now constitute a large enough market for books aimed at their
special interests and with appropriate vocabulary levels or subject matter, in Spanish or other languages when necessary, to support either
mass distribution or the initial publication of books intended for mass
distribution.

What I have been saying is that quantitatively the sale of books in the
United States is quite large. Contrary to the general impression, it is in
fact perhaps the highest per capita in the world. Commercial distribution is larger than library distribution in large cities. (Statistics, both of
book sales and of library circulation, are seriously inadequate. But it is
a fair estimate that the annual sale of adult books, other than textbooks
and encyclopedias, to individuals in the United States is roughly six
books per capita, measured against the adult population. Library circulation figures are at approximately the same level; but book sales are
much larger in large cities than elsewhere, and library circulation per
capita is smaller in large cities than in small ones.) Yet book publication,
and more specifically book distribution, is effective only in serving a
rather narrow segment of the population very near the top of the socioeconomic and educational pyramid. Book publishing and book distribution, I have pointed out, are very sensitive and flexible in their response
to demand—even small, specialized, and minority demands—far more
responsive than other media. But it is necessarily to *demand*, rather than
to *need*, that the industry responds. The upper strata of this pyramid
are aware of the benefits and satisfactions they can obtain from books
and have the sophistication and means to demand the books they want.
It is easy to publish for this group, and the books they need do exist.
In small towns and rural areas, there may not be enough members of
this class to support an adequate book distribution, but in the largest
cities this is no problem. The highly educated man of means in New
York, Chicago, or Boston easily commands an almost infinitely rich
informational and cultural resource in books.

A poor and undereducated Negro, Puerto Rican, or recent white immigrant in the same cities may have a far more desperate need for kinds of
information available through print. But he is not aware of the need, or
of the fact that print can serve it, or of how and where to get the materials that can help him; nor does he have money to buy them. Without

the intervention of some social instrumentality, his need is not translated into a demand that can play a role in the economics of book publication and distribution. There is little effective incentive, for example, to publish in Spanish for the Puerto Rican population of New York, or to produce vocational training materials aimed at similar groups, or to produce material for general sale outside the schools that treat subjects of adult interest with simple vocabularies.

In particular, there is little incentive to produce such materials in the massive quantities and to give them the mass distributions that would be required to bring the price very low and physically to reach out to the groups needing to be served.

What are the implications of these facts for the library? I think there are two. One is that the library should be the social instrumentality that can translate the needs of the culturally deprived, of the non-book-using urban groups, into a demand, just as the school is, or ought to be, the instrument that translates into a demand their needs for formal educational materials. The library has the ability to perceive their needs, the sophistication to know what kind of printed materials can serve them, and the means to enter the marketplace to buy them. If libraries are really interested in buying materials in some quantity specially intended to serve the needs of presently non-book-using groups, publishing will rather sensitively and quickly respond to that demand. But if no social instrumentality performs this service—and none will unless the library does—the needs of these groups will remain unexpressed, and materials will simply not be published to meet them.

Beyond providing the demand that will stimulate publishing, libraries have the further indispensable function of providing the channel through which books may be brought to presently non-book-using groups. (I should point out that the "non-book-using" group of which I am speaking here embraces not only the seriously disadvantaged groups elsewhere referred to but also a large proportion of the high-school-educated, stably employed, reasonably prosperous elements in the society who, for one reason or another, cannot easily, or do not, make use of books.) The library is already the most comprehensive book-distributing instrument in the country. It has been estimated that, at least in smaller cities, about 25 percent of the population make some use of the library, as compared with a possible 11 to 20 percent who buy the paperbounds, 3 to 5 percent who belong to book clubs, and less than 1 percent who patronize the bookstore. And it has been pointed out that the necessity for a very large market tends to press book clubs and paperbounds upward rather than downward in the socioeconomic and educational pyramid, since the larger markets are in the middle to upper reaches of that pyramid, in spite of the smaller absolute sizes of the strata at those levels. Hence there is little practical hope, even if more materials appealing to the non-book-using elements in the population were available, that those elements would soon come to make up a sufficiently dense market to support mass-market distribution methods. It is therefore up to the library not only to demand suitable materials for that audience but also to reach that audience with them.

In spite of splendid efforts undertaken in many cities, the library does not do so very effectively now, as the 25 percent figure given in the preceding paragraph indicates. In the socioeconomic and educational structure, the library remains primarily a middle-class institution. The reasons are obvious. Public institutions respond to a calculus of demand —as contrasted with a calculus of need—almost as sensitively as does the private economy. The middle-class housewife knows she wants books and what books she wants and knows the library is the place to get them. She will use them if they are in the library and demand them if they are not. The Puerto Rican laborer is not able to assert—nor for that matter is he interested in asserting—such a demand. Because the groups in the society to whose demands the library responds are substantially the same groups as those to whose demands the book industry is also responding, the library intensifies without broadening the demand for books (except—and they are important exceptions—children's books and serious nonfiction) and spends some part of its resources in filling needs, for example, for detective stories and light fiction, that could just as easily be met at the bookstore or newsstand or through the book club. It provides a service that parallels as much as it complements the provision of books through private channels. Meanwhile, both library and industry, for somewhat different but in both cases rather compelling reasons, are likely in the future to have to give even more limited attention to serving the unexpressed needs of the disadvantaged groups.

In the absence of a clear policy determination on the part of the urban authorities who supply libraries with funds, this situation is reasonably certain to get much worse. There are two reasons for this. One is that over the next decade the library will undoubtedly have to enter into an increasingly fierce competition with other social service institutions for state and local funds that will be quite inadequate to meet a whole range of explosive social needs. Relatively, at least, it is more likely to have to curtail the range and quality of its services than to be able to expand them broadly.

The second reason is that urban public libraries are already nearly collapsing under a new wave of demands from groups requiring a highly sophisticated book service, at the opposite end of the spectrum from the needs of the groups I have been discussing. I refer, of course, to the student demand for public library services, which is already the most pressing of the problems of the urban public librarian today. In large part this is now a high school problem, directly traceable to the poor quality of high school libraries, their unavailability in evenings and on weekends, and the more demanding level of high school assignments. But increasingly it will become a college problem. Enrollment in colleges is expected to double in the coming decade. Most of this increase will take place in urban institutions in which the students live at home. For reasons of convenience and because of the almost certain inadequacy of the library resources of the new or rapidly expanded urban colleges, most of these students will make heavy use of urban public library resources, already used to their uttermost. The consequence is almost certain to be an even further concentration of the acquisitions policy, staff services, and general policy attention of the urban public library upon the needs of a very restricted sector of the intellectual elite. In the absence of a clear policy decision to the contrary, the public library is likely to be incorporated more and more fully into the network of institutions serving research and higher education, to the necessary neglect of those now having limited access to books and limited competence to use them. The probable trend of urban public library service hence will be to reinforce further the book services available through academic libraries and the book trade, rather than to complement those services by vigorous attention to the otherwise unserved. I do not mean to suggest that it is undesirable that the public library play a major role in providing an intellectual elite with complex and sophisticated printed materials. On the contrary, that is an obvious and socially indispensable function for it to perform, and indeed it may well be the most socially efficient use of limited resources. I do mean that unless a radical increase in public library resources can be obtained and unless pressures on public libraries can be reduced by greatly improved school and college library service, any substantial enlargement in the service to present nonusers will be tragically impossible.

This is, of course, only one aspect of a major problem in what might be called the distribution of intellectual wealth in our society. We have seen the problem rather clearly internationally. It has been fourteen years since President Truman delivered his "Point Four" address setting forth the urgent necessity of measures that would enable the then underdeveloped coutries to participate in the advanced technological society of Western Europe and North America. Since that time uncounted billions of dollars have been spent, principally by the United States but also by the other Western powers and by Russia, to achieve that objective. Yet at the end of fourteen years the gulf between the fully developed and the underdeveloped countries is not smaller but far greater— the gulf in education, in technology, and in standard of living. For every painful yard the underdeveloped countries have progressed, the United States and Western Europe have advanced an easy mile. Nor does there seem to be any practicable way of reversing this process save by a cataclysm that would reduce us all to a primitive equality.

Something similar may be happening within our society. There has always been a stratification of education and trained intellectual competence, more or less correlated with a stratification of income. But in earlier times this was a stratification within a more or less integral society, in which the component parts were reciprocally necessary to each other, in which there were more or less commonly accepted goals, and in which there was a good deal of internal mobility independent of formal education. Today we have to some extent divided internally into two societies: one—at whatever level—participating productively in, and enjoying the fruits of, an extremely high technology; the other largely excluded from that technological order, both as producers and as consumers.

The boundary between these two societies is defined principally by the presence or absence of a realistically effective literacy. The test of useful participation in the technological society is the ability to use efficiently the bodies of print in which the knowledge and procedures of that society are recorded and by which they are conveyed. As those bodies of print and their content become more and more complex, the capacity to use them becomes more difficult to acquire, and the barrier between the two societies becomes more forbidding. At the same time the plight of those excluded becomes more desperate, as employment opportunities narrow and as political comprehension of the actualities of the advanced society dims.

This dichotomy is given a further explosive potential by the facts that today it falls largely along racial lines and that it is most evident in large cities where the extremes of the two societies live side by side in painful contrasts of security, competence, and wealth.

Yet our national policies have the result, if not the object, of further widening this division. Partly impelled by our competition with the Soviet Union, we are devoting many billions of dollars annually to research and development activities that increase the level of complexity of our technology. Billions more go into the development and installation of systems of automation that replace the less skilled. Our principal educational investment in dollars over the next decade will go into the doubling of our facilities for college education, a benefit that can serve only the effectively literate. A doubling of the college-educated class will, of course, further lessen the social utility of the uneducated and enlarge the areas from which they are effectively excluded.

In comparison, the investment of thought and resources in solving the problem of incorporating within the literate culture those now excluded from it is small, though, I hope, growing.

The library has always served as one of the means by which unusually gifted and unusually motivated children could escape from the limits of a disadvantaged background and find their way into the literate society. For thousands of individuals in the past it has quite literally opened doors to a new world. Now the developments that have made the non-literate class obsolete and functionless require, not an avenue of escape from that class for exceptional individuals, but rather an instrument for transforming the class itself. This is a new and vastly heavier responsibility for the library, as it is for the schools and the other instruments of society with which it must serve.

The effective dissemination of print through the efforts of the private sector of the economy is confined and will continue to be confined to the middle and upper segments of the socioeconomic and educational pyramid, for only there does a demand exist that is adequate to sustain the machinery of distribution. Therefore, there necessarily rests on the public sector, on urban schools and on the urban public library, the responsibility for expressing a demand for materials needed by the segments of society not now effectively literate and for providing a channel of distribution for those materials. This is a responsibility in some degree counter to the pressures on the library to serve the highly literate segments of the society—pressures that will become far more intense with the anticipated more than doubling in urban college enrollment. Yet a failure to discharge this responsibility could, by omission, contribute one more element to an already potentially explosive social situation.

5 Partnership Federalism and the Civilizing Function of Public Libraries

John E. Bebout

Public libraries that are worth their salt are no longer the somewhat cloistered institutions of local cultural benevolence that many of them once were. They should have quiet corners in which a boy or a girl, man or woman can be alone for a while with a chosen book and his own probing or soaring thoughts. As institutions, however, they are caught in a vast web of governmental organizations and practices—national, state, local—that has come to be called partnership federalism. The nation is just beginning to become aware of the complex system of intergovernmental relationships that has evolved out of the relatively simple concept of federalism embodied in the Constitution of 1787. Libraries, quantitatively miniscule elements in the system, have hardly sensed the implication of this evolution for either their institutional integrity or their function in society.

To be sure, local libraries have known for a long time that they could borrow books from afar through rudimentary state library agencies. In recent years they have become aware that a trickle of money for libraries has begun to flow from Washington and that an increasing number of the states were appropriating modest sums for grants-in-aid to public libraries. Moreover, library associations and leaders in the profession have taken the initiative in shaping this trend and in urging more extensive national and state involvement in making full-scale library service available to all Americans.

However, old habits of thought and practice established in a more parochial era are hard to shake. Like the tradition of the "little red schoolhouse," that of the "independent" library still has value, but it is utterly inadequate armor for the battle for recognition and support in the modern arena of intergovernmental and interagency relationships. It is important for librarians to understand this arena, both to ensure the healthy survival of the library institution and to discharge their share of the responsibility for the continuing education of citizens on the nature of American democracy and what it takes to operate it.

The principle of partnership in the government of the Union, established by the Constitution, makes every citizen responsible to both national and state governments and divides the tasks of government between the nation and the states. This arrangement in its early operation was relatively simple, because the emphasis was on the division of powers between nation and states rather than on the sharing of responsibilities for related functions. National and state governments worked for the same people, but in distinctly separate functional areas. In addition to being responsible for foreign affairs and the national defense, the national government exercised power over a limited number of domestic matters specified in the Constitution. The states were left with all powers not delegated to the federal government or denied by the Constitution to the states. This division left to the states the lion's share of the business of domestic government, including responsibility for the local governments through which much of this business was conducted. The states were expected, through the militia system, to share in the national defense, and they were expected to assist in the enforcement of the laws of Congress, which were declared to be the supreme law of the land. On the other hand, there was little or no involvement expected of the United States government in the vast area of domestic affairs left to the states.

Perhaps the most notable example of national concern for a state function was in education. The founders of the Republic were profound believers in the importance of education to a free people. This belief was expressed in the Northwest Ordinance, adopted before the Constitution, which set aside land for the states to be used for the support of public schools. However, this national act did not entail any continuing participation by the national government in the school system.

The written constitutional blueprint for American federalism has changed very little in nearly two centuries. The working constitution, under the impact of territorial expansion, economic depression and development, war, and technology has become a quite different thing. In response to broadening concepts of the general welfare and the national interest, the original division of powers between nation and state has been replaced by an intricate melding of national, state, and local powers and capacities in a working partnership to meet the governmental needs of its people. In the process America has truly become a nation.

The forces that have brought the national government increasingly into domestic affairs showed themselves in the demand for national action in the areas of economic regulation and conservation during the Progressive Era following the turn of the century, in the need for national action to meet the problems of individual and family welfare and of economic stability exposed by the depression of the 1930s, and in the equally insistent need for national action after World War II to cope with problems of urbanization and technological change. Each of these eras also laid new burdens on state and local government and intensified intergovernmental relations. Paradoxically the greater the expansion of national domestic programs, the greater has been the expansion of the state and local sector. The net result is that by any measure of taxing, spending, personnel employed, or sheer bulk of governmental activity, the domestic role of state and local government has undergone greater expansion than that of the national government.

While the principle of partnership federalism was inherent in the Constitution of 1787, and indeed in the Articles of Confederation, the extensive practice of it is of recent development. Patterns of partnership, which in this urban age are of the very essence of the system, began to appear while America was still predominantly rural and heavily agricultural. The intergovernmental system of educational and technical programs in aid of agriculture and improvement of rural life, which began with the passage of the Morrill Land-Grant College Act of 1862, is the best example of the emerging partnership. One aspect of this system, the Cooperative Extension Service, which achieved its present form in the Smith-Lever Act of 1914, involves a partnership of national, state, and county governments. The program provides financial support from all three levels. The U.S. Department of Agriculture sets goals, and the State Agricultural College and Experiment Stations provide technical assistance. The partnership is further extended to include organized agriculture and local volunteers. Hence, like many recent programs in the urban area, the Cooperative Extension Service is not only an intergovernmental partnership but also a public-private partnership. Later farm programs of the New Deal added new dimensions to intergovernmental and public-private partnerships.

This system, with its deep involvement of the national government at the grass roots of domestic affairs, was supported by a three-part rationale. First, there was recognition that the condition of agriculture and rural life was a matter of national concern. Second, there was acceptance of the view, ably promoted by rural-oriented politicians in both the state and the nation, that farmers and rural communities were disadvantaged in their dealings with powerful corporate and urban segments of the nation. Third, there was the implicit assumption that the problems could not be solved by state or local action alone. The same rationale underlies the whole vast superstructure of partnership federalism that has evolved since World War II to meet the needs of a predominantly urban society.

It is natural that the modest beginnings of intergovernmental dealings on behalf of libraries were primarily for the benefit of rural or small-town areas. County libraries and "traveling libraries" were encouraged by the states and assisted by state public library agencies. The entry of the national government into the field occurred during the Depression with the creation of a small library branch in the Office of Education to gather data and promote coordination between the public school system and the public library. In 1946 the American Library Association began a ten-year period of lobbying for a five-year rural demonstration program for places of 10,000 population or less, which was finally established in 1956. In 1964 the legislation for the program was amended to eliminate the population limit. Amendments passed in 1966 to the Library Services and Construction Act not only continued the modest federal subvention on a matching basis through the states for library services but also offered incentives for the creation of library networks to give all persons in an area the benefit of specialized and differentiated capacities of libraries in the region. One year earlier, through the Higher Education Act of 1965 and the Elementary and Secondary Education Act, more generous but still modest federal programs of support for university and school libraries were inaugurated.

In the meantime, partly because of the federal incentives, states began to get somewhat more deeply into the library business. Today almost half of the states have interstate compacts that permit rendering of services across state lines. Nearly all the states have some kind of state library plan, though many of the plans have not yet been implemented. As of the fiscal year ending in 1969, all but eighteen states provided some support for local public library services. Only ten states, however, appropriated as much as a million dollars for this purpose, including Hawaii, which has a completely integrated public library system. A number of states have fairly well-developed regionalization programs with state support related to the level of specialized service offered by the designated libraries.

The New Jersey Library Aid and Development Program enacted in 1967 is an example of the type of program that may be in the future of most of the nation's public libraries. New Jersey offers per capita aid for local library service through a sharing formula that increases state support as local tax support rises. The plan provides additional support for "area libraries," which contract to provide substantial reference and book services throughout the area. It also provides special support to four major research libraries to extend services statewide: the Newark Public, Rutgers University, Princeton University, and State libraries. Finally, it provides a small sum for emergency aid and incentive grants; these funds have been used to promote cooperative activities among libraries. While New Jersey's appropriation under this act made it the third biggest spender among the states for public library services in 1969, exceeded only by New York and Pennsylvania, it has so far failed to meet the level of per capita aid promised by the act of 1967. With $5,000,000 appropriated, it fell nearly $3,500,000 short of full funding in fiscal 1970. Thus it has followed the national government in under-funding modest programs laid out in plans and statutes.

I do not intend to suggest here that the New Jersey plan, even at full funding, is necessarily ideal. It seems doubtful, in any event, that the regional and research libraries are adequately recompensed for their service or that there is sufficient incentive for phasing out or consolidating weak units. Tying the level of state aid to local tax effort offers an incentive for local support, but in a state with a grossly inequitable property tax system it does not assure equal service to all comers. In view of recent court decisions on school financing, the relating of state support to local tax effort may have to be abandoned in favor of a scheme designed solely to assure overall service equity. Indeed, a veritable revolution in New Jersey's method of supporting public services appears to be in the making. A state court has declared the reliance on the property tax for the bulk of public school support to be in violation of the state constitution. The court gave the legislature until January 1973 to produce a more equitable system. This decision was followed by a report of the State Tax Policy Commission recommending a state income tax, a statewide property tax, and other changes in the tax and expenditure structures that would reverse the state's historic policy of loading the major part of the cost of government on the local property taxpayer. This has great potential importance for the future support of libraries. It is, moreover, a good example of the kind of public policy development that libraries should be ready to help their clients put into perspective during the discussion stage.

The small beginnings of library involvement in the web of intergovernmental relationships suggest some of the understandings and principles on which partnership federalism rests. They may be summarized briefly:

1. Recognition that there is an active national interest in human conditions throughout the country, which demands substantial equality of opportunity for self-development for all, with special attention to the needs of underprivileged and otherwise handicapped persons and groups and to depressed areas

2. Recognition that economics and technology know no political boundaries

3. Recognition that disparities in the fiscal and other capacities of state and local governments make them unable to meet the national need for equality of opportunity without help from Washington in the forms of technical assistance, money, and the setting of standards and goals

4. Recognition that local governments, although legal creatures of the states, are in fact partners of both state and nation, not mere agents, in supplying domestic government

5. Adherence to a policy of encouraging initiative and innovation in all levels and sectors of the system and of using state and local government in the delivery of services

6. Recognition of the need for developing new patterns of regionalization—interstate, intrastate, and even intracity—for the planning of policies and programs and delivery of services

7. Recognition of the special problems of governance in metropolitan areas in which the web of government is most complex and in which the functions and frustrations of interrelationships are most intense.

If these principles are not fully realized in practice, they at least characterize a concept of American federalism that seems to be emerging. I have been calling it "partnership" federalism. Others have called it "cooperative," "creative," or "new" federalism. President Lyndon B. Johnson's expression "creative federalism" suggests the dynamic qualities inherent in its pluralism and the capacity, it is hoped, to fuse a multiplicity of local initiatives and energies in building the national purpose and strength needed for survival in an age of unprecedented complexity and fluidity.

Librarians and their cohorts need to understand these concepts if they are to play a significant role in this venture. The federal partnership is not a company of saints vying with one another to make sacrifice for the common good. The playing field is rough. The rules are complicated, changeable, and sometimes contradictory. The goals are often obscure, the goalkeepers frequently anonymous, and the rewards uncertain. It is no game for the weak, the timorous, or the uninformed. It is being played for the common good, however variously that common good may be understood by the players. Libraries *should* have much to contribute to the clarification of goals and the knowledge of the rules by which a civilized society must live and evolve.

Here are a few suggestions for urban librarians, their board members, and friends on how they can participate in and contribute to this partnership:

1. The staid politics of the library board dealing at arm's length with city hall and local philanthropists is not enough. Library boards must play real city hall politics, plus statehouse and Congressional politics, as well as the politics of interagency grantsmanship.

2. They must learn to maximize the effectiveness of limited resources. This means a constant reappraisal of the goals, methods, and distinctive role of libraries in an expanding and increasingly competitive information marketplace. Library leaders must also be prepared to negotiate appropriate divisions of functions and responsibilities not only with one another but also with still other, often more powerful, trading partners, including public and private information or data systems and the schools and universities. It necessarily means regionalization of many library services and phasing out of obsolete or nonproductive units or services.

3. Libraries must learn to obtain an increasing share of their support from state and national sources. This means that they must join actively in the national quest for viable priorities, both public and private, and for a better system of funneling resources into the public sector.
4. Librarians must develop ingenious and effective ways of educating their clienteles on the nature of partnership federalism and on its demands on American citizens.

Some of these points can be illuminated by a review of the famous Newark, New Jersey, library crisis of 1969, which was a one-month wonder and a long-term worry for librarians everywhere. On February 10 the City Council voted to cut off funds and close the Newark Public Library, one of the most prestigious in the country. On March 11 the Council voted to restore the appropriation. What happened between those dates is instructive. Only a few highlights can be related here.

In terms of the human condition of most of its inhabitants, Newark is one of the most debilitated cities in the country. With a tax rate of $9.19 per hundred of true value of ratable property, it is one of the most heavily taxed cities in the nation. It would be hard to find another with so wide a gap between the need for basic services and for physical and human renewal and the resources available to meet that need. New Jersey, with no personal income tax except for that from interstate commuters, has a highly regressive tax system. State aid for education and other service needs that tend to be concentrated in the old central cities is close to the lowest in the country.

The Newark Public Library has long been one of the city's proudest possessions. It has always been innovative and versatile. It serves as a cultural center, with art, music, film, and other programs for young and old. It has a strong preschool program, and it stocks public, private, and parochial school libraries with about 75,000 volumes, with weekly deliveries. Special services are supplied for business, labor, industry, and education. Branch libraries serve as community centers and sometimes provide secretarial or technical assistance for community councils.

For an annual city appropriation of about $2,100,000, this looks like a pretty good bargain. The fact is that through its years of early prosperity and later depression Newark has made a handsome gift to a much larger multicounty region, most of whose inhabitants have for many years been far better able to pay for culture than the people of Newark.

In view of these facts, it is not too hard to understand the impulse that led to the February 10 action of the City Council. Why did the Council backtrack one month later? Basically, their reversal was based on evidence of the many-faceted services that had endeared the library to so many people and institutions. The library's strong and dedicated staff and loyal board teamed up to rally the natural supporters. The response was astonishing in the breadth and depth of concern shown by schoolchildren, adults, businesses, the press, and numerous organized groups. All elements of the college community—students, faculty, and administrators, including Newark College of Engineering, Rutgers–Newark, and Essex County College, with a student population of approximately 21,000—gave strong support. Organizations of various political orientations, in terms of right to left, were on the bandwagon.

The library leadership was sophisticated enough to tell the City Council that it understood the city's plight and to offer help in publicizing that plight and gaining financial assistance. Members of the legislature canvassed the possibility of special state aid, but the library leadership preferred to stand with other libraries in working for full funding of the existing state aid plan. Friends of the library outside the city were asked to direct their pleas to the governor and the legislature. In any event, there is no doubt that the existence of the 1967 state aid plan, which at half-funding brought $320,000 to the Newark Public Library, made it harder than it would have been otherwise for the Council to persist in nonsupport. Those state funds plus $33,000 in federal money helped to make the point that Newark was not alone in support of the library. After the crisis, but not because of it, the library received a federal grant of $100,000 for its role as Metropolitan Regional Library for the 4,000,000 people living in the Northern New Jersey metropolitan region.

Some lessons in this experience are perhaps obvious in the telling. The following are worth stressing:

1. The Newark Public Library entered the struggle for survival from a position of strength based on wide public recognition of the breadth, excellence, and relevance of its services to virtually all segments of the community. There is no substitute for this asset.

2. Politically sensitive leadership and a staff that can identify with the

condition and needs of the community as a whole are equally important.

3. The existence of state and federal support is a very important factor.
In the long run, it may well be the crucial factor in ensuring the survival
of many fine libraries.

4. The importance of the library's service to children of all ages can
hardly be overestimated. This point deserves some elaboration.

This service not only made the children vigorous and effective lobbyists for the library appropriation but also engaged the efforts of parents
and parent organizations. Despite federal appropriations for school and
college libraries, the Newark schools and colleges in the area recognized
that the Newark Public Library's superior reference and research capacity was of great importance to them and their students. Modern teaching methods that de-emphasize old-style textbooks and stress research
papers and reports make it difficult for each school, college, or even a
struggling university to keep up with the library needs of its students.
The Newark Public Library provided an indispensable back-up service
for these institutions.

These observations call attention to an aspect of partnership federalism
of crucial importance to librarians: the relationship between libraries
and school, college, and university government. For partnership federalism, it must be remembered, involves not only the vertical relations of
federal, state, and local governments and their agencies but also the
lateral relations of governments and agencies at the same level. The
appropriate role of the public library in relation to education in schools
is a matter of current controversy. The Newark example suggests, however, that it would be a mistake for public libraries generally to opt out
of serving students as students, leaving the "burden" almost entirely to
special institutional libraries. Such a course would seriously narrow the
constituency of an institution that badly needs a truly community-wide
support to survive.

This is not to say that the public library should be expected to be *the*
school or college library. There is no excuse for the establishment of a
new community college with hardly even token provision for a college
library, as occurred recently in one of the country's largest school districts. This lapse, quite properly, elicited a strong resolution of protest

from the regional library association, which pointed out that the existing high school, college, and public libraries in the district were not equipped to meet the needs of the more than 5,000 students already enrolled in the college. On the other hand, it would appear to be elementary good sense in any metropolitan region to plan for the public, school, and college library needs of the area together, on a total system basis, with a view to arriving at an optimum allocation of responsibilities designed to achieve the benefits of scale, specialization, and accessibility for all users. One wonders, in view of the old, not new, American concept of the community school, whether school libraries might serve as branch outlets of the public library for adults as well as children. A partnership between the public library and the school would seem to be the surest way to obtain maximum support for meeting all the library needs of all the people. This partnership can be achieved without a merger of public and school library systems or any loss of identity by the public library. Public libraries have more to gain from alliance with the strength of the total educational enterprise than from aloofness from it.

A little earlier I suggested that libraries need to do a better job of educating for citizenship in the complex, pluralistic republic that we call the United States of America. Benjamin Franklin, Thomas Jefferson, and other founders of that republic believed that libraries, as well as schools, were essential to the education of a free people. They had in mind not only general education for competence and enlightenment but also education directed to the responsibilities of citizenship.

In some ways education for citizenship is a more difficult task in this country than in most others, because the nature of our system makes the calling of the complete and effective citizen a particularly exacting one. Our system of partnership federalism is in itself more puzzling to Americans than are the systems of many other countries to their citizens. The problem only begins with the fact of multilevel citizenship. It is compounded by the separation of powers among executive, legislative, and judicial branches; by the bicameral system and the whole gamut of so-called checks and balances; by the Congressional committee structure and the complex relationships of senior committee members, functional bureaucrats, and private interests, at national, state, and local levels; by the fractionation of the executive in most state, county, and local governments; by the tens of thousands of local jurisdictions, which even in a single metropolitan area run into the scores or hundreds; by the fact that many of these local governments—county, city, town, school district, special district, and others—overlap so that generally the citizen is responsible to and for at least three and usually more of them; by the consequent multiplicity of elective offices faced by a single voter, to say nothing of the numerous referenda on state constitutional and local charter amendments, bond issues, tax levies, and other matters; and by the great variety of arrangements for selecting the people's representatives in the various jurisdictions that comprise the whole system known as American government. The problem of the mobile citizen who moves from one town or state to another is complicated by the bewildering lack of uniformity among states, counties, cities, school districts, party organizations, and the like, which means that much of the civic learning acquired in his last place of residence must be unlearned and replaced in his new home.

These conditions account, at least in part, for the apparent indifference of many citizens and for the chronic frustration felt by many others. By the same token, they place a very great responsibility on such educational institutions as schools and libraries. If one judges by the record, the way that responsibility is being met leaves a great deal to be desired. The library's role in civic education is in some ways more complex and demanding than that of the schools because it extends directly to people of all ages and stations and because it must be specifically related to the changing demands upon the citizens as the civic and political calendar unfolds.

This is not the place to outline a program and strategy for civic education through libraries. A few hints may suggest some of its possible dimensions. The first observation is that the library needs for its own institutional purposes much of the same information on the current civic scene that it should be imparting to the public. For both purposes it needs a better early warning system of impending developments and of documents relating to them than most libraries now have. Libraries have well-established methods of learning about new books and periodicals. They can easily find out about public documents that appear in official lists, and selected libraries are "depositories" for some of those documents. The trouble is that state and local governments neither maintain nor publish comprehensive lists, and many of the most educational documents and reports disappear before most people, including librarians, become aware of them.

Incidentally, the word *depository* is a bad one. Certainly part of the job of a modern library is, like that of the medieval monasteries, to hold treasures from the past on deposit for use in the future. Unfortunately, much of the material is really not worth the space for deposit, at least in many places, while some gems that should be on display are hidden away under uninformative labels in files or stacks. The depository function needs constant reappraisal not only to relieve many libraries of unprofitable burdens but also to see that more libraries obtain materials of lively current interest that now never reach them. Librarians could well take the initiative in seeking a continuing cooperative study of the problem with appropriate national, state, local, and academic agencies.

Librarians realize that there is another dimension of the problem of access to material useful for civic enlightenment even more baffling than that of public reports. That is how to lay hands on material issued by private and voluntary organizations that often do not consider the library's possible interest in it. Consequently, the study of access to public documents should be supplemented by a somewhat similar inquiry with private groups. In both the public and private sectors it will be found that one difficulty lies in the inadequate provision for printing and digesting for popular use precisely the kinds of materials that could be most helpful to the questing citizen. Librarians should have good advice to offer on this subject. As it is now, citizens have to depend too much on the spotty and otherwise inadequate coverage of the news media. If all elements in the communication system could join in exploring this problem, each could increase its own effectiveness in meeting the public's right to know.

The library's role in civic education, even more than in other areas, should be an active, not a passive, one. It is not enough to have on deposit a report of, say, a commission on reform of the welfare system, just in case a citizen might ask for it. Part of the job is to handle such a report so that a potentially interested citizen who did not learn about it in some other way may learn about it through the library. There are many ways to do this, including a listing in a periodical report on new acquisitions of civic interest, translation into some sort of visual display, and use in a library-sponsored forum or discussion.

A library might maintain a civic corner with a civic calendar, shifting displays on timely subjects, and lists of materials available from the library or other sources. It should include basic, easily understood materials on the nature of our system and on such specific aspects of it as are found in League of Women Voters "Know Your State" and "Know Your Town" studies, with particular attention to avenues for citizen access. The library could use newspapers, radio, and television to extend this service to people who seldom enter its doors. The civic calendar and other aspects of the civic information system should be geared to the timing of issues as they emerge for citizen concern and action at all levels of government and community organization. All of this can be done in a balanced nonpartisan fashion that could help counteract the biases that creep into the information activities of less objective media.

Of course, many of these things are being done, more or less systematically, by many libraries. The fact is, however, that a failure to perceive this function on a scale appropriate to its importance has kept many librarians from giving it the attention it deserves.

The time has come, as we approach the two-hundredth birthday of the Republic, for a new Declaration of the Civic Purpose of American Public Libraries. That declaration should recognize the special importance of civic education in the American system and its increasing importance in this age of growing complexity and accelerating change. It should relate the inevitable continuing revolution of today and tomorrow to the revolutionary purposes of the founders who saw in the fate of the American system a new hope for all mankind. *Civic* should mean *civilizing*. The library is a repository of accumulated knowledge, thought, and feeling from the past. Its immediate role is to help people relate this inheritance to the study of the future. In a sense, the library is a window on the future, illumined in part by light from the past. It should promote understanding of the essential continuity, rather, the essential unity, of past, present, and future. Behavior in terms of this understanding is of the essence of civilization, or of that liberating, progressive order that is essential to the good and the better life.

The declaration should not be limited to high-level generalization. Like the Declaration of Independence, it should include a bill of particulars on the people's right and duty to know, suggesting some of the things on which the complete citizen must have constantly updated knowledge and some of the ways in which the library should help him get it.

As for the civilizing function of the library, which is the context in which civic education belongs, no one has put it better than Philip Roth in an article in the *New York Times*, March 1, 1969. Mr. Roth, whose book *Goodybye, Columbus* was set in part in the Newark Public Library, was inspired, or provoked, into writing the piece by the Newark Library crisis of 1969. It read, in part, as follows:

When I was growing up in Newark in the forties we were taught, or perhaps just assumed, that the books in the public library belonged to the public. Since my family did not own many books, or have very much money for a child to buy them, it was good to know that solely by virtue of my citizenship, I had the use of any of the books I wanted from that grandly austere building downtown on Washington Street, or the branch library I could walk to in my neighborhood. But even more compelling was this idea of communal ownership, property held in common for the common good. Why I had to care for the books I borrowed, return them unscarred and on time, was because they weren't my property alone, they were everybody's. That idea had as much to do with civilizing me as any idea I was ever to come upon in the books themselves.

If the idea was civilizing, so was the place, with its enforced quiet, its orderly shelves, and its knowledgeable, dutiful employees *who weren't teachers*. The library wasn't just where one had to go to get the books; it was as much a kind of exacting haven to which a city youngster willingly went to get his lesson in restraint, to learn a little more about solitude, privacy, silence and self-control.

And then there was the lesson in order. The institution itself was the instructor. What trust it inspired—in oneself and in systems—to decode the message on the catalogue cards; then to make it through the network of corridors and staircases into the stacks; and there to find, exactly where it was supposed to be, the right book. For a ten-year-old to be able to steer himself through thousands of books to the very one he wants is not without its civilizing influence, either. Nor did it go for nothing to carry a library card around in one's pocket; to pay a fine; to sit in a strange place, beyond the reach of home or schools, and finally, to take back across the city and into one's home a book with a local history of its own, a Newark family-tree of readers to which one's own name had now been added.

If the American system is to succeed over time in both liberating and harnessing the creative and cooperative, rather than the destructively competitive, impulses of its people, it will be because they become increasingly civilized in the sense suggested by Mr. Roth's testament to the library. No system of government relies more fully on the civilized behavior of its citizens. No institution has more, proportionately, to offer the cultivation of this behavior than the public library.

6 Some Alternatives for the Public Library

Edward C. Banfield

The public library has more users and more money today than ever before, but it lacks a purpose.[1] It is trying to do some things that it probably cannot do, and it is doing others that it probably should not do. At the same time, it is neglecting what may be its real opportunities. What the library needs is, first, a purpose that is both in accord with the realities of present-day city life and implied by some general principles and, second, a program that is imaginatively designed to carry its purpose into effect.

This paper will begin with a brief look at the principles justifying *public* action. (Why should a public body distribute reading matter and not, say, shoes?) In the light of these principles, it will then consider what the public library has been, what it is now, and what it ought to be.

Some General Principles

Economists offer several justifications for governmental intervention to set the demand for a commodity or good (in this case library service).[2] One justification exists when the good is of such a nature that it cannot be supplied to some consumers without at the same time being supplied to all—examples are national defense and air pollution control; in such cases, it is impossible for the distributor of the good to charge a price for it, since he cannot withhold it from anyone who refuses to pay the price. Therefore (apart from philanthropists) only the government, which through its tax power can coerce everyone into paying, is in a position to offer the service. Clearly this justification has no application to libraries.

Another justification—and one that presumably *does* apply to the library—exists when the public will benefit in some way if the consumer consumes more (or less) of the good than he would if the government

An earlier version of this paper appeared in *The Public Library and the City*, ed. R. W. Conant (Cambridge, Mass.: The MIT Press, 1965). The revised version, which appears here, was prepared for *Urban Government*, revised edition, ed. Edward C. Banfield (New York: The Free Press, 1969).

did not concern itself in the matter. If my consumption of a good—my immunizing myself against disease or my sending my children to school, for example—confers benefits of some kind upon the community at large, the government ought, in the community's interest if not in mine, to see to it that I consume a proper amount of it. In order to encourage consumption of such "merit goods" (to use an economist's term), the government may employ subsidies.

That consumption of certain goods confers benefits upon the community does not automatically justify government subsidies, however. No doubt, it is a good thing from a public standpoint that I eat well, have a safe roof over my head, and go to the doctor when I am sick. But if I am compos mentis and not indigent, the chances are that I will look after these matters without any encouragement from the government. The public does not have to pay me to eat; I will do so both because I must in order to stay alive and because I enjoy eating.

Public intervention to set the demand does not necessarily involve public production or distribution of the good. The school board sets the demand for school books, but it does not hire authors to write them, and it does not operate its own printing press. The Air Force sets the demand for planes, but it does not manufacture them.

By the same token, that a good is produced or distributed under public auspices does not imply the necessity of a public subsidy for the people who consume it. The function of the government may in some instances be merely to make up for a deficiency in the private market by offering consumers a good that from the standpoint of the community they ought to have and that for some reason no private enterprise offers. If no one saw fit to go into the shoe business, the government would have to. But if it went into the shoe business, it would not have to give shoes away or sell them for less than the cost of manufacture.

The Nineteenth-Century Purpose

Let us now look at the public library of the past in the light of these principles. In the very beginning, libraries were private associations for the joint use of a facility that was too expensive for any but the well-off to own individually. Some state legislatures conferred on the associations certain corporate powers, including the power to tax their members provided that a two-thirds majority concurred. They did this on the grounds that benefits to the community at large would ensue—that is, that library service satisfied a "merit want." "These libraries," Franklin remarks in his autobiography, "have improved the general conversation of Americans, made the common tradesmen and farmers as intelligent as most gentlemen from other countries, and perhaps have contributed in some degree to the stand so generally made throughout the colonies in defense of their privileges." Early in the nineteenth century charitable societies were formed in the larger cities "to furnish wholesome religious, moral, and improving reading of all kinds to the poor, cheaper than they now get fanatical or depraved reading." There were complaints that the books circulated were not improving enough (a director of the Astor Library in New York wrote that "the young fry . . . employ all the hours they are out of school in reading the trashy, as Scott, Cooper, Dickens, Punch, and the 'Illustrated News' "), to which the reply was made that "if people will not come to your library you may as well establish none." No one, however, would have justified a charitable library on the grounds that it provided entertainment.[3]

Later on, the corporations thus created were made public and were supported in part by taxation of the whole public. This was about the middle of the last century, when bright and ambitious farm boys who had mastered the 3 Rs but not much else were flocking to the cities to seek their fortunes. "Mechanics libraries" were established to afford these Alger characters opportunities to pick up by home study the small amount of technical knowledge that then existed. Such libraries were not supported in full by the public—philanthropists provided most of the support—but they were tax exempt and they enjoyed other advantages. There were good reasons for giving them these advantages: anything that encouraged self-improvement on the part of the "respectable poor" tended to increase the productivity and wealth of the community. Besides, to the Anglo-Saxon Protestant elite that ran the cities, self-improvement appeared good in and of itself.

It was not until near the turn of the century, however, that most sizable cities had public libraries in the present-day sense. There was no doubt about the public purpose of these libraries. They were to facilitate the assimilation of European immigrants into the urban, middle-class American style of life.

Many of the immigrants were highly receptive to what the library offered. Many of them came from cultures that respected books and learning; with few exceptions they were eager to learn the language and customs of their new country and to get ahead in a material way. There was, accordingly, a high degree of harmony between the public purposes being sought through the library and the motives and aspirations of its potential clientele.

Times Have Changed

Today the situation is entirely different. The Horatio Alger characters and the immigrants have long since passed from the scene. There are, to be sure, more poor people in the large cities than ever (they are not as poor in absolute terms, however, and they constitute a smaller proportion of the metropolitan area's population), and the movement of the poor from backward rural areas of the South and Puerto Rico into the cities is likely to continue for some time to come. The present-day poor, however, represent a new and different problem. Their poverty consists not so much of a lack of income (although they lack that) as of a lack of the cultural standards and of the motivations, including the desire for self-improvement and for "getting ahead," that would make them more productive and hence better paid. "The culturally deprived of today's cities are not on the bottom of a ladder; they do not even know that one exists," the editor of a bulletin for librarians, and coeditor of this volume, has written in an article extremely apposite to the present discussion.[4] Many of the poor are "functionally illiterate," some though they have gone to, or even graduated from, high school. Giving them access to books will not accomplish anything.

Assimilating the lower class into the working and the middle classes may be a public purpose of the highest urgency. (Some people, of course, assert that lower-class values—certain of them, at any rate—are as worthy of respect as any others.) But however compelling the case for assimilation is thought to be, the question has to be faced of whether the library is a fit instrument for the purpose.

Certainly no one believes that the library is now of any service to the lower class. By and large, libraries are of the middle class and for the middle class. With rare exceptions, librarians have the wrong skin color, the wrong style of dress and make-up, the wrong manner of speech, and the wrong values (among other things, they think that people should be quiet in the library!) to be acceptable to the lower class. The feeling is mutual, moreover, for most librarians are probably no freer of class and race prejudice than are other middle-class whites. The consequence is that the lower class is repelled by the library or would be if it ever got near it.

A few library boards have tried to change this but have not had much success. Some will say that their methods have not been sufficiently ingenious: they should establish storefront libraries and staff them with lower-class librarians, preferably radical ones; they should employ super-salesmen to go from door to door selling cheap reprints, and so on.

If one believes that lower-class adults can be enticed to read, there is much to be said for making this a primary purpose of the library and for trying any approach that offers the least promise. It may be, however, that the educational level of the lower class is so low and its demoralization so great that no efforts on the part of the library will have much effect. Something much more fundamental than library service may be needed—for example, compulsory nursery school attendance from the age of two or three.

Not being able or willing (or both) to serve the lower class, the public library has tended to make itself an adjunct of the school, especially of the middle-class school. Children have always been an important group of library users, but in recent years they have become the principal clientele of the public library in many places. Children sent by teachers to use books in connection with course assignments crowd some libraries after school hours to such an extent that adult users have to leave. (In certain Los Angeles schools, teachers require each pupil to borrow at least one book a week from the public library!) Here and there libraries have been forced by the sheer weight of the children's numbers to place limits on service to them.

One reason for this invasion is that, thanks to the "baby boom" of a few years ago, there are more children than ever. Another is that the schools do not have adequate libraries of their own. Still another reason is that it has become fashionable among teachers to require research papers (in some places third-graders swarm into the public library to do "research") and to assign, not a single textbook, but a list of readings, some in very short supply, selected by the teacher from a variety of sources.

Public libraries were not designed for large numbers of children and are usually not staffed to handle them. The wear and tear on books, librarians, and innocent bystanders is therefore very great. In Brooklyn, it was recently reported, book losses—not all of them caused by children—run to 10 percent of the library budget. In some places rowdyism is a serious problem.

In fairness to both the children and the adults, the schools ought to have adequate libraries of their own. Children should not be excluded from public libraries, however—it is a good thing for them to go now and then to a place with a decidedly adult atmosphere—but they should not be sent there to do assignments; they should go to the public library on their own initiative to find books that please them and in the expectation of entering a world that is not juvenile.

The Light Reader

Apart from schoolchildren, the most numerous category of library users consists of light readers, especially middle-class housewives. The books these readers borrow are not *all* light, of course, and even the ones that are light are not the very lightest; public librarians do not buy out-and-out trash. Nevertheless, a considerable part of the circulation is of romantic novels, westerns, detective stories, and books on how to repair leaky faucets, take off excess fat, and make money playing the stock market. About one-half of the books public libraries lend to adults are fiction, and most of these are probably light fiction. (Unfortunately, libraries do not use more precise categories than "fiction" and "nonfiction" in their record keeping.)

It is hard to see how encouraging light reading can be regarded as a public purpose. That the housewife finds it convenient to get her detective story from a public, rather than a rental, library is certainly not a justification for the public library. Her neighbor, who may not care to borrow books and whose income may be less than hers, will be coerced into paying taxes to support a facility that is for her convenience. Why should he be? Whether she gets to sleep by reading a novel, by watching the late show, or by taking a sleeping pill—indeed, whether she gets to sleep at all—is a matter of indifference to him and to the community at large.

If it could be shown that light reading leads to serious reading, a justification for public action would exist. In the case of uneducated people who are introduced to books by the library, such a showing might possibly be made. But it is highly unlikely that it can be made in the case of the middle-class readers who constitute most of the adult library users. For the most part, light reading leads to nothing except more light reading.

Unless reason can be found for believing that light reading confers some benefit upon the community, the public library should leave the light reader to the rental library, the drugstore, and the supermarket. If for some reason these readers *must* be served by the public library, they should be charged the full cost of the service, including, of course, a fair share of the rental value of the library building and site. Charging the full cost of service would soon put the public library out of the light reading business, but this would prove to be a benefit even from the standpoint of the light reader. He would find that when the public library stopped competing with rental libraries by giving its service free, they and other profit-making enterprises (the paperback counters of the drugstore and supermarket, for example) would fill the gap and give him better service than he got before. If there is a demand for thirty copies of *Peyton Place*, the rental library makes haste to put that many on its shelves. The public library, not being under the stimulus of the profit motive and (let us hope) feeling itself under some obligation to serve more important purposes, buys only one or two copies of such a book if it buys any at all. This, of course, accounts for the more than 3,500 rental libraries (not to mention the drugstore and supermarket counters) that are competing successfully with the tax-supported libraries.

The Serious Reader
The proper business of the public library is with the *serious* reader and—assuming that the library cannot be an effective instrument for educating the lower class—with him alone. "Serious" reading is any that improves one's stock of knowledge, enlarges one's horizons, or improves one's values. Reasonable men will disagree as to where the boundary

should be drawn between light and serious reading; that does not render the distinction invalid or useless, however, although it will lead to some practical difficulties.

The commonsense assumption is that all serious reading confers some benefit upon the community. This would be hard to demonstrate in a rigorous way (imagine trying to specify the amounts and kinds of benefits conferred upon various sectors of the community by, say, so many man-years of novel reading, so many of historical reading, and so on); but the difficulty, or impossibility, of demonstrating it does not mean that the assumption is wrong.

That an activity confers benefits upon the community does not, however (as was remarked before), constitute a sufficient justification for publicly supporting it. Perhaps those who read serious books would read as many of them if public libraries did not exist. (Indeed, conceivably they might read more of them, for if an existing institution did not stand in the way, a new and more effective one, public or private, might come into existence. Any foreigner who has observed the operation of the government salt and tobacco monopoly in Italy will agree that other and better ways of distributing these commodities are possible. To the Italian who has never been abroad, however, the idea of putting the government out of the salt and tobacco business might seem preposterous. "How then," he might ask, "could one possibly obtain these indispensable articles?") Most serious readers have adequate or more than adequate family incomes; it seems likely that if they had to pay the full cost of their reading they would not read less. If this is so, there is no reason for the public to subsidize their reading.

The relatively few serious readers who are poor—so poor that to pay for library service would entail a sacrifice of something else that is necessary to an adequate standard of living—present a problem. They would of course be given service at reduced rates or free. This is widely done by colleges, and there is no reason why there should not be "library scholarships" for all who need them. If such an arrangement involved use of an objectionable means test (would it be objectionable to give service free to all families with incomes of less than $5,000 if the user's statement that he belonged to that category were accepted without question?) or if the costs of record keeping were unduly high, the sensible thing would be to make the service—the standard service, not necessarily special services—free to all.

If it is decided that serious reading must be subsidized in order to secure for the community all of the benefits that it wants, it need not follow that the best thing for the library board to do is to own and circulate a collection of books. There may be much better ways of accomplishing the purpose. Perhaps, for example, those who have responsibility for allocating the library fund—let us now call it the "fund to encourage serious reading"—would get a greater return on the investment by inducing the local supermarket to display a big stock of quality paperbacks and to have one-cent sales of them now and then. Or, again, perhaps the fund would best be used to subsidize the rent of a dealer in used books who, because of the ravages of urban renewal or for other reasons, could not otherwise stay in business.

Some Illustrative Ideas

If one assumes, however, that such radical innovations are out of the question and that the practical problem is to make some minor changes in the existing institution, what might be done?

Here are a few suggestions.

1. Provide soundproofed cubicles that readers may rent by the week or month and in which they may keep under lock and key books (subject to call, of course), a typewriter (rented, if that is what they want), and manuscripts. Nowadays few people have space at home for a study. Many libraries have reading rooms, but there are no places where one can read, let alone write, in privacy and comfort. (A habitual smoker, for example, cannot read if he is not permitted to smoke.) The New York Public Library on 42nd Street is probably the only public library with cubicles (they are supported by an endowment); there is a long waiting list for them.

2. Offer the services of a "personal shopper" to take orders by phone and to arrange home deliveries and pickups. Many readers are too busy to go to the library, especially when there is no more than an off-chance that the book they want is in. The personal shopper could also arrange fast interlibrary loans and for the photocopying of hard-to-get, out-of-print books. (Publishers naturally object to the copying of copyrighted

material. But perhaps they could be persuaded to give libraries general permission to make one copy per library of works that are not available for sale.) A fair number of the larger libraries have had "readers' advisers" ever since WPA days; the advisers' time is usually entirely taken up by children, however; in any case, only handicapped persons are assisted in absentia.

3. Buy a large enough stock of *serious* books so that no reader will have to wait more than, say, two weeks for a copy. Bentham's remark about justice can be paraphrased here: "Reading delayed is reading denied."

4. Display prominently and review in library newsletters those current books that are not widely reviewed by "middlebrow" journals. Many people suppose that all worthwhile books are listed, if not actually reviewed, by the better newspapers and magazines. This is not the case. Scholarly books are ignored as often as not; some of them are unknown to most serious readers. The natural tendency of the library is to make a fuss about the very books that the ordinary reader would be most likely to hear of anyway. It should try instead to make up for the deficiencies of the commercial institutions by calling attention to the less advertised books.

5. Maintain up-to-date, annotated bibliographies of the sort that would help introduce a layman to a specialized field. A physician, let us suppose, wants to know what social science has to say that is relevant to problems of medical organization. What books and journals should he look at first? If the library had a file of reading lists, course outlines, and syllabuses used in colleges and universities, together with bibliographical notes and articles from academic journals, he could be helped to make his way into the subject. A good many of the better libraries have materials of this sort—more materials, probably, than most of their serious readers realize. Even so, there is probably a good deal of room for improvement in both the quality of the materials that are collected and the methods by which they are made known to library users.

6. Offer tutorial service for readers who want instruction or special assistance. Perhaps the physician would like to discuss his questions with a social scientist. The library might have a social scientist on its staff or it might bring one in as a consultant from a nearby college or university. The tutor would be available for an hour's discussion or, at the other extreme, to give a short course.

99 SOME ALTERNATIVES FOR THE PUBLIC LIBRARY

7. Have a mail-order counter supplied with a directory of all books in print, a list of available government publications, and the catalogs of some dealers in used and hard-to-find books. A librarian should be on hand to help buyers find what they want. In the many towns and small cities that are without proper bookstores, this kind of service might go a long way toward making up for the lack.

The Library's Failure Is Typical
The library is by no means the only public institution that with passage of time has ceased to serve its original purpose and has not acquired a new one that can be justified on any general principles. Very likely it could be shown: (1) that the professionals most involved, and a fortiori everyone else, have given little serious thought to the nature of the purposes that presumably justify not only public libraries but also public parks, museums, schools, and renewal projects (to mention only a few activities of the sort that are in question); (2) that such purposes as might plausibly be advanced to justify such activities are ill-served, or not served at all, by the activities as presently conducted; (3) that these purposes could usually be better served by the market (rigged perhaps by public authorities) than by public ownership and operation; (4) that in most cases using the market would result in greater consumption of the good and in less waste in the supplying of it (public institutions tend to offer too much of those goods that are in light demand and not enough of those that are in heavy demand); and (5) that certain goods not offered by private institutions are not offered by public ones either, in spite of the fact that increased consumption of these goods would confer relatively large benefits upon the community at large.

To find the reasons for this state of affairs, one must look deep into the nature of our institutions and of our political culture. Organizations tend to perpetuate themselves and therefore to embrace whatever opportunities come along, however unrelated these may be to any previously stated purposes. Public organizations, moreover, often exist as much to symbolize something as to accomplish something. These are only two of many considerations that doubtless should be taken into account.

Notes
1. For evidence, see the report of the eighty-fourth annual conference of the American Library Association, *New York Times*, July 4, 1966, p. 40. The theme

of the conference was "Libraries for a Great Society," and the president of the association announced that an inventory of public and school library needs made by the U.S. Office of Education and the association revealed that $3.1 billion would have to be spent to bring the nation's libraries to the level of "adequacy" and operating budgets would have to be raised $1.2 billion a year to keep them there. "These are enormous figures, of course," he said, "but our wealthy nation can easily contribute all that is called for and then some." With regard to the library's purpose, he seems to have said nothing.

2. See Richard Musgrave, *The Theory of Public Finance* (New York: McGraw-Hill Book Company, 1959), Chapter 1.

3. David B. Tyack, *George Tichnor and the Boston Brahmins* (Cambridge, Mass.: Harvard University Press, 1967), pp. 208–211.

4. Kathleen Molz, "The Public Library: The People's University?" *The American Scholar* 34, no. 1 (Winter 1964–1965): 100. The author wishes to express his appreciation of Miss Molz's criticism of an earlier draft of this paper.

7 The Public Library in Perspective

Jesse H. Shera

John Keats, in a mood that might be characterized as somewhat less than inspired, penned the lines:

The sun from meridian heights
Illumined the depths of the sea,
And the fishes, beginning to sweat,
Cried, "Damn it, how hot we shall be."

These words, which are not entirely metaphorical but can be taken with a certain degree of literalness, describe the plight of the public librarian today; for he, like the fishes, is learning what it is to be in hot water. Caught in a paradoxical time of inflation and deflation, and with the current concept of the public library being brought into question, the public librarian finds his institution squeezed between rising costs and shrinking income. Thus, it is more important than ever that he understand his responsibilities and the role of the organization of which he is a part. To comprehend fully that role, he must begin with the historic origins of the public library itself.

The American public library was born of the Renaissance, was nurtured in the Enlightenment, and came to fruition in the early years of the Republic when democracy, supported by universal public education, seemed the perfect answer to every social ill. Like so many of today's public services, public libraries began as voluntary associations, little groups of individuals who banded together to form "social libraries" so that they might secure collectively the books that individually they could not afford or were denied because of a very severely limited book supply. Benjamin Franklin founded his Junto to provide young artisans an opportunity to discuss the important social current of the day; his Library Company was designed to provide books and even scientific apparatus, to enrich the intellectual lives of the young artisans of Philadelphia, to familiarize them with the best thought of the ages, and in other ways to improve their careers.

The public library, then, has its origins in voluntary associations of the community's ambitious intellectuals who wanted to procure for themselves access to those books that up to that time had been available to only an economically privileged few. The principle of voluntary associations, the importance of which Tocqueville was the first to point out, was peculiarly American, and these loosely formalized structures are, as Hannah Arendt has said, "*ad hoc* organizations that pursue short term goals and disappear when the goal has been reached."[1] Historians of American librarianship have tended to neglect the role of the voluntary association in the emergence of the public library. To quote Tocqueville, "In no country in the world has the principle of association been more successfully used or applied to a greater multitude of objects than in America";[2] and again, "nothing . . . is more deserving of our attention than the moral and intellectual associations of America."[3] These voluntary library associations, of which Benjamin Franklin's Philadelphia Library Company appears to have been the first on this side of the Atlantic, exemplified a contractual relationship, a social covenant modeled, not on the Hobbesian form wherein the individual concludes an agreement with a secular authority to ensure his safety, for the protection of which he relinquishes all rights and powers, but rather on Locke's aboriginal contract, which brought about an alliance among all the individual members who had contracted for their form of organizational control after they had mutually bound themselves for the purpose of achieving certain ends. This contract limited the power of the individual member but kept intact the power of society. Often these voluntary associations were eventually taken over and operated by local government, and, as will be seen later, this trend did occur in the case of the public library.

The voluntary associations formed for the support of library book collections, which flourished and spread rapidly along the Eastern Seaboard from New England to the Carolinas during the end of the eighteenth century and up to the period of the Civil War, assumed a variety of corporate forms: joint-stock companies, simple membership associations, and other variations of collectivization. During the Colonial period these associations were often chartered individually by the Crown, thus making them legal corporate entities, and after the formation of the Republic, by the governments of the several states. By the beginning of the nineteenth century a few state governments, notably in New York

and New England, enacted general permissive legislation that allowed
the organization of library associations without the need for special
legislative action for each individual company. Thus these so-called
social libraries were permitted to register a corporate name, hold real
and intangible property, elect officers, sue and be sued, adopt a corporate seal, and otherwise conduct themselves as legal entities. At the
outset, the collections of these social libraries were quite general, but
not many decades had passed before they began to assume, in some
instances, specialized functions to meet the needs of a particular clientele. Thus there emerged the mercantile libraries for the merchants'
clerks, libraries for mechanics' apprentices, libraries for lawyers, minis-
ters, doctors, and other professionals. There were children's libraries
and, especially in the state of Michigan, libraries exclusively for women.
A variety of means was employed for the support of these voluntary
associations: the sale of stock was subject to an annual "tax" on each
share, the returns providing a continuing, though modest, income for
the purchase of new books. Membership fees were an obvious and preva-
lent source of revenue, and the annual auctioning of new books for the
privilege of being the first, or early, borrower was not uncommon.
Income was also collected from social events and raffles, and, in a very
few instances, even the principle of the tontine was employed until it
was prohibited by law.

Yet the means of support, however ingenious, was always inadequate,
so that by the middle of the nineteenth century it was becoming increasingly clear that the shifting sands of voluntary association provided an
unstable foundation for library demands. Even such relatively prosperous associations as the Library Company of Philadelphia, the Boston
Athenaeum, and the Redwood Library of New Port, Rhode Island,
more than once came dangerously close to bankruptcy. Tax support
from the local treasury was the only viable alternative. So social libraries, which in their heyday formed something very closely akin to a
modern public library system, all but disappeared. Often their books
were scattered and lost after initial enthusiasm had waned, or they were
taken over by the community to form a public library as a legitimate
part of local government. The Salisbury, Connecticut, town library of
the early 1800s and the town library of Peterborough, New Hampshire,

which flourished in the 1830s, were but harbingers of what was inevitably to come; and when the Boston Public Library opened its doors in 1854, the doom of the social library was all but sealed.

The annals of the public library and its precursors, then, recapitulate those of many public services today. The voluntary associations played an important role in the inauguration of such services as care for the poor, the provision of a municipal water supply, the fighting of fires, police protection, and other social functions that today are taken for granted as proper responsibilities of the municipality, county, or state. Thus, the library became a recognized part of the public sector and was sanctioned by legislative fiat. The principle of voluntary association passed from the actual *formation* of libraries to consideration of the best means for improving the utility of libraries (witness the Librarians' Conference of 1853) and then to the *promotion* of libraries as a civic good and an instrument of social reform.

Sidney Ditzion has shown in his *Arsenals of a Democratic Culture* that those who were promoting the public library during the closing decades of the nineteenth century charged the public library, by implication if not by positive injunction, with the responsibility to provide those materials and services that would enable the user to perform adequately his obligations as an enlightened citizen. An enlightened citizenry, these advocates of the public library rightly argued, was essential to a democracy, and it was the major role of the library to see that the responsible citizen was provided with the basis for his enlightenment.

It is important to remember, however, that the public library did not come into being as a result of a popular, or grass-roots, movement. One cannot but wonder what the future of even the tax-supported public library might have been without the tremendous stimulus given to it by the philanthropy of Andrew Carnegie and a multitude of lesser donors. That there are public libraries today is largely the result of the work of a few individuals who believed in them, worked tirelessly for them, and enlisted the support of benefactors of great, or even modest, wealth. That this accomplishment occurred is the result of the American faith in the importance of universal popular education and a sense of local pride—a belief, even by those who never darkened its doors, that a public library, "is a good thing for a community to have."

Though the association libraries had been economically impoverished, their book collections were directly responsive to the needs and desires of their clientele. In this sense, they approached the most efficient type of library—the personal library of the gentleman scholar. But in the origins of the public library there exists a paradox, an aristocratic or elite institution grafted upon a democratic cultural base. This paradox is further intensified by the fact that the public library is now part of the public sector, as a heritage from the private sector, and the public sector is unbounded, that is, not sharply defined. America has always been ambivalent about books and reading, a curious mixture of veneration for the scholar with an often ill-concealed contempt for "book larnin'." Small wonder that the public library became uncertain about where it stood, or what it was supposed to be doing.

Librarians have tried to escape from the dilemma of choosing between the needs of the elite and those of the populace by insisting that they should serve the "general reader"; but there is no "general reader" any more than there is an "economic man." Every reader is unique, special, or atypical. To chart a course for the public library in the troubled waters of a society that has no clear-cut goals of its own requires a skill that probably transcends that of any navigator. Public librarians only intensified their problems when, at the turn of the present century, they ceased thinking about their role as masters of the bibliographic resources of the culture and became professionally self-conscious. One could well argue that the birth of the American Library Association and its chapter satellites in the states, another manifestation of Tocqueville's voluntary associations, was a professional step. In short, the public librarians began to think, not of function and service, but of status. It was no accident that the organization was named the American *Library* Association. The library as organization became the focus of the librarians' collective thought. Thus, the American Library Association, like other voluntary associations, emerged as a pressure group, a lobby. At that point the librarians turned a corner and began to proselytize. They even erected library schools, as sacrifical goats, to atone for their professionals sins. To express this transformation another way, the public library movement in the United States passed from the earlier biblio-centered, or centripital, organization to one that was promotional, or centrifugal-centered; and in this transition the true objectives of the public library, for example, the classic statement set forth as the first report of the Boston Public Library, were obscured.

"Americans still regard association," again to quote Arendt, "as the only means they have for acting, and rightly so. In short, as soon as several of the inhabitants of the United States have taken up an opinion or a feeling which they wish to promote in the world, or have found some fault they wish to correct, they look out for mutual assistance, and as soon as they have found one another out they combine. From that moment, they are no longer isolated men but a power seen from afar, whose actions serve as an example and whose language is listened to."[4] As Tocqueville has said, "the citizens who form the minority associate in order, first, to show their numerical strength and so to diminish the moral power of the majority."[5] To be sure, it has been a long time since moral and intellectual associations could be found among voluntary associations—which, on the contrary, seem to have been formed only for the protection of special interests, of pressure groups and the lobbyists who represented them in Washington.

What then, one may properly ask, is the purpose of the public library? To answer such a question it is necessary to look first at the generic role of the library, what the library can and should do and what no other agency in society does, or at least can do as well. The function of the library, regardless of its nature or clientele, should be to maximize the social utility of graphic records for the benefit of the individual and, through the individual, of society. The library, as a social invention, was brought into being because graphic records are essential to the development and progress of culture; hence it is important that the citizen have access to those resources that will best enable him to operate effectively in his several roles as a member of society. The public library, as its name implies, has been predicated on the assumption that it could meet this objective for all strata of the population. It was probably the concept of a "general reader" that pushed public librarians into professional self-consciousness and made them no longer bibliographic specialists, or experts, but administrators and promoters, thus shifting the emphasis from the library as intellectual resource to the library as organization, until today the most striking characteristic of the public library is that it lacks a sense of direction. The situation is intensified by the confusion of the typical public librarian, and the consequences of this uncertainty cannot be avoided by saying that because the public library is part of the public sector it is necessarily unbounded.

If the public library cannot develop a clearly defined and generally recognized sense of social purpose, society is not likely to continue to support it. Policy should lie in the area where cognition—the understanding of the facts—and conceptualization—or judgment—join, but librarians, despite pretensions to "research," have not sought out the priorities with sufficient thoroughness and objectivity, and those that have been accepted have not been judiciously evaluated; hence policy has been all but neglected.

With librarians in such a state of confusion it is not surprising that Kathleen Molz has lamented:

Society, with its . . . view that the public should get what it pays for, has so chipped away at the concept of the public library that, in all too many communities, it has become little more than an informational hodgepodge, furnishing its staff and resources as a solver of riddles for the community's contestants, a reference arm for the burden of community homework, and a supplier of cheap best sellers for the titillation of the middle class.[6]

Yet, twenty years before she wrote, the accuracy of her statement was amply revealed by Bernard Berelson's study, *The Library's Public*, for the Public Library Inquiry.

Public librarians have failed to grasp the importance of the fact that the public library began as an "elite" enterprise and that every attempt to superimpose it on a mass population has failed or, at best, has had a kind of half-success, so long as a philanthropic agent gave it support. When the public library began to relinquish its appeal to serious reading interests and substituted for this traditional role the accumulation of trivia, in the hope of attracting more readers to its doors, it dissipated its resources, forsook its ancient responsibilities, and betrayed its heritage. A public library cannot contribute to the enlightenment of a responsible citizenry and at the same time stock its shelves with tawdry fiction that can be purchased at every corner drugstore or newsstand.

A generation ago Douglas Waples told a conference at the University of

Chicago that over the cash registers in many restaurants hung a sign that read, "We have an agreement with the banks—they will serve no food and we will cash no checks." Waples, in a spirit not entirely facetious, proposed a comparable sign for the public library, "We have made an agreement with the drugstore—it will keep no books of lasting value and we will keep nothing else." Robert D. Leigh, when dean of the School of Library Service at Columbia University, denied Alvin Johnson's thesis that the public library is "the people's university," saying that it is "the *library* of the people's university." Of course, an agency such as the library can change its function, but it should be aware of what it is doing and what the consequences may be. The public library cannot, and should not, try to pander to every reading taste, or lack of taste, for if it does it will be like the fabled chameleon, which turned red when put on a red cloth, green when on a green cloth, but died of vexation when placed on a Scotch plaid.

To say that the public library exists for the benefit of the serious reader is not as snobbish as it may sound. The public library should, of course, be freely available to all the people, but we as librarians should not be surprised or dismayed if it is used by only a relatively small proportion of the people. Nor should we so betray our professional responsibilities that we load its shelves with inferior reading matter. Such a policy brings discredit upon us as librarians and will end in futility. Ardent zealots, in their enthusiasm for the preservation of "intellectual freedom," have so distorted their laudable objective that many are now fearful of excluding any book, however trivial or unworthy, for fear of being charged with practicing censorship.

To the protests of the young activists at the ALA convention in Atlantic City in 1969, William S. Dix, in his inaugural address as president of the association, replied:

Libraries do many things, and we who work in them have many tasks, but central to everything that they and we do is the contact between reader and book. It is to facilitate and stimulate this contact that we exist. I submit that our most effective response to the challenge of these difficult and exciting times may be to do better—much better—what we have always tried to do.

"To do better . . . what we have always tried to do." But over the years the public library has tried to do many things: "self-improvement," adult education, "Great Books" discussion groups, storytelling hours, civic meetings, motion picture programs, outreach to the disadvantaged, aid to the immigrant, courses aimed at the eradication of illiteracy, and on and on. One can properly argue that all of these things are good in themselves, but whether or not they are appropriate to the public library or whether they could be better done by some other agency has not seriously been examined by the community. Instead, there has been a tendency for the library to hop on every bandwagon that seems even remotely associated with the use of books, in the hope of widening the library's popular appeal and hence strengthening public support for increased financing. Many of these ventures have met with indifferent success, and it is doubtful whether they have contributed in any important way to the improvement of the reputation of the library as a social or community force. Rather than dissipating their energies in these marginal activities, librarians might better invest their time in attempting to make the public aware of the potential the library has for assisting the patron in his serious reading interests and needs.

One can argue that, in a sense, the public library has been oversold or at least sold in the wrong way: sold in the manner promoted by National Library Week. Librarians have generally found it easier to promote than to produce—easier to create expectations than to develop a staff with the expertise to fulfill them. "Society is our trustees; it is to society that we are responsible," Dr. Francis Peabody once told the medical profession, and what he said of medicine is equally true for librarianship. Consciously or unconsciously, Dr. Peabody voiced sound general systems theory. When a subsystem fails to produce in the way the larger system requires and in terms of that system's orientation, the subsystem is either modified or abolished. Most librarians will readily acknowledge that the library is but one segment of a system that is the communication network of society; but, failing to heed the tenets of systems theory, they are not aware that if society discovers a more effective means for gaining access to recorded knowledge than that provided by the public library, the public library will be rejected. In short, the public library has a perilous knife-edge to travel and the public library may fail.

Not all the blame for the library's shortcomings, however, can be

placed on the librarians. In the final analysis, it is the library trustees
who must assume the responsibility. The community generally fails to
provide a local library board with competence and insight appropriate
to its responsibilities. All too often board members are political appoint-
ees who are neither qualified for their tasks nor aware of their need to
seek professional advice from librarians and other specialists. Library
trustees are involved in, or make, decisions on the choice of a head
librarian; the location and construction of the physical plant; the allocation of resources; the responsibility for determining whether, how,
and for what amounts they should use pressure on local authorities for
the release of funds for library support; and all other matters subsumed
under the heading of "policy." The key decisions, then, are beyond the
control of librarians, however well informed and well intentioned they
may be—even to the matter of a choice of a director of the system in
which they operate. It is for this reason that inappropriate decisions are
often made, and the individual librarian is powerless to do much about
the predicament in which he finds himself.

Long before Bernard Berelson wrote of the library's public or Kathleen
Molz nailed her thesis to the library's paneled door, Mr. Dooley, that
perceptive critic of the American scene, addressed his friend Hennessy
on the same subject:

"Has Andhrew Carnaygie given ye a libry yet?" asked Mr. Dooley.
"Not that I know iv," said Mr. Hennessy.
"He will," said Mr. Dooley. "Ye'll not escape him. Befure he dies he
hopes to crowd a libry on ivry man, woman, an' child in th' counthry.
He's given thim to cities, towns, villages an' whistlin' stations. They're
tearin' down gas-houses an' poor houses to put up libries. Befure another
year, ivry house in Pittsburgh that ain't a blast-furnace will be a Carnaygie
libry. In some places all th' buildin's is libries. If ye write him f'r an
autygraft he sinds ye a libry. No beggar is iver turned impty-handed fr'm
th' dure. Th' panhandler knocks an' asts f'r a glass iv milk an' a roll.
" 'No sir,' says Andhrew Carnaygie, 'I will not pauperize this onworthy
man. Nawthin' is worse f'r a beggar-man thin to make a pauper iv him.
Yet it shall not be said iv me that I give nawthin' to th' poor. Saunders,
give him a libry, an' if he still insists on a roll tell him to roll th' libry.
F'r I'm humorous as well as wise,' he says."
"Does he give th' books?" asked Mr. Hennessy.
"Books?" says Mr. Dooley. "What ar-re ye talkin' about? D'ye know
what a libry is? I suppose ye think it's a place where a man can go, haul

down wan iv his favorite authors fr'm th' shelf, an' take a nap in it. That's not a Carnaygie libry. A Carnaygie libry is a large, brown-stone impenethrible buildin' with th' name iv th' maker blown on th' dure. Libry, fr'm th' Greek wurruds, libus, a book, an' ary, sildom—sildom a book. A Carnaygie libry is archytechoor, not lithrachoor."[7]

Today one can say with some truth that the library trustees stand in loco "Carnaygie."

Almost forty years ago the present writer argued that librarianship was suffering from the absence of a philosophical frame of reference for what it was attempting to do. He was told that a philosophy was indeed a very fine thing to have, though it wasn't really necessary, and that librarians were too preoccupied with trying to keep alive in the face of the Depression to worry about theory. Today the profession is paying the penalty of that neglect at a time when the current concept of the public library is being challenged on every hand.

A *paradigm*, as the term has been used by Thomas S. Kuhn in his stimulating and provocative study *The Structure of Scientific Revolutions* may be described as that body of techniques, principles, and theory by which a science—and, by extension, any human activity— is understood or defined. It is closely akin to Kenneth Boulding's "image." Thus a paradigm is, in fact, the scientific community's image of a science. The paradigm of phlogiston, for example, was shattered by the discovery of oxygen, the paradigm of Newtonian physics suffered a comparable fate with the work of Einstein, and the whole paradigm of physiology was transformed by Harvey's discovery of the circulation of the blood. In short, an old paradigm is shattered when it comes into conflict with a new paradigm, and what Kuhn says of the paradigms of science can generally be applied to the social sciences as well.

Today the paradigm of the public library, ill-defined though it may be, is being threatened by the new paradigm of information science, of which automation and systems theory are but manifestations. Any such challenge, of course, results in temporary confusion and turmoil, a period of unhappiness, in which those who earn their living from the old paradigm feel themselves insecure in, or "bewitched, bothered, and bewildered" by, the transition that is taking place. A society has a tremendous inertia built into it, an inertia that, in many instances, has been centuries in the making; so it is not surprising that society yields but stubbornly to any change. Often this inertia is sanctified by a whole body of religious belief and moral or ethical imperatives, which heighten the sense of disorientation and doubt.

The problem of dislocation arises not so much from the fact that our society is changing (society has always changed, often drastically in the past) but that the rate of change is accelerating, and there is real doubt as to whether society can redirect its values with sufficient rapidity to keep pace with the rate of change without catastrophe. One blinding flash over the sands of Alamogordo, and nothing would ever again be quite the same. There has always been a generation gap, but it is quite possible that never before have the young pressed so insistently and with such determination upon the heels of the old. It has been charged that man has too much knowledge, more knowledge than he can possibly assimilate and use, and the invention of new and devastating instruments of international homicide is cited to prove the point. Therefore, it has been argued, there should be a moratorium on science, which stands in the eyes of the public as a symbol of many of our social ills. Few arguments could be more fallacious; the defense against "too much knowledge" is more knowledge of the right kind. Man does not knowingly commit evil if he can rightly foresee the consequences of evil. Thus one may paraphrase an old horse-trader's observation about the animal that is his medium of exchange: Men are not by nature mean, but many men are stupid or ignorant and that makes them mean. The fault, dear Brutus, is not in knowledge but in ourselves that the world trembles on the brink of possible catastrophe.

Never, perhaps, has knowledge of information been more vital to the survival of the human race than it is today. On all sides our society is beset by social ills: overpopulation, war, destruction of the environment, racial conflict, prejudice, anti-intellectualism; one could go on and on. All the knowledge and wisdom that we can command will be required to solve these problems; certainly solutions will not be found through simple legislative action. As Vannevar Bush has written in *Pieces of the Action:*

We smile to ourselves as the cosmologists get this universe all sorted out to their satisfaction, and then find quasars which make them start all over again. The physicists build atom-smashers a mile long and discover so many sub-particles that they don't know what to do with them. The logicians struggle to pin down their language so that it will finally be precise, and then question whether it means anything whatever.

We cure disease and face population explosion. We struggle to modify our legal and political systems to cope with the changes all about us, and the changes outpace us and leave us still tangled. We make progress, lots of progress, in nearly every intellectual field, only to find that the more we probe, the faster our field of ignorance expands.[8]

But this distinguished honorary chairman of the board of the Massachusetts Institute of Technology and former president of the Carnegie Institution of Washington would not for a moment suggest that there should be any interruption in the growth of man's knowledge or a cessation in man's exploration of his physical and social environment. Indeed, he might agree that information and recorded knowledge may now be too important to be left to conventional methods of treatment. In fact, it was he who, a quarter of a century ago, envisaged the coming of Memex, that personalized information retrieval system that would, in a sense, make every man his own librarian.

Certainly one must admit that librarians have not done a very good job of disseminating information despite their dedication to their tasks. All too often they have indulged themselves in wishful thinking and self-delusion about what they are doing. They have talked optimistically about bibliotherapy, for example, without much evidence concerning the effect of reading upon human behavior. The present writer worries when librarians attempt to "play social worker," armed with nothing but a few books and a burning desire to "do good."

If one accepts the doctrine that the policy of any organization should be the product of a knowledge of the facts that relate to the organization, interpreted in the light of understanding and judgment, then it must follow that we need a far better knowledge and understanding of the facts that relate to the public library than we now possess. That knowledge of the facts probably can best be obtained through programs of well-directed research. We are not among those who believe that research is the only source of truth, and we have no intention of defending—if defense is possible—much of that amateurish counting that passes for library research. We are here arguing for research by scholars in many disciplines: anthropology, sociology, psychology, linguistics, and the physical sciences, all of which should be meaningfully related to and brought to bear upon library functions and operations. In recent years librarians have talked much about research, even to the point of making it a fetish, a tendency that has been stimulated by federal largess. But librarianship has never been research oriented, and librarians' attempts to engage in research, especially that relating to the public library, have been far from impressive. Moreover, the little valid research that has been done has not filtered into practice.

With the exception of Berelson's *The Library's Public*, there has been little significant research on the public library since the early work of Douglas Waples and some of his students at the University of Chicago. But today such research should be conducted by librarians with substantial assistance from a wide variety of other disciplines. The absence of a factual base for public library policy and operations is amply exemplified by a metropolitan library that, in developing a branch library to serve in a predominantly black community, staffed it with blacks, placed on its shelves Afro-American literature, and otherwise tried to make the installation attractive to its anticipated clientele, but located the facility next door to the district police station. The results were disappointing. The main users of the library proved to be little old ladies from a "retirement home" a short distance away. Attempts to extend library service to the disadvantaged have suffered because of a lack of information about what their book needs are. As a result of professional isolation, librarians continue to address themselves to such problems as the psychological factors that stimulate college graduates to choose librarianship as a career or how best to determine the extent and nature of in-house use of open-shelf collections.

There is good reason for suggesting that librarians, alone, cannot engage in the kind of research that the library needs. At least as a beginning, the librarian must look to research in other disciplines that promises to be applicable to research in librarianship and encourage research investigators in those disciplines to pursue inquiries that are relevant to libraries. But most important of all, perhaps, is the need for librarians to rid themselves of the notion that research, however trivial, is essential to professional status and must be practiced, however poorly conceived. For this miscarriage of research the library schools must bear much of the blame, for they have yielded both to pressures from the academic community and to a desire for status within their universities by undertaking programs of inquiry for which neither students nor teachers were qualified. Unfortunately, these schools have been aided and abetted by university administrations, the Office of Library Education, and the Committee on Accreditation of the ALA. If the blind do not stop leading the blind, education for librarianship will sink ever deeper into the slough of mediocrity.

The degree to which all library activities are dependent upon developments in other segments of society is clearly suggested by the fact that librarianship does not stand alone; it is derivative, created not of and for itself but for some particular need for recorded knowledge. It is a subsystem within the larger communication system of society, and its purpose is to preserve, service, and disseminate the social transcript for the benefit of a particular clientele or clienteles. Therefore, because it serves the needs of society by meeting the needs of the individual, it must understand the communication system of the individual and of society. But the communication system within the individual is basically the province of neurophysiology and psychology, and within society, of anthropology, sociology, linguistics, and communication theory. In addition, the public library must look to political science and public administration. This listing is by no means complete, but perhaps it is enough to be suggestive. Certainly it is enough to indicate that a public library is much more than an operating system of clerks, catalogers, reference librarians, public service librarians, children's librarians, and custodial personnel, all presided over by an administrative staff.

This nation has always felt a deep concern for the education of its youth. Some Colonial acts in support of education precede even the Continental Congress and the Constitution itself. Education provided the individual with occupational mobility; it was the road to the top, to success and economic reward. The truth would make men free and keep them free. To be "the crowning glory of our public schools" was the role that Horace Mann saw for the public library of mid-nineteenth-century America, and a century later Alvin Johnson saw it as "the people's university," the one place in our society to which people could turn for continuing education beyond the years of formal study. There

116   JESSE H. SHERA

is no doubt that the school and the library should work in the closest possible harmony. The present writer is not one of those who believe that the public library should surrender its services to children and youth to the school library; the two have been created for quite different purposes, and a consolidation would result only in further confusion. Nevertheless, it is the responsibility of the school to foster and encourage an intellectual quality that will assist the individual to use the public library to the fullest possible extent. That the library touches such a small proportion of the total population is more the fault of the school and the community than it is the failure of the library to reach out into those segments of the population that it does not now serve. A public library in a community can be a powerful intellectual force, but it cannot shape society in the way that the school can, though it can work with the school in the molding of the young. The library is an auxiliary agency.

Scholarship, bibliography in its broadest sense, and not social action, is the province of the library. I have every sympathy for the young protest movement that has been so conspicuous among librarians, but I have also been depressed to discover how little these young activists know about the social problems against which they batter their fists. They have read Eldridge Cleaver's *Soul on Ice*, and Jerry Rubin's *Do It*, and perhaps other works of protest, but their reading of them has a kind of "modish" quality, and their reading in other areas is remarkably slight. Often they are too busy protesting to absorb the intellectual content of the library's merchandise. Professor Fred A. Hargadon found this reading profile to be true for many of the high school graduates applying for admission to Stanford University, and it is disturbing to discover that much the same can be said for many young librarians after four years of college and a year of professional education.

But here again one finds a paradox. Professor Hargadon's observations have been amply substantiated, but there are others in higher education who have found not only that students are seeking admission to college in larger numbers than ever before but also that a high proportion of them are strongly motivated, deeply concerned about the ills that beset mankind, serious in their intent to obtain the best education available, and well prepared academically for their college careers. Eric Sevareid aptly set forth these contradictions to his television audience on September 14, 1970: "At the top level," he said, "these students may well be the best ever, except perhaps for the returned GIs after World War II, the best informed and the most mature. At the bottom level, which includes unprecedented numbers driven in by parental and social pressures and fear of the draft, they pretty surely are the worst ever, the most self-indulgent, the most illiterate and lazy-minded. So the pressure is intense, not to drive them up to the old standards of performance but to drive the standards down to their level. Some, however unprepared, will rise and make it by their own hard efforts. A great many will end up with degrees and no education worth the name." Once again we must face the question of who *should* go to college and accept the reality that not everyone should. Democracy has set itself an impossible task in attempting to provide every child with a college education. There is an *educational* Gresham's law, too, for cheap education will drive out good, and if this law is permitted to operate, the public library cannot but face a seriously shrinking clientele or lower its standards of excellence to meet demands for mediocrity. One cannot deny the fact that the future of the public library is closely linked with the future of our educational system.

The library cannot truly be said to lead society, but it can and should help to prepare the leaders for their future role. Society must somehow create the goals that it will seek. Unfortunately, as Heinrich Rickert pointed out over a half century ago, *"Es gibt keine Wissenschaft, als Wissenschaft* . . . [There is no science, as science, that teaches man what he should be or what he should want] ." Yet, despite the truth of Rickert's observation, the public library along with the rest of the educational system is not making men as hospitable to knowledge as they should be. This lamentable situation may help to explain why the public library has not defined its purpose as it should, but it scarcely excuses the organization for dissipating its powers in areas where it is ill-prepared to serve. Librarianship as a profession cannot escape the fact that the library is a bibliographic system brought into being to meet man's need for access to the social transcript.

What, then, can be done to restore the librarian to his ancient and honorable position as a bibliographic subject expert? How can we realize the admonition of Ortega y Gasset, in his "Mission of the Librarian," written in 1934, to look to the future and "create a new bibliographic technique . . . that will raise to its highest power the labor begun by librarians some centuries ago"?[9] How can the confidence of the public library as a house of intellectual activity be restored? The answer is simple, but its implementation is difficult, and, Janus-like, it looks in two directions—toward professional education and toward administrative practice.

If the present writer could, free from all financial restraints, create one library school of his dream, he would first insist that no student be admitted to the school who had not demonstrated the possession of a sound general education supplemented by subject specialization in a respected and respectable academic discipline to at least the possession of a master's degree, and preferably beyond. These students would be enrolled in a curriculum emphasizing intensive study in subject bibliography and bibliographic organization. The graduates of such a school would be scholars but not necessarily all research investigators. Research would be reserved for only those who had a sincere interest in it and an intellectual fitness for it. Once these graduates entered the field of practice, they should be regarded at a level commensurate with their contribution. They should be recognized for what they would be—true librarians in the highest sense. The routine of the library's operations could be left to the clerks, technicians, and an administrator or two.

This picture is, of course, an oversimplification to demonstrate where the future of the public library must lie if it is to survive. Not until librarians prepare themselves as bibliographic specialists and the public recognizes them for what they are worth will confidence in the library be restored and the public library perform its social role. Yet the sad fact remains that these graduates of our dream library school would be handicapped by their very competence; they probably could not find employment in any but the largest research or metropolitan public libraries. Even if they did secure a position, it would come at a substantial economic sacrifice. The country doctor does not need to know less about medicine than his big-city colleague, but he too must often provide his services at a financial disadvantage. "We all die of a lack of information," a former dean of the medical school at Case Western

Reserve University once told us, to which we replied, "But cancer and heart disease always get the recognition." What *are* the costs of ignorance of the recorded word? What *is* the value to society of a literary masterpiece? How *much* ignorance can society allow to persist? How *can* the librarian bring people and graphic records together in a fruitful relationship for the benefit of society? Unfortunately the answers to these questions are often securely concealed and little sought out.

Perhaps it is largely true that the good librarian, like the good teacher, is born rather than made. Perhaps there is a "books-to-people" sense, a kind of bibliographic spark if you will, that cannot be taught, or at best can only be improved through the right kind of education. There is some evidence for this. The little lady librarian in the high-necked dress, upon whose slender shoulders has been heaped so much derision by her "more professionally trained colleagues," was, in her own way, a true bibliographer. We once wrote of her in an essay entitled "The Quiet Stir of Thought; or, What the Computer Cannot Do":

She may not always have been able to tell you why she did what she did, nor is it likely that she could articulate her philosophy of librarianship, even though it was certainly latent within her. She was possessed of a sense of the rightness of what she did; she flew by the seat of her— should one say "petticoat" or "slip"? She knew what her goal was and how to get there. She would never have defined the role of the librarian, as we have, to serve as a mediator between book and reader for the maximum benefit to society, yet that was exactly what she did. She couldn't have distinguished Cobol from Fortran, or a collator from a key punch. To her, Peek-a-boo was a game little children play, and she wouldn't have known what one meant by the systems approach. She had no need to make such distinctions; but what is far more important, she knew her book stock and she knew her clientele, and she could bring the two together in a fruitful and often exciting relationship that many of her patrons have never forgotten.[10]

The professional success achieved by this popular stereotype of the librarian derives most of all from the art implicit in her sense of oneness with her patrons. To achieve her innate sense of psychological affinity with those who sought her aid was no mean accomplishment.

"Will you play upon this pipe?" Hamlet asked of Guildenstern, presenting him with a recorder. "My lord, I cannot," was the courtier's response.

"I pray you." "Believe me, I cannot." "I do beseech you." "I know no touch of it, my lord." " 'Tis as easy as lying; govern these ventages with your fingers and thumb, give it breath with your mouth, and it will discourse most eloquent music. Look you, these are the stops." "But these cannot I command to any utterance of harmony, I have not the skill." "Why, look you now, how unworthy a thing you make of me! You would play upon me you would seem to know my stops you would pluck out the heart of my mystery you would sound me from my lowest note to the top of my compass; and there is much music, excellent voice, in this little organ, yet cannot you make it speak. 'S blood, do you think I am easier to be played on than a pipe? Call me what instrument you will, though you can fret me, you cannot play upon me."

For three-quarters of a century or more our lady has been both the archetype and the backbone of the public library movement, and what is needed today is her modern counterpart—dedicated, knowledgeable, and qualified to meet contemporary needs. Let us not sell her short; rather, let us bring her up to date and, having done so, reward her with the trust and recognition she deserves. Her intellectual descendants can save the public library, and the public library is worth saving.

The library as the repository of recorded knowledge is an instrument of latent power for the dissemination of either good or evil; like Shelley's West Wind, it is both "destroyer and preserver." Reading is not an act of unmitigated good; it can be harmful and misdirected as well as beneficial. "Man must tame the book," wrote Ortega in the essay quoted earlier. So too, the library can become an agency for the propagation of false values and error. Indiscriminate "blanket" ordering of books and the increasingly popular networks of libraries and information systems, about which so much has been heard in recent years, can, by their very effectiveness, be used by those who would destroy the foundations of democracy and become instruments for the growth of dictatorship. Library networks are made to order for thought control, and the public library can easily become the target of those who would suppress intellectual freedom in order to shape the populace in their own image.

Anyone who has done much reading in the literature of "futurology" knows that we may be moving into a strange and unhappy new world that scarcely exemplifies the "gracious living," of which so many dreamed at the close of the Second World War. There has been considerable concern over "future shock," that is, the sociological and psychological consequences of man's failure to adjust to rapid change. But some scientists are now coming to believe that the reverse of this thesis may be true and that increasingly our problems derive from the inability of technology to keep pace with the social demands that are being placed upon it. Society cries out for solutions to problems that the scientist is unable to solve. If this interpretation is correct, it then follows that the need for information, at least so far as science is concerned, is vital. Derek Price may well be right in stating that science will someday be inundated by the proliferation of its own publications to the point that further advance will become impossible.[11]

There are many forces in society today that are eroding the character of the public library: the loss of cohesive social values; changes in the life-styles of the population; the weakening of the family and community unit; the rising outcry for change in education, especially higher education; the fragmentation and ephemeralization of the learning experience as reflected in the flickering shadows of the television screen; the proliferation of "things" made possible by the burgeoning of scientific and technical innovation and augmented by pressures from the marketplace for "progressive obsolescence" in a throw-away age; and the perils of the self-fulfilling prophecy of the futurologists. All of these forces and characteristics of contemporary society, and many more, will shape the future of public education and the public library, while weakening financial support for both.

In this uncertain world, balanced precariously between menace and promise, the public library must prepare itself for the possible coming of a new "Dark Age" when it may be required to succor the world of learning and relate itself to the elite, as did the monastic libraries of the medieval world. Can the public library's board of trustees and the public librarian of today be trusted to carry the flickering lamp of learning into the winds of a barbaric storm?

The public library does not have to die, but if it is to save itself, it must examine more critically than it has in the past what it is doing and what it should do if it is to be something other than "archytechoor" or an "informational hodgepodge." Whatever the future may hold for the public library—whether good or ill—for the public librarian, as for Keats's fishes, between the present and the unknown there will be a lot of perspiration.

Notes

1. Hannah Arendt, "Reflections—Civil Disobedience," *New Yorker* (Sept. 12, 1970), pp. 102–103.

2. Alexis de Tocqueville, *Democracy in America*, tr. by Henry Reeve (New York: Vintage Books, 1945), v. 1, p. 198.

3. Ibid., v. 2, p. 118.

4. Hannah Arendt, "Reflections," pp. 102–103.

5. Alexis de Tocqueville, *Democracy*, v. 1, p. 203.

6. Kathleen Molz, "The Public Custody of the High Pornography," *The American Scholar* (Winter 1966–67), p. 103.

7. Finley Peter Dunne, *Mr. Dooley on Ivrything and Ivrybody* (New York: Dover, 1963), pp. 225–226.

8. Vannevar Bush, *Pieces of the Action* (New York: William Morrow, 1970), p. 236.

9. Ortega y Gasset, "The Mission of the Librarian," *Antioch Review* (Summer 1961), p. 153.

10. Jesse H. Shera, *"The Compleat Librarian" and Other Essays* (Cleveland and London: The Press of Case Western Reserve University, 1971), p. 173.

11. Derek J. deSola Price, *Science since Babylon* (New Haven: Yale University Press, 1961), pp. 92–124.

III The Public Library in the Metropolis

8 America Is an Urban Society

John E. Bebout and David Popenoe

As a general background to this discussion of the problems and prospects of library service in metropolitan areas, including most importantly the need for research, it seems useful to present some of the broader characteristics of urban society. The modern metropolis, which is the environment upon which this report is focused, is the physical form of human settlement that has become dominant in highly urbanized societies such as the United States. It is both a product and a producer of the society of which it is a part, however, and it cannot be fully understood apart from its own larger environment.

Although there have been cities of sorts within the present domain of the United States since Colonial days, until quite recently the United States had been primarily a rural nation; and until even more recently most Americans had maintained an essentially rustic frame of mind. A very few of the leaders of the country at the time of the Revolution, Hamilton and Samuel Adams, for example, might have qualified as urban men; but most of them, like Washington and Jefferson, were essentially rural people. Casual observation indicates that a large proportion of the people making the most important decisions, public and private, in the United States today have rural backgrounds and once thought of themselves as country boys or girls. The rapid pace of urbanization puts a great strain on our institutions and on those responsible for policy and program development. It accounts, in considerable measure, for the doubts and discontents of librarians over such matters as the appropriate functions, locations, and service methods of libraries; the nature of library education; the financing of libraries; and the relations between libraries and other public and private institutions.

Like many other words, *urban* and its derivatives, *urbanization* and *urbanism*, often confuse conversation as much as they inform it. They certainly mean very different things to different people. Even the Census Bureau has had a hard time making up its mind how to divide the

This paper appeared in *Research on Library Service in Metropolitan Areas: Report of a Rutgers Seminar, 1964/65*, Ralph Blasingame, Director.

people of the United States between rural and urban. Thus, according to a definition used through the 1940 census, the United States became a predominantly urban country in 1920 when the Bureau found 51 percent of the people living in urban areas. Under this definition, urban territory was defined as incorporated places of over 2,500 inhabitants. Since 1950 the census has included as urban some unincorporated territories in standard metropolitan areas, now known as Standard Metropolitan Statistical Areas (SMSAs). The 1970 census introduced a new way of distinguishing between urban and rural residence. The urban population now comprises all persons in "urbanized areas" and all other persons in other places of 2,500 or more, whether incorporated or unincorporated. "Urbanized areas" contain a central city or "twin central cities" (for example, Champaign and Urbana, Illinois) of 50,000 population and the surrounding territory that meets certain criteria of density.

There is a growing tendency to think of urban America primarily as that part found in the Standard Metropolitan Statistical Areas, which can roughly be defined as metropolitan regions that contain a central city or twin central cities of 50,000 population, the same nucleus required for an urbanized area, and the surrounding or contiguous substantially urbanized county or counties (or towns in New England). Thus, the Buffalo SMSA embraces Erie and Niagara counties. If earlier census figures are adjusted to match the current definition of the Standard Metropolitan Statistical Area, they show that the United States became predominantly a metropolitan nation in 1940, when 51 percent of the people were found to be living in what the census would now define as metropolitan areas.

There are problems with these shifting statistical definitions of rural, urban, and metropolitan areas. Thus, the census now lists as rural certain parts of Standard Metropolitan Statistical Areas and even of some "extended cities" that do not meet density criteria. For example, the San Bernardino and Riverside, California, SMSA includes vast areas of mountain and desert extending to the Arizona border, while the Utica-Rome area in New York includes hundreds of square miles of forest land in Herkimer County. The "urbanized area" is essentially a sociological concept, whereas the Standard Metropolitan Statistical Area, comprising whole cities and counties or towns, is essentially political. However, there is substantial congruence between the two sets of areas. It can well be argued that some more or less isolated places of more than 2,500 population, primarily serving an agricultural hinterland, are more rustic than urban in basic attitudes. However, the numbers involved are small and are more than offset by nonfarm people with an essentially urban orientation living in "rural" areas. The continuing decline of agriculture as a way of life is dramatic. Between 1960 and 1970 the farm population dropped from 15,635,000 to 9,712,000. As a percentage of total U.S. population, the drop was from 8.7 percent to 4.8 percent. For over a generation now, the United States has been incontestably not only an urban but also predominantly a metropolitan nation.

The 1970 census shows that of about 204 million people, more than 149 million, or just over 73 percent, live in urban places, while approximately 136 million, or 66 2/3 percent, live in metropolitan areas. Moreover, 74 percent of the population increase since 1960 has been in the Standard Metropolitan Statistical Areas. Thus, all indications point to a continuation of the urban trend.

It is unnecessary to attempt either a rigorous definition of urbanization or a clear distinction between it and such closely related phenomena as industrialization and bureaucratization. If the world *urban* is confusing, even controversial in some contexts, nevertheless, we have come by a fairly satisfactory understanding of what we mean when we say that we are living in an essentially urban society. Implicit in the concept is the recognition that ours is a "modern" industrial society, dynamically charged by a rapidly developing technology. The word *urban*, however, stresses certain aspects of that society, particularly those having to do with the way people concentrate or cluster in different areas for purposes of living, working, and engaging in social and intellectual intercourse. This chapter deals with ways in which increasing numbers of Americans, and some of the basic activities they perform, are distributed and mixed among recognized urban concentrations. Its primary concern is with the frictions and problems generated by the impact of changing aspects of the urban scene on the older institutions and ideas with which people attempt to cope with new situations.

The principal aspects of the nation's urban configuration that will be considered are:

1. Urban-rural relationships and distinctions
2. Central city-suburban differences
3. The national and regional distribution of urban areas
4. Intrastate urban patterns

These aspects are chosen partly because together they contribute to a fairly rounded, however gross, picture of urban America today, but mainly because they all affect the nature of our urban problems and the means available for solving them.

Because the transition from rural to urban has been going on during the lifetime of many adults now living, and because of its galloping pace, it is no wonder that there has been a decided lag in intellectual, emotional, and institutional adjustment to the altered nature of the American scene. It may be hard for young people to realize that in the early years of the century there were more horse-drawn than motor-driven vehicles on the streets of every American community. By the same token, it is hard for older people to keep up with the implications of the coming of the automobile, to say nothing of the jet airplane. It is important for everyone, young and old, to understand that the urbanization of the United States, a phenomenon that is more and more being matched throughout the world, is essentially machine-made and the product of applied science. The one machine, more than any other, that has brought this about is the internal combustion engine, especially as it has powered automobiles and farm machinery. This engine not only made a massive urban development possible, but also, to a large extent, determined the nature and many of the details of that development, especially its almost formless, lateral spread.

The pace and magnitude of the urban trend would not have been nearly so great if we had not learned to produce more food for more people on less land with less and less manpower. The result is that, although we tend to think of farming and "the country" as going to-gether, considerably less than one-fifth of the people now living in so-called rural areas live on farms. Along with the increase in productivity of farm labor has come an increase in corporate, as opposed to family, farming and a narrowing of the social, cultural, and economic distance between the agricultural and other segments of society. Revolutions in transportation, communication, and homemaking have brought everyone closer to the city and have brought many urban amenities to people living outside the city. As factories move into the field, and fields come to be managed more and more like factories, traditional ideas about the distinction between urban and rural become less relevant to reality. In short, while American society is becoming quantitatively more urban, it is everywhere becoming qualitatively more *urbane*—if we may use the word *urbane* to denote qualities hitherto pertaining mainly to the urban condition.

At the same time, the society shows an increasing concern for preserving certain aspects of the rural scene because it is increasingly felt that a great urban society needs open space and the opportunity to enjoy and commune with nature. A massive urban society has a special need to avoid such disruption of the ecology of the planet as to make it uninhabitable. Hence, an increasingly important goal of an urbanizing society is the preservation of the countryside. Long ago, it was observed that the voters of the Bronx were the most consistent defenders of the provision of the New York Constitution requiring that the Adirondack and Catskill state forests be kept "forever wild." This is because those areas were deemed to be as important adjuncts of the city as Central Park itself. Another illustration of the way in which urban men are assimilating rural land into the urban system is the increase in the number of two-home families, families with urban houses or apartments who acquire a second home "in the country." Thus Vermont, the only state north and east of West Virginia that is still listed by the census as rural, is more and more becoming inhabited, for at least part of the year, by city people who have acquired Vermont farms as occasional refuges from the city. This has led former Governor Hoff of Vermont to observe that his state can be best understood, in some of its aspects, as a suburb of Boston, New York, and Montreal. As a result of all these trends, the old urban-rural dichotomy is becoming less important. The way in which urban settlements are distributed around the country and the differentiations and relationships within and among those settlements are much more significant for the future than is the age-old and somewhat synthetic distinction between the country bumpkin and the city slicker.

Aside from social and economic distinctions, which exist in greater or lesser degree everywhere, one of the oldest divisions in urban society is between city and suburb, between the older, generally more thickly settled central areas and the newer, more sparsely settled, but nevertheless urban, outer or fringe areas. Until fairly recent times, the city was the seat of prestige, the chosen home of the rich, the powerful, and the more highly cultured. Contrast this with the current stereotype of the old, decaying central city and the new, shiny suburbs, the preferred abiding places of those who can afford the choice. Whereas people used to be proud to claim to be city dwellers, many persons rightly listed by the census as urban, who happen to live in suburbs, will hotly deny the urban label.

In order to provide a basis for some understanding of the variety of conditions, tensions, and problems that characterize urban metropolitan United States, it is necessary to resort to some statistics. Unless specially trained, most of us tend to be bemused by a parade of numbers. However, in an increasingly interdependent world we must resort a great deal to numbers to convey essential information, and we must learn to react emotionally as well as intellectually to numbers if the society is to act effectively on problems of interdependence. It is a responsibility of the library not only to make statistics available to its clients but also to help them interpret statistics in human terms. While urban America has been growing at an explosive rate since the Second World War, the old central cities have, in most cases, grown very little except where they were able to annex or consolidate with fringe territories, as in Indianapolis and Jacksonville. An increasing number of cities have been experiencing a decline in relative, and even in absolute, numbers. The 1950s saw the peak of SMSA growth, with a rate about double that of the rest of the country. During the decade, the population increase within SMSAs but outside central cities more than quadrupled the central-city rate. Between 1960 and 1970, the population within SMSAs continued to grow faster than the rest of the country but at a somewhat lower rate than earlier (about half again). Within SMSAs, however, the population outside the central cities grew at more than five times the rate within those cities (25.6 percent compared with 4.7 percent). Moreover, of the 230 SMSAs defined by the 1960 census, 1970 figures show that 102 experienced an actual loss in central-city population (as much as 23 percent in the cases of Atlantic City and Savannah), and another 69 suffered a relative loss compared with the rate of growth for their SMSA as a whole. The same pattern will certainly continue, and the urbanization of the country will mean, in terms of traditional thinking, its increasing suburbanization. In short, the suburban or fringe areas are growing rapidly at the expense of central cities and of many small towns and rural communities.

Before examining in more detail the divisions within metropolitan communities and how they affect the urban condition, we need to see how urban America is distributed over the face of the land. When one thinks of the phenomenal concentrations in the Northeast, around the Great Lakes and the Gulf of Mexico, and in the Southwest, in contrast to the great open spaces over which one flies across the continent, one tends to think of urbanization as a highly regionalized phenomenon. This impression has a good deal of validity, but it needs correction. The fact is that urbanization has reached into all sections of the country. The 1960 census listed one region, the Eastern South Central, containing Kentucky, Tennessee, Alabama, and Mississippi, as being predominantly rural; and it found 11 states with rural majorities. Since 1960 even this region has become predominantly urban, and Kentucky, Arkansas, and Idaho have moved into the urban category, leaving only 8 rural states out of 50: Vermont, North Dakota, South Dakota, West Virginia, North Carolina, South Carolina, Mississippi, and Alaska. Anyone familiar with the concerns of state and local policy makers and educators in a number of the remaining rural states, for example, the Carolinas, knows that they are heavily preoccupied with urban problems and with the increasing urbanization that they anticipate. The wide distribution of the urban condition is indicated by the fact that there are only three states that do not contain all or part of a Standard Metropolitan Statistical Area. These states are Alaska, Vermont, and Wyoming. Alaska, it should be noted, is in this group only because of the arbitrary effects of definition. If the city of Anchorage were to annex just a few of the people living in the surrounding, built-up fringe area, or to combine with its embracing borough, it would go over the 50,000 mark and be the center of a recognized metropolitan area considerably larger than a number of those in the older states. The number of SMSAs per state in the remaining 47 ranges from 1 to as many as 23 (in Texas). There are also at least 27 bi- or tristate SMSAs.

Another significant aspect of the national pattern of urban settlement is the way in which it has developed in ribbons or strips, sometimes extending hundreds of miles across several states. The best advertised of these strips, often spoken of as "megalopolis," a name attached to it by Jean Gottmann, can be traced on the map from Portsmouth, New Hampshire, or Portland, Maine, as far south as Norfolk, Virginia. There are a number of such developments along the Great Lakes, and it takes little imagination to see these running into each other from New York State to Wisconsin, across northwestern Pennsylvania, northern Ohio, southern Michigan, and northern Indiana and Illinois. One can see a spur of this region running along the western side of Pennsylvania and into West Virginia. Urban development along the Gulf Coast from Florida to Texas, though not yet continuous, gives every indication that it will become so. The other most massive urban developments are, of course, in the Los Angeles and San Francisco areas of California. Still others may be discerned in a number of other regions, including central North Carolina, central and southwestern Ohio, northern Kentucky, and the Northwest. Even the fairly widely separated cities along the eastern slope of the Rockies, from Wyoming to New Mexico, can be thought of as developing a distinctive urban region of their own. Each of these urban regions contains several Standard Metropolitan Statistical Areas, with their innumerable local jurisdictions. Many of them are interstate; some are international.

The regional distribution of growth is both an indicator and a cause of changes in the distribution of political power, economic resources, and the demand for public services. During the last decade, the strong growth areas have been the South Atlantic, Mountain, and Pacific areas, all showing rates substantially above the national rate of 13.3 percent. Particular states in other areas also showed high growth rates: New Hampshire and Connecticut in New England, New Jersey in the Middle Atlantic, and Texas in the West South Central. The vast central region, roughly between the Mississippi River and the Rocky Mountains, is thinning out, relatively overall and absolutely in hundreds of counties, in scores of small towns, and in two whole states (the Dakotas). A map showing growth rates by counties indicates that the concentration of population is increasing mostly around the outer edges of the country, including the northern edge along the Great Lakes.

Both the distribution and spread of urban settlements and the diversification within them have, as will be shown in succeeding chapters of this volume, important implications for concerned citizens and responsible policy makers in many areas of the public, private, and voluntary sectors of the society, including libraries.

In view of the nature of our governmental system, which places a primary responsibility on the states for the government of local communities and for the solution of community-related problems, it is important to have some understanding of the urban pattern state by state. It has already been pointed out that statistically most states are now urban and that virtually all of them have urban developments that are important enough to be of substantial statewide, sometimes interstate, concern. There was a time, in a number of states, when a single city was large enough and powerful enough to come very close to dominating the state; and there were people who predicted that more states might come under the control of a single city or of a big-city coalition or alliance. The more urban the several states become, the less likely is large-city control of state governments. Through 1950 the city of New York did contain a majority of the population of the state of New York, but by 1960 New York City's share had dropped to 46.4 percent; by 1970 it was down to 43.2 percent. That share will continue to drop rapidly. Anyone familiar with New York urban politics knows that, despite some common interests, large cities from New York to Buffalo do not easily join hands for political control. The same truth can be illustrated by Pennsylvania, Ohio, California, and many other states. The big-city component of any state is fractionated and is growing weaker as it becomes, compared with the suburban and urban fringe component, a smaller element of the state as a whole. Only 21 states now have a city with 15 percent or more of the state's total population. In New Jersey, the most densely populated state in the Union, the six old central cities, Newark, Jersey City, Paterson, Camden, Elizabeth, and Trenton, with over 100,000 population each, together contain only

15.3 percent of the people, and like the large cities in New York, they
are scattered all the way across the state.

There are states, however, in which there is a single SMSA or a group
of two or more contiguous SMSAs with more than half of the population. There are nine states in which a majority of the people live in one
SMSA. From east to west these are Rhode Island, New York, Delaware,
Maryland, Illinois, Colorado, Utah, Arizona, and Hawaii. Almost half of
the people of Minnesota live in the Minneapolis–Saint Paul SMSA. In
addition, Massachusetts, Connecticut, New Jersey, Michigan, and California have continuous metropolitan regions of two or more SMSAs
containing more than half their populations. Since all these metropolitan
regions, except in Hawaii, are governmentally fractionated, they do not
have the political weight in the state that single cities of equal size would
have. However, the major metropolitan concentrations in several of these
states, in Illinois and California, for example, have a profound impact
on the politics and government of the state. In New York, notably,
metropolitan development has led to assumption of state responsibility
for various regional functions through special authorities. In addition,
the various ways in which urban and metropolitan populations are
distributed within the states have different effects on politics and governance and on the way in which citizens can best be served. Think, for
example, of the political and service implications of these diverse patterns: virtually continuous urbanization as in Connecticut and New
Jersey, the state with a dominant metropolitan region as in Colorado
and Illinois, the bipolar state like Pennsylvania or California, and the
multinucleated state like Florida, Ohio, or Texas.

It is not possible to filter out strictly urban problems from the limitless
universe of human problems. However, if we think of urban problems
as those posed or shaped by the conjunction of distinctive and largely
new urban conditions with the existing institutional and ideological
apparatus through which we seek to solve common problems, we can
discern two related clusters of issues that can be identified with the
results of urbanization. These are:

1. Environmental and physical: impact of urban development on basic
resources like land, air, water, and living organisms and the use of those
resources to meet such needs as living and working space, transportation,
and production of goods essential to urban society

2. Social and human: effects of diverse and changing mixes of people
and activities in different segments of the urban-metropolitan scene.
The impact of problems in these areas on the existing resource and
institutional base has made physical and, more recently, social planning
into household words, if not yet highly effective operating realities. It is
significant that both kinds of planning are products of the new urban
era. They were virtually unheard of, except among utopians, in an
earlier age. The emergence of planning as a proper social concern and
public function is a reflection of the fact that man is a problem-solving
animal except in a condition of stasis, which is virtually impossible
under present conditions. If American man has, somewhat belatedly,
discovered the urban society, it is because it has forced him to face up
to some new and challenging problems.

All forms of life are dangerous. Man is the most dangerous form of all
because only man commands the ultimate power to destroy the planet.
Contrariwise, only man has the capacity consciously to manage the
environment so as to prolong and improve the conditions of life. The
concentration of rapidly expanding populations in urban areas has, for
the first time in history, forced man to face up to his ultimate potential
for destruction or creation. So far, he has not faced up too impressively,
but he has made a start. Here we can note only a few major problems
stemming from the confrontation of urban man and his environment
and point to a few effects of the structure of urban America on the way
in which libraries, and other old institutions, must be shaped and used
if man is to solve the problems and not be dissolved by them.

The periodic water shortages in different parts of the country are a
good example of a crisis created by urbanization. Water supply used to
be a strictly individual or family matter. In time it came to be a matter
of municipal concern in areas too built-up to permit everybody to
obtain water from his own brook, spring, or well. Now with the spreading of urban concentrations over vast intermunicipal, interstate, and
international regions, the competition for water is leading cities to reach
out across two or more watersheds. The problem of water supply can
be solved only on a regional basis and only through the participation of
all levels of government, under some discipline imposed by no lesser
authority than that of the nation itself. The same can be said of the
related problem of water pollution and of the not dissimilar problems

of the pollution of land and air by wastes and by chemicals that are used primarily for supposedly desirable purposes, but which, in the process of achieving these purposes, may have dangerous side effects. Neither the flow of water above the ground or under the ground nor the sweep of the winds across land or sea respects municipal, state, or national boundaries. An automobile, a brushfire, or an open hearth, no matter where it is, makes its contribution to the accumulated pall of carbon dioxide in the upper atmosphere. Atomic waste wherever generated may contribute to the radioactive component of the polar ice pack. Obviously it will take, not just local, but national and world strategies to monitor and control such largely city-generated alterations in the planetary environment.

When it comes to the man-made facilities deemed necessary or desirable for urban living, we find that an increasing number of them can neither be built nor maintained on a strictly local basis. Consequently, the United States government has invested in experimental work to develop a high-speed ground transportation system to connect the principal centers in the East Coast megalopolis from Boston to Washington. Whereas once the New York subway and elevated railway system constituted in itself a fairly effective metropolitan transportation system, it is now evident that a metropolitan system for the New York area cannot be maintained without the collaboration of three states and the United States government. Electronic communication by telegraph, telephone, radio, television, and man-made satellites long ago got beyond the power of local communities and local authorities to control.

Around the turn of the century, states began to get seriously into the highway business, first with very modest subventions for county and local roads and then with the beginning of state highway systems. In President Eisenhower's administration, the government moved massively to develop a national-state highway system because, extensive as state activities in the field had been, even with some federal support, they had failed miserably to keep up with the automobile and had left too many bottlenecks, particularly on national cross-country routes and at the entrances to big cities.

Land use controls, traditionally left in local hands, have been fairly ineffective, even within a single municipality. One reason for this failure is the pressure of the regional market on municipalities that are in competition with one another for a strong tax base. States that have not weakened their own powers through constitutional limitation are reluctant to use their power to override entrenched local interests, except occasionally in connection with the location of a state highway or other facility. In consequence, the national government is getting more involved in the effort to introduce order and reason into urban development. Beginning with national support for local planning provided by Section 701 of the Housing Act of 1954, the United States has moved a long way toward a requirement that effective metropolitan planning be a prerequisite for the location of national, state, and local facilities. Policy makers have gradually come to realize that the federal government, either on its own or in collaboration with state and local governments, is responsible for a great variety of physical facilities and programs that, if planned and developed in some kind of harmony, could have a great influence on the future shape of urban America. These programs include, but are not limited to, transportation by air, land, and sea; control of pollution of water and air, of strips of land along the highways, and of other land that borders on federal facilities; and supervision of hospital and other health facilities, defense installations and contracts, housing and urban renewal projects, and educational facilities of various kinds and levels. Moreover, the planned management of these programs is an essential tool for the development of new cities or towns.

All of this does not mean that there is no role for local governments, however fractionated, or for the state. It does mean that in the matter of physical facilities and programs affecting the physical environment, urban America must more and more expect to be served and governed by a collaborative effort of national, state, and local governments. The facts previously set forth regarding the distribution of urban settlement throughout the country should be enough to make this necessity clear. The smoothness and efficiency with which this collaboration proceeds and the amount and nature of local participation in it will depend partly on the level of national statesmanship and partly on the capacity of people organized in state and local communities to contribute vision and initiative, rather than parochial obstructionism, to the effort.

Another cluster of human needs and activities that are affected, and sometimes compounded, by the nature of urban settlements is primarily social and cultural. These are sometimes thought of as including health, which has already been briefly dealt with, living conditions, which are related in part to housing, and a host of other needs or interests generally lumped under the broad headings of welfare, education, and employment. All of these, of course, are affected by the way in which physical facilities are planned and deployed.

Essentially the same conditions that have made it necessary to deal with the physical aspects of the city on a much broader base than the single municipality make it equally necessary to do this with respect to the human service needs of urban society. Unfortunately for people living in America today, the problem of meeting these needs has been greatly complicated by what can be described as the ghettoization of race and poverty. There is no need to repeat here the statistics that demonstrate that poverty, inferior education, disrupted or nonexistent families, diseases of various kinds, mental illness, drug addiction, malnutrition, delinquency, unemployment or underemployment, and various other socially pathological conditions are heavily concentrated in central cities, and especially in decaying segments of those cities. Whereas at the turn of the century most Negroes were rural people, now the vast majority are city people and constitute a very large proportion of the poorest and most depressed people in the country. Despite efforts to counteract it, the urbanization of social problems continues. It has a profound effect on the financing and delivery of library and other services and requires an experimental approach to the problem of adapting these services to the style and needs of the people.

The cities in which these conditions are concentrated are quite incapable of dealing with them on the basis of their existing jurisdiction or resources. The very concentration of these problems in the city, many of them exported from rural America, reduces the city's fiscal and personal resources for meeting them. While the exclusiveness of the suburbs, enforced in varying degrees by law, by the market, and by organized snobbery, makes it impossible for the cities to export their problems to other areas, at the same time it intensifies the hopelessness of the unfortunate ones and reduces their ability to respond to well-meaning efforts to increase their upward mobility.

For the same reason that the states were not able by themselves to deal with such physical problems as highway development or pollution control, they have proved equally incapable by themselves of mounting an effective attack on these primarily human problems of the older cities and some of the older suburbs into which the problems have spilled. The United States government began to respond to locally based social needs during the Depression. As a result, we have permanent and expanding programs in the areas of social security, housing, urban renewal, and employment. It is only during the past decade that, in the Civil Rights Act, in the Economic Opportunities Act, and in a growing list of acts relating to health planning, libraries, education, and other human needs, the United States government has begun to show a comprehensive and, it is hoped, effective concern for urban problems of this nature. These programs provide national leadership and investment in collaborative efforts involving national, state, and local governments, as well as private agencies and interests of various kinds. The federal anti-poverty program typifies this method. These and other programs are concerned with rural as well as urban areas. But urban people will, in the long run, benefit by any effective attack on rural poverty, ignorance, or deprivation, since rural problems, if untreated in their rural environs, tend to move to the city.

The United States did not become a truly urban nation simply as a result of the location in urban areas of 51 percent, or even 70 percent, of its people. If it is today an urban nation, it is because it has come to think in terms of urban reality and is beginning to act nationally with intelligence and energy on crucial urban problems.

One reason why national policy has been urbanized more rapidly than policy in most of the states is to be found in the compositions of the national and state legislatures. Members of the United States Senate are elected from their states at large. Since an overwhelming majority of the states are predominantly urban, the senators must pay serious attention to the overall urban needs and problems of their states. This is true even of senators from states with urban minorities, because they must cater to urban as well as rural voters. In most state legislatures, however, even under reapportionment urban legislators tend to represent small segments of large urban communities, a fact that will continue to emphasize narrow rather than broad urban interests. Reapportionment of state legislatures will help states rise to urban statesmanship only if the urban people who live outside the central cities send representatives who will assume a generous attitude toward the needs of the whole urban society. For it is the suburbs, not the old cities, that are benefiting from reapportionment. Finally, it is worth noting that it is no accident that there are more urban-minded governors than legislatures, because like a United States senator, a governor is elected by the whole state.

In any event, it is certain that the more comprehensive and less parochial view of urban America that is possible from the national capital will always be needed for leadership and for the fair allocation of resources to meet problems that cannot be contained or fully managed in the patches set apart by local and state boundaries. Only the nation can tap the necessary fiscal and intellectual resources on a sufficient scale and deploy them over large enough areas to cope with many of the problems discussed in this chapter.

Fortunately, since complete centralization in a country so vast and varied as America would be a horror, it is a firm national policy to govern the United States as far as possible through state and local institutions. Deficiencies in state and local ability to tax a fair share of the wealth of the country in order to meet their respective needs are increasingly being made up by national support of locally administered programs. Just as important as money for the maintenance of constructive local initiative and influence is the supply of leadership and knowledge. The English complained for a time of a "brain drain" of scientists attracted by the more glittering opportunities they saw on this side of the Atlantic. State and local governments and even local voluntary institutions suffer a similar "brain drain" because of the higher pay and supposedly wider opportunities offered by large private business and by the national government. If the national policy in favor of local self-government is to be successful, it will be necessary to counteract this "brain drain."

Fortunately some of the newer national programs in the areas of research and education are calculated not only to improve the skill and prospects of the underprivileged but also to help those who have the capacity to advance in the higher educational system. Increasing attention is being paid to continuing education, including education for community and public leadership in an urban society. Libraries are involved, but their potential role in the universal education of the future is far from being fully realized.

Behind a well-trained and well-informed leadership there must be a well-educated citizenry. Thomas Jefferson, in a rural age, understood this need and argued for a comprehensive educational system. We may, under the impact of urban reality, be on the threshold of answering Jefferson's call. Responsible self-government is possible only if large numbers of people have a sound education and continuing access to the founts of knowledge that contribute importantly to their understanding of both national and social problems. Education and information are necessary and powerful driving forces in a society such as ours. Libraries, therefore, are both increasingly important and increasingly interlinked with many other specialized intelligence units in a society of complex interdependencies. Like the metropolis itself, the library will not only be a shaper of modern society but, to an accelerating extent, will be shaped by it. The ability of libraries to meet the challenges of urban change, particularly in metropolitan areas where the great bulk of our population lives, will undoubtedly affect the speed with which improvements in society can be achieved and the quality of living that such achievements will bring to all of us.

9 Trends in Urban Politics and Government: The Effect on Library Functions

Robert H. Salisbury

This essay was originally written in the early 1960s, and as such it reflects the perspectives of that decade. In important respects its interpretation of urban political trends failed to recognize or anticipate the dominant issues of the years that followed. Poverty and race were mentioned, but they were not given appropriate emphasis as the central issues with which cities—and public libraries—have since been compelled to deal. Riot, assault, and urban violence generally were not seen as persistent conditions of the contemporary city. The ineffectuality of urban renewal and public housing was not yet appreciated.

When I was asked to revise the essay, I was at first tempted to redo it entirely so as to purge it of all its myopic misunderstandings, yet the blind spots of the early 1970s would surely have marred the result. The plain fact is that social scientists are not very good at forecasting the future. Our hindsight is much better than our prevision. Consequently, I have chosen to exercise hindsight and to interpolate remarks and emendations into my original statement.

There would, of course, be no point in preserving the original argument if it had no substantial value. I believe that despite its errors, principally those of omission, the central themes are still valid. Public libraries still face some critical choices of strategy. Should they "go metropolitan" and follow their traditional book-reading clients to suburbia? Should they become data banks for metropolitan business? Should they be linked more closely to the schools in an effort to salvage the minds and hearts of the ghetto? Should they serve as cultural adornment, instrument of economic growth, intellectual welfare agency? The choices are not absolute or clear-cut, but decisions must be made concerning which emphasis to pursue. Librarians, along with other community leaders, will make the choices, and this essay attempts to define and evaluate some of these choices.

It is very difficult to distinguish trends in the development of urban

An earlier version of this paper appeared in *The Public Library and the City*, ed. R. W. Conant (Cambridge, Mass.: The MIT Press, 1965).

political patterns. Cities are so diverse that comparative statements about cities in general have no predictive power. Dahl's study of New Haven suggests some interesting historical patterns; other students of political science, including myself, could generate hypotheses from their knowledge of particular cities. But comparative study to establish common patterns of development and to isolate crucial variables has been largely neglected so far. We must rely on a rough summation of single-community studies, which, because of differing methodological approaches, are not always comparable. The severity of these limitations is lessened only by the success of an individual scholar's guesswork, and that is a notoriously unreliable basis for analysis.

Yet even while the difficulties are recognized, some things can be said about trends in urban political and governmental development. A number of demographic points, although familiar, bear restating.[1] In the past two decades core cities in the older metropolitan centers either lost population or gained only a tiny fraction. Their suburban areas continued to grow rapidly, as did core cities in the West and Southwest, but the population figures dramatized what many had observed and worried about for some time: core-city decay. The loss of population was compounded by the fact that the remaining core-city residents were increasingly the very poor, inhabiting slums or public housing and helping to speed the disintegration of the city's physical plant. A shrinking tax base was called on to support increasing demands for public services. The latter were partly demanded by the low-income population of the city and partly sought by other interests as a means of staving off further decay.

The efforts to cope with problems such as urban renewal, juvenile delinquency programs, and "gray area" education are all too familiar. The question here is what the socioeconomic changes in the large city have meant for the political system. At one level the changing population of the city has contributed to a breakdown of the traditional structure of organization politics in the city. One consequence of this change is that a large portion of the city's residents are not integrated into the political system. Without an active party organization, there are no institutional channels through which lower- and lower-middle-class residents may express their interests. The significance of the change lies

not merely in the nonintegration of the citizenry. As the party professionals have lost power, the governmental system has gained it.

If the party organization is withering away, who controls this enlarged
governmental apparatus? The party was the effective mechanism by
which candidates were recruited for public office, and it also provided
a general posture toward policy questions. If party is no longer effective
and the organization, where it exists at all, must follow rather than lead,
who does decide public policy? Or, more accurately, who decides who
decides?

I would suggest that in city after city we are witnessing a reconvergence
of political and economic power. The fragments of city history bearing
on the point pretty generally agree that prior to the late nineteenth-
century flowering of the machine, political office and authority, such
as they were, were dominated and even held by the civic elite. The
merchants moved in and out of city hall and demonstrated that the
notion of a pyramid of power culminating in somebody's bank or board
room had both reality *and* reputation. The rise of machine politics,
based on the growing low-income population of the industrializing city,
had the effect of divorcing political and economic power, giving to each
a secure and autonomous base and forcing each to bargain on the points
of their interdependence.

Not only is the political machine withering, the economic and social
elite is, too. Certainly in many of the older cities (and only a community that is a century or so old could have gone through these cycles)
the civic notables have seen their local investments threatened. Some,
of course, have been removed from active power by virtue of mergers
and amalgamations that make former notables into local branch managers with limited stakes in the local scene. Those who remain, however,
have a heightened sense of involvement in and responsibility for their
community's economic and social well-being. The remaining notables
actively invest time, money, and prestige in urban revitalization.

They do not hold office, of course. Few notables could win elections
in communities inhabited predominantly by low-income people. There
must be political leadership separate from the notables, but collaborat-
ing with them. Candidates for public office today are not dominated by
a strong party organization, which frees them to work with the civic

elites. I recognize that I have not answered the question: Whence do political leaders now come? The answer is that no effective mechanisms now function to provide political leadership.

A third element in the recasting of urban politics is the rise of "the experts," those technical specialists who preside over the details of operation in each of the major areas of city activity. In an increasingly technological society, possession of expertise has become a genuine component of power. As politicians seek ways to win over the electorate and the notables seek to protect their interests, they must rely on systematic empirical knowledge. More and more, the planner, the economist, the social worker, the public health expert, and other specialists set the agenda for city action and specify the means of accomplishing its tasks.

Thus, the city is faced with an increased dispersion of power. It is not simply a perspective altered by a decade of urban strife that suggests that the power of "the Establishment" to act effectively is over. The assertive self-consciousness of urban blacks and, more recently, of city employee unions has displayed this fragmentation of power vividly indeed. The claims of these groups to be heard, to participate in decisions, and to prevail have come to have great weight. They have added further complexity to that pluralistic struggle that is the community political process. For the most part the new issues placed on the urban agenda by these newly emergent contenders for power have not displaced older questions. Instead they have added the issues of poverty, race, and labor relations to the still nagging conflicts over traffic, taxation, sewage disposal, and mass transit. The list of public problems grows longer and more insistent, while the power to deal with them seems to grow ever more elusive.

Leadership—coordination of efforts, communication with the public that must support bond issues, recruiting of personnel, etc.—lies largely in the hands of elected officials, chiefly the mayor. Part-time personnel and substantial financial resources must come from the civic elites, as must private investment to supplement public undertakings. Substantive planning of programs is the job of the professional. Thus, the new collaborative grouping is hardly a power monolith. Power is too broadly shared for each individual group to accomplish the tasks it sets itself. In short, the capacity to achieve power may be inadequate. But what capacity there is lies chiefly in the hands of these three groups, working more or less together.

What is the relevance of these developments for the public library? The library serves the city and is affected by the city. Thus librarians must understand what is happening to the library market and to the system that controls it. In the past, exchanges between librarians and political scientists fortunately involved men who took a modern, or behavioral, approach to political questions. Oliver Garceau's study[2] exemplified an approach to politics that is widely current today. Garceau and, more recently, Morton Kroll[3] have discussed the relationship of the public library to the community power structure. Garceau places considerable stress on the tactical issues facing library leaders as they compete in the urban environment for scarce fiscal resources.[4] These enduring issues will be the focus for the remarks that follow.

Most public libraries operate under boards appointed by the city's political leadership; I shall take this pattern to be standard for purposes of this discussion. Although some libraries are financed through special library taxes, it is exceptional when a library does not have to compete with other public agencies for public money. Even where there is a special minimum library tax, bond issue funds must be sought for new construction in competition with other projects. Thus the library is competing for scarce resources, and this is its inescapable political problem.

In any competition for scarce resources, an institution such as the public library must consider what claims it can persuasively make on public funds. In general the limits are set in three ways. One limit is established by the place of the library in the system of community power. Where does the library fit into the urban alliance of economic, political, and technical resources? A second limit is established by the library's public. To what extent are the voters sensitive to library needs—and willing to support them? Note that this point is a different and perhaps secondary question. My thesis is that general public opinion, apart from the power system, counts for much less in securing financial support than our civic mythology suggests. It is not irrelevant, but without support from the power system public opinion is unlikely to be effective. On the other hand, without broad public support, the power system may be unable to secure the necessary electoral approval of tax rates and bond issues.

A third limit is less subject to manipulation. It is the limit of fiscal capacity, which I shall not discuss in detail. The library's share of public revenue is sufficiently small so that marginal adjustments in library money have only a slight relationship to changes in the city's fiscal picture. It seems fair to say that while a shrinking tax base will, of course, hurt the library, the library's relative share of the public money can potentially be altered, regardless of the overall size of the pie, with only a small effect on other city services.

It should be added that despite the infusion of modest federal and state funds, the overall fiscal position of urban public libraries is worse today than it was a few years ago. From the perspective of this discussion the main reason is the rapid rise in the priority given to claims on the urban budget from the black community, the public schools, and city employee groups. The first two of these claimants are not entirely remote from the programs of the public library, of course, but in the present climate library spokesmen will need to rest a larger part of their case for more money on the services provided to blacks and schools.

Let us turn our attention to the first two points: the library's relationship to the power system and the library's relationship to its clientele. Since the mayor often appoints the library board, it is structurally possible for the library to be linked to the centers of community power. The question is: Whom does he appoint and why? We are not concerned here with the ways in which the board may or may not shape library policy, but rather with its potential role in the political process. Kroll found that housewives comprised a large proportion of the board members in the Northwest and that, while they were not themselves powerful, they were reasonably close to those in power. This may not be an entirely inaccurate statement for the rest of the nation. Board members tend to be close to or acquainted with the civic notables, so that they can establish working contacts if they wish. They are unlikely to have equal access to those segments of the community with numbers but relatively little power: organized labor, blacks, or political parties.

With the technicians I suspect that a similar relationship exists. That is, the professional librarians, as technicians, can have contacts with other agencies of government, if they try. Contacts with land clearance or housing officials or with welfare agencies are, I would guess, under-developed, but not impossible to establish.

How well the library will fare in the competition for public money depends on how effectively the lines of communication with those who have power over community resource allocation are developed. How would such contacts work? Suppose the library professionals found that existing facilities, especially the branches, were being overrun by adolescents who, especially in the poorer neighborhoods, tended to be rowdy. Possible responses include more rigorous policing, more restricted use, or possibly a flight of facilities to more safely middle-class areas. All or any of these steps might be taken within the library's existing resources and on its own initiative. Alternatively, library personnel might initiate conversations with school, planning, and welfare officials. Some recognition of the general problem of weakened family structure in lower-class neighborhoods might be achieved and physical facilities and programs jointly worked out whereby the library is made an integral part of antidelinquency and antiblight programs. The library might then be able to extend its service in ways that not only complement the work of other agencies but also rank higher in present-day priorities for public money than do books alone. Implicit here is the notion that cooperative alliances with professionals in other public agencies contribute to multi-pronged attacks upon multifaceted social problems and, in the process, increase the bargaining power of the library in getting appropriations.

These contacts will be crucial when bond issues are necessary for new construction or renovation. The librarian may be able to speak expertly about use patterns and location, but if he cannot also relate those questions to larger issues of city policy, he loses not only effectiveness but also his standing as an expert. If he cannot discuss the contribution of a new branch to neighborhood conservation or the effect of a new central building on downtown redevelopment, his advice will and must be ignored. Libraries do not rank at the top of any city's agenda. It is therefore the task of the librarian to develop the arguments and evidence showing the possible contribution of library service to the functions that outrank it. Again, this is primarily a technical task calling for an exchange between professional librarians and other professionals.[5]

What of the board in this process? Obviously, whenever board members are able and willing to interpret and relate library needs to other community needs they may contribute to the political strength of the library's case. But insofar as the library's case is a technical case, it will be presented by technicians and largely for technicians. The board's function would seem to consist largely of linking the library with other civic needs at another level, that of the civic notables. It is with this group that the board's contacts are likely to be closest; the natural alliance has only to be cultivated, and those committed to the library will have to do the cultivation.

One consequence of the convergence of urban power is that civic institutions are working in closer harmony than they once did. Library boards might be wise to seek out other public institutions in a similar power position and with a similar claim to public prestige and attention. Cooperatively, they might get more support from either notables or the public than could be achieved separately. In 1961-1962, for example, the Saint Louis Public Library collaborated with the city's zoo and art museum in a campaign to increase the tax levies supporting the three institutions. This campaign involved securing state legislative authorization and city council and voter approval. The last two stages were carried on in conjunction with school tax and bond issues and a dozen other city bond proposals, including one for branch library construction. This combination of issues aroused far more interest and commitment from civic notables than the library proposal alone could have done. There seems little doubt that, to some extent, the latter rode the coattails of the bigger proposals. (The most prominent matter was a proposed new stadium.) This package campaign was headed by a long roster of civic notables and planned by a broad group of professionals in various public agencies. The pattern is fairly well established in Saint Louis now and may contain lessons for library officials elsewhere.

Until now we have said very little about the library's clientele and its political uses. One reason for this is my conviction that the library's political prospects are so intertwined with those of other city agencies and programs that any effort to differentiate a library public will and should be costly. The library's constituency is a peculiarly mixed one. On the one hand, the library has been the preserve of the educated, like art museums and universities, attracting the time, money, and energy of a few devoted spirits and the more passive approval of the WASP. On the other hand, it is a refuge of the adolescent, the elderly, and the underprivileged. It attempts to serve the masses and at the same time to nurture the occasional creative individual who escapes there. In recent years librarians have sought to be helpful to any group, in an effort to build as broad a base as possible. At the same time, they have seen their traditional clientele move to the suburbs and have felt the mixed effects of the decline of philanthropy and the rise of taxation as the source of their income.

My personal priorities in a list of library functions would put service to organized groups at the bottom and service to adolescents and senior citizens at the top. Particularly in the older cities, where the middle-class exodus is most marked, the traditional prestige of the library as a civic "good thing" may no longer have much relevance. An effective library program may serve a major welfare function for adolescents and may provide necessary encouragement to the rare creative person among them. My point here is not that a program designed principally for adolescents and senior citizens will bring political rewards. These groups will not, even if they could, vote for increased library service to a much greater extent than their general socioeconomic position would lead them to do. Rather, a program of this kind will provide an empirical basis for the professional librarians' argument as they present their case for more public money to other technicians in city agencies. To get the power they need to broaden their resources, librarians must recognize that their function is not simply to get people to read books. Books are the means, of course, but the ends include the prevention of delinquency and blight; and librarians must be self-conscious about these ends and how they may contribute to them if they are to work more effectively.

There is a theme touched on here and referred to earlier that I would like to elaborate. It strikes me that public schools and public libraries share a common political position. They are both asked to serve masses of people, many of whom are not enthusiastic about the service. Both institutions justify their claims on public money largely in terms of (1) the numbers of service units provided (so many children in school, so many books in circulation) and (2) the transforming quality of the experience to the child or reader and, ultimately, to the society in which he or she lives. Most people are not transformed or even marginally affected by reading a book. But some are, and more might be if the library were set up to identify and nurture more fully than now that small minority for whom the encounter with books can indeed be transforming. Good reader clubs and Saturday story hours are not enough, of course, and all the other imaginative ideas so far attempted to attract and hold the nascent intellectual of the urban ghetto need to be multiplied many times.

The schools must play a crucial role in helping to identify the children most likely to benefit from these opportunities, and school officials must join public librarians to develop complementary programs of encouragement. But the fundamental strategy involved is to design library services and facilities, or an important part of them, to give maximum support to providing intellectual nourishment, physical retreat, and, perhaps, psychological salvation to a comparative handful of ghetto kids. It is an elitist strategy, and it seems to me that libraries cannot avoid a fundamentally elitist course. The schools must "process" the masses even though they *educate* only a minority. The library does not confront the mass in its full and sometimes awful magnitude, and it cannot if it would. But rescuing a dozen children a year in each city of America would be no small contribution to the commonweal. Underlying this strategic view, in turn, is the feeling that it is the quality of individual lives that counts and that should provide the criterion for designing and judging social policy.

A further point may be made: If the library is integrated into the notable political and technical establishment, its ability to win public support will be equally integrated. In the Saint Louis example, mentioned earlier, votes on the several tax and bond issue questions did not vary more than 3 or 4 percent, with the library proposals, having received little special notice, following the patterns set by other more prominent issues.

Another political concern of interest to librarians is governmental reorganization. The issue has two main facets: (1) changes in the internal structure of city government and (2) the matter of metropolitan government. An important concern of librarians has been whether introduction of a city-manager form of government would constitute a threat to the autonomy, and hence the power, of the professional librarian.[6] It has been feared that a manager, oriented toward the scrutiny of details of operating procedure, might interpose his judgment concerning, say, personnel selection or book acquisition without having enough appreciation of the substantive issues of librarianship. A political mayor, it is thought, would be less likely to interfere at this level. As experienced librarians know, there is no guarantee that public libraries fare any better (or worse) under elected local officials than they do under professional, appointed ones. Although few city managers are professionally trained in areas of city service such as the library, welfare, and education, they are trained in the technical areas of budgeting, personnel, and sometimes engineering. Actually, the manager stands in the same relation to the librarian as any administrator does to his operating personnel. His sympathetic understanding of their needs and problems is as good as the professional librarian's ability to communicate with him and command his respect. His perspective is shaped by his training and his job specifications, and neither attaches a high priority to libraries. By the same token, however, the traditional autonomy of the librarian, assured of financial support sufficient to maintain a kind of genteel poverty, has preserved the institution from "interference" from administrators in the past. The library, like an industry protected by tariff walls, has had a chance to mature.[7] Now it must compete more directly with other increasing demands on public money and attention. Successful competition will depend less on the structure of government than on the persuasiveness with which the library can be linked functionally with other city needs and programs.

Metropolitan reorganization presents a different set of questions. One side of this issue involves the level at which service can most efficiently be provided. Earlier discussion tried to arrive at a model allocation of financial responsibility among federal, state, and local authorities (for example, 10 percent, 25 percent, and 65 percent, respectively). Similar ideal allocations for servicing could be made. In either case, a metropolitan library agency might fall between the state and local categories. A metropolitan library is clearly a means of extending service to newly developed suburban areas as well as of broadening the tax base for libraries throughout the metropolitan area. Libraries are in the same position as schools, police, or other services commonly discussed whenever reorganization on a metropolitan basis is suggested.

There is a complicating factor where libraries are concerned, however. To a significant extent, the increasing suburban population is composed of middle-class people, many of whom have left the core city. If the core-city library "goes metropolitan," it implies that service emphasis will continue to be given to the relatively well-educated, middle-class homeowners who traditionally have constituted the public library's adult clientele. Direct competition between two rather different types of programs is likely to develop. If, however, separate library organizations serve the city and the suburbs, the core-city library may concentrate on its special clientele, while the suburban library may continue more directly in the public library tradition. It seems likely that the separate structural devices would be useful, perhaps essential, as a means of differentiating the attention and programs of librarians. Somewhat greater differentiation would, in turn, improve the bargaining power of the library when it seeks its share of the tax money.

One dimension of the relation of the public library system to the metropolitan area involves the potentialities of the library as a central data bank. Core-city libraries have long served as resource facilities for the local business community, of course, and in one sense the concept of a central data bank is simply a more sophisticated version of this traditional service. But the modern data bank serves a vastly larger volume of information needs than the reference librarian could ever handle, and it does so by means of computer technology of vastly greater cost. To invest the necessary money and energy in servicing the need for a metropolitan data bank would, I think, inevitably subtract from the resources available for the ghetto effort discussed earlier.

This consideration reminds us that the library is and has long been a multipurpose institution, serving diverse publics and clienteles with quite distinct services. Perhaps more explicit consideration should be given to dividing some of these functions into separate institutional units. Is there any eternal virtue in providing neighborhood reading centers for book distribution, scholarly research facilities, and business reference services within the same organizational framework? I do not propose an answer, but I do ask the question seriously, and so should librarians. And they ought not to rely on the comfortable bureaucratic responses.

Throughout this paper I have assumed that politics involves the allocation of scarce resources and that, for any particular group or institution, the primary political problem is how to maximize its share of the scarce resources, notably money. There are those whose conception of "the political" is more normative and who ask not, Who gets what? When? And how? but, What is just and good? To the latter question librarians must have answers, but unless they are effectively linked with power, their answers remain academic in the most futile sense of the term.[8]

Notes

1. A convenient summary of these data with a discussion of their impact on library service may be found in the issues of *Library Trends* (July–October 1961), ed. Frank L. Schick.

2. Oliver Garceau, *The Public Library in the Political Process* (New York: Columbia University Press, 1949).

3. Morton Kroll, *The Public Libraries of the Pacific Northwest* (Seattle, Wash.: University of Washington Press, 1960).

4. Garceau observes that public libraries "have scarcely commenced the transition to a public service institution actively sponsored by a broad range of power groups in the community," *The Public Library*, p. 104.

5. A striking example of the apparent failure of librarians to integrate their plans with other elements of a city program is reported by Roger B. Francis, "Public Library Site Controversy," *Library Journal* (February 15, 1959). In this case the library board was able to "resist political pressure" and go ahead with its own plans and its own money. In many communities the latter element would not be present, and even in South Bend one wonders how much damage the library's "resolute firmness" may have done to larger redevelopment plans.

6. See Carlton B. Joeckel, *The Government of the American Public Library* (Chicago: University of Chicago Press, 1935), pp. 161-169; and James A. Ubel, "Library Board Forms," *Library Trends* (July 1962): 33-34.

7. Herbert Goldhor makes this point using the same simile in *A Forum on the "Public Library Inquiry,"* ed. Lester Asheim (New York: Columbia University Press, 1950), p. 11.

8. In stressing the importance of power, I do not intend to disparage the efforts of librarians to win friends in other, less political ways. "Friends of the Library" may often serve a helpful function as links to the larger community and/or as supplementary sources of financial help. See, for example, the discussion by Guy B. Garrison, "Friends of the Library: Who Are They?" *Library Journal* (September 15, 1962): 2985-2989. In larger cities, however, "friends" can be of marginal help, at best. Too many other structures of influence exist with greater power and larger stakes for friends to sell the community the case for greater library support.

10 Trends in Urban Fiscal Policies: The Effect on Library Functions

William F. Hellmuth

This chapter explores the financial capacity of local governments to provide public library service needed by various types of communities. It also considers financing of libraries by state and local governments, especially in metropolitan areas.

Local Government Finances

The direct general expenditures of local governments have been rising rapidly since World War II. For example, these expenditures increased 374 percent between 1952 and 1969-70, from $17.4 billion to $82.6 billion. The central city and older suburbs have spent their funds differently from the newer suburbs. In the older cities the increases have been relatively large for welfare, health and hospitals, public safety, housing and urban renewal, and education. Capital outlays have been used to renovate and replace the existing plant. The largest capital outlays for new facilities have been for highways and freeways, parking facilities, housing and urban renewal, and education.

In the newer suburbs, large capital outlays have been made for the construction of new schools, streets, police and fire stations, water, storm, and sanitary sewer systems, and other services needed by new communities. Increases in current operating expenses have been largest for schools, with both current and capital expenditures per pupil usually higher than in the city.[1] Capital outlays for schools have been higher since buildings must accommodate large increases in population, while the central-city school systems frequently need to accommodate only small increases and neighborhood shifts in population.

At first glance, the difficult fiscal situation facing local governments in metropolitan areas seems suprising as the metropolitan areas generally have the highest incomes and greatest taxable wealth of any areas in the United States. Average incomes in the major metropolitan areas are distinctly above the national average, with median family incomes of

An earlier version of this paper appeared in *The Public Library and the City*, ed. R. W. Conant (Cambridge, Mass.: The MIT Press, 1965).

$10,261 in 1969 against $7,982 in nonmetropolitan areas.[2] Assessed property values and retail sales per capita in metropolitan areas exceed the national average. Thus the economic base and the potential local tax base available to support activities of local governments in metropolitan areas appear to be adequate.

There are significant limitations, however, on the ability of these local governments to raise revenue. State laws and state constitutions limit the taxing and borrowing capacities of the local governments, so that even though a government operates in a relatively rich and high-income area, it often lacks the legal power to tax this wealth and income. Further limitations exist because the many governments in the metropolitan areas compete with one another to keep their own tax rates low in order to attract industry, shopping centers, and other businesses.

The local property tax has traditionally been the major revenue source of local governments. Although the property tax base has been expanding as a result of new construction and increases in the value of property, this expansion has not kept up with the increased need for revenues. This need has led to a significant increase in the average tax rates. The property tax still accounts for more than 80 percent of all taxes collected locally, but other taxes, fees and charges, and grants from state and federal governments are rising in both amount and relative importance as sources of revenue.

In recent years, local governments have been given the power to levy more local nonproperty taxes and to add incremental rates to existing state taxes for local purposes. As illustrations, many local governments in Pennsylvania, Ohio, and New York levy income taxes, while local governments in California and Illinois impose an additional municipal or county rate on state sales taxes. Among local governments, large cities have been most active in developing other local tax sources in addition to the property tax. Thus in 1969–70 while all local governments collected about 85 percent of local taxes in the form of the property tax, cities with populations exceeding half a million obtained 60 percent from the property tax and 40 percent from other local taxes, such as sales and income taxes.

Among local governmental jurisdictions fiscal imbalance between the need for expenditures and tax sources is a pressing problem in most metropolitan areas.[3] Imbalance may exist for a number of different reasons. In a metropolitan area some communities may be primarily residential, consisting of modest homes, many children, and very limited commercial and industrial development, leading to low taxable values per capita against large expenditure needs. Other communities may have large shopping centers and manufacturing plants with relatively few residences, generating high taxable values per capita against small expenditure needs. Few residential communities are rich enough in terms of the average value of homes to be able to support high-quality services without a major effort in the form of high tax rates. Imbalance may also exist because rapid growth creates a great need for capital outlays rising more rapidly than the tax base. Some jurisdictions have imbalance due to small size. One village in the Cleveland area, which undoubtedly has counterparts in most metropolitan areas in the country, has an area of less than one-half of a square mile and a total tax base of only about $1 million. To maintain a police force with one officer on duty at all times would require a tax rate for this function alone of more than 30 mills.

The decline in the ability of central cities to raise revenue is often due to a decline in the tax base relative to financial need. Available evidence indicates that local taxable capacity (as measured by taxable property values per capita) is higher in the suburban ring than in the central cities. Netzer concludes that "this is especially true of the older metropolitan areas, particularly those in the Northeast and Midwest such as New York, Philadelphia, Newark, Chicago, Milwaukee, Cincinnati, and Toledo."[4] This decline in the tax base usually reflects a move of middle-income families, retail shopping areas, and manufacturing plants from the central city to the suburban ring. On the other hand, there is a large migration into the central city of individuals and families with limited skills and lower educational levels, due in part to cultural, social, political, and economic disadvantages and discrimination. The central city and older suburbs thus bear disproportionately the heavy costs of the entire metropolitan area for welfare, traffic congestion, and slums, while suffering a relative decline in their tax base.

Various steps have been taken to reduce imbalance. In some states, state aid has been designed to assist in equalization. Often, however, state aid does not reduce the imbalance between needs and resources in the different jurisdictions. A few areas, such as Miami–Dade County, Jacksonville, Nashville, and Indianapolis, and also Toronto, Canada, have established a form of metropolitan government, with some functions performed and financed on a county-district-metropolitan-wide basis.

In summary, the trends in metropolitan fiscal problems are rising expenditures, increasing pressure on revenue sources to keep up with the needed spending, and imbalances between revenue sources and need in different jurisdictions of the same metropolitan area. The economic interdependence of the jurisdictions is increasing, but the increase is not always reflected in political cooperation and consultation.

Effect of Urban Fiscal Policies on Library Functions

State and local government spending has risen very rapidly over the past fifteen years, both for libraries and for all functions, as shown in Table 1. Total spending for local libraries quadrupled over this period, from $154 million in 1955 to $700 million 1969–70.

This sharp upward trend apparent in spending data expressed in current dollars is substantially reduced when adjusted to allow for population growth and inflation. Spending on a per capita basis expressed in dollars of constant purchasing power is probably the best measure of real resources provided or quality of library service. When adjusted for the increase in population, spending more than tripled between 1955 and 1969–70, from $0.93 to $3.44 on a per capita basis. Inflation also has substantially reduced the real purchasing power of the dollars spent for libraries, with both rising salaries and wages for library staff and the increasing cost of books and periodicals contributing to this reduction. (These increases are measured approximately by the price index for goods and services purchased by state and local governments, which increased about 75 percent between 1955 and 1969–70.)[5]

After adjusting the per capita spending on libraries for inflation, the increase in dollars of constant purchasing power per capita was only 98 percent. In other words, real expenditures per capita for libraries approximately doubled over the past fifteen years.

Total spending for libraries increased at a faster rate than state and

Table 1 Expenditures for Libraries and Total Expenditures for State and Local Governments from 1950 to 1969–70

Year	Library Expenditures (in millions of dollars)				Total Direct General Expenditures (in millions of dollars)			Per Capita Library Expenditures (in dollars)	Per Capita Total Expenditures (in dollars)
	Total	State	Local	Cities	State and Local	State	Local		
1952	n.a.	n.a.	111	100	26,098	8,653	17,444	0.71	166.29
1955	154	7	146	128	33,724	11,190	22,534	0.93	204.05
1957	n.a.	n.a.	199	145	40,375	13,647	26,729	1.17	236.98
1960	278	17	261	185	51,876	17,784	34,092	1.54	288.23
1962	340	20	332	211	60,206	20,375	39,831	1.83	324.00
1964–65	444	30	414	267	74,678	26,273	48,405	2.29	384.62
1965–66	486	37	449	282	82,843	29,162	53,680	2.48	422.97
1966–67	518	49	469	305	93,350	34,249	59,101	2.62	471.79
1967–68	573	52	521	341	102,411	38,446	63,966	2.87	512.41
1968–69	634	55	579	370	116,727	43,244	73,483	3.13	578.14
1969–70	700	54	646	407	131,332	48,749	82,582	3.44	646.20

Note: For 1962 and earlier years, data are for governmental fiscal years ended within the indicated calendar year. Subsequent to 1962, financial data are for the fiscal years that close within the twelve-month period ending June 30.
Sources: U.S. Bureau of the Census, Census of Governments, 1967, Vol. 6 Topical Studies, No. 5, *Historical Statistics on Governmental Finances and Employment* (Washington, D.C., 1969); also *Governmental Finances* (annual series). When the two sources showed minor differences, the data were taken from the *Historical Statistics* volume. A complete census of state and local governments is taken every five years in the United States. The most recent one, in 1967, provides an excellent source on the financing of public libraries.

local government general expenditures, so that expenditures for all libraries as a percentage of all state and local spending also increased. We must remember, though, that expenditures for libraries are "fiscally insignificant," accounting for less than $.60 out of every $100 spent.

The various factors that contribute to growing government expenditures—an increasing population, especially the young and the old, rising prices, and prosperity—also contribute to growth in libraries. The population has been increasing most in the age groups under twenty and over sixty-five. These groups are especially interested in libraries; the young use the libraries for education and pleasure, and the elderly have the leisure time. Other age groups are also using libraries more, both for self-education and for recreational reading and other activities.

Various governments finance public libraries in the United States. Excluding school and university libraries, which are generally not classified as public libraries, state governments, counties, municipalities, townships, and special districts all provide financial support for public libraries. For 1966-67, the last year when a census of governments was carried out, Tables 1 and 2 show that of the $518 million spent on public libraries, states spent $49 million and local governments $469 million. Of the latter amount, cities financed $305 million, counties $69 million, and townships and special districts smaller amounts.

It is clear from these tables that in most areas library service is provided by municipal or county governments. There were also 410 special library districts in 10 states in 1966-67. About a third of these districts operate in metropolitan areas. The North Central area has most (359) of these districts, with over half (222) in Indiana and most of the others in Missouri, Illinois, and Ohio.[6] As indicated in Table 2, these districts spent $28.9 million, or about 6 percent of the total expenditures for libraries in 1966-67.

Expenditure amounts include both current operations and capital outlays. Of $305 million spent by municipalities for public libraries in 1966-67, $251 million was for current operations, $51 million for capital expenditures, and $2 million for intergovernmental expenditures. Further detail is available only for 1966-67 for capital expenditures, of which $40 million was spent for construction, $8 million for equipment, and $4 million for the purchase of land, including existing structures.[7]

Table 2 Expenditures on Public Libraries by Local Government Jurisdictions within and outside of Standard Metropolitan Statistical Areas, 1966–67

	Total (in millions of dollars)	Per Capita (in dollars)
U.S. (total)	469.3	2.40
Within SMSAs (total)	377.3	2.90
Counties	69.7	–
Municipalities	255.8	–
Townships	22.9	–
School Districts	–	–
Special Districts	28.9	–
Outside SMSAs (total)	92.0	1.40
SMSAs as Percentage of United States Total	80.4	120.8

Source: U.S. Bureau of the Census, Census of Governments, 1967, Vol. 5, *Local Governments in Metropolitan Areas* (Washington, D.C., 1969).

Data on local library employment and payrolls are available for 1970. All employees of local libraries numbered about 79,000 or 56,545 in terms of full-time equivalent employees, with annual payrolls of about $350 million. The average earnings were $513 per month for full-time employees.[8] Given total library expenditures of $700 million for 1969–70, as shown in Table 1, the amount of payrolls shows that roughly half of all library budgets goes for wages and salaries.

State and local expenditures for libraries vary widely among states on a per capita basis and also as a percentage of total spending by these governments, as shown in Table 3. While spending for libraries averaged $2.62 per capita throughout the United States in 1966–67 and such spending in the median state was $2.43, the per capita amounts ranged from highs of $7.01 in the District of Columbia and $5.05 in Massachusetts to lows of $1.03 in South Carolina and $1.08 in Georgia. By

Table 3 Library Expenditures of State and Local Governments Per Capita and as Percentage of Total Expenditures, by Regions and by States, 1966–67

	Per Capita Expenditures (in dollars)	Ranking According to Per Capita Expenditures	Library Expenditures as Percentage of Total General Expenditures
United States Average	2.62	–	0.6
Median State	2.43	–	–
Regions			
Northeast	3.14	2	0.6
North Central	2.49	3	0.6
South	1.78	4	0.4
West	3.63	1	0.6
States			
Alabama	1.52	43	0.4
Alaska	1.36	46	0.1
Arizona	2.43	26	0.5
Arkansas	1.17	49	0.3
California	4.02	7	0.6
Colorado	2.32	27	0.4
Connecticut	4.35	5	0.9
Delaware	1.98	35	0.3
District of Columbia	7.01	1	1.2
Florida	1.88	36	0.4
Georgia	1.08	50	0.3
Hawaii	4.92	3	0.7
Idaho	2.50	25	0.6
Illinois	2.62	24	0.6
Indiana	2.76	21	0.7
Iowa	2.82	18	0.6
Kansas	2.15	30	0.5
Kentucky	1.68	40	0.4
Louisiana	2.04	34	0.4
Maine	2.19	28	0.5
Maryland	3.99	8	0.9

Table 3 (continued)

	Per Capita Expenditures (in dollars)	Ranking According to Per Capita Expenditures	Library Expenditures as Percentage of Total General Expenditures
Massachusetts	5.05	2	1.1
Michigan	2.80	19	0.6
Minnesota	2.70	22	0.5
Mississippi	1.68	40	0.5
Missouri	2.78	20	0.7
Montana	3.82	10	0.7
Nebraska	2.17	29	0.5
Nevada	4.54	4	0.7
New Hampshire	3.55	12	0.8
New Jersey	3.73	11	0.9
New Mexico	1.80	37	0.3
New York	3.30	13	0.5
North Carolina	1.23	48	0.4
North Dakota	1.75	38	0.3
Ohio	1.60	42	0.4
Oklahoma	2.05	33	0.4
Oregon	2.88	16	0.5
Pennsylvania	1.42	44	0.4
Rhode Island	2.63	23	0.5
South Carolina	1.03	51	0.3
South Dakota	2.15	30	0.4
Tennessee	1.74	39	0.4
Texas	1.37	45	0.4
Utah	2.88	16	0.6
Vermont	3.28	14	0.6
Virginia	2.06	32	0.6
Washington	3.89	9	0.7
West Virginia	1.32	47	0.3
Wisconsin	3.17	15	0.6
Wyoming	4.34	6	0.6

Source: U.S. Bureau of the Census, Census of Governments, 1967, Vol. 4, No. 5, *Compendium of Government Finances* (Washington, D.C., 1969), Tables 35, 36.

regions, spending was generally highest in the West, followed by the Northeast, both well above the median, and then the North Central, and last the South, with relatively wide spread among the different areas.

Relative to total general expenditures, library expenditures averaged 0.6 of 1 percent on a national basis, with the range from highs again for the District of Columbia and Massachusetts of 1.2 and 1.1 percent, respectively, to lows of 0.1 of 1 percent for Alaska and 0.3 of 1 percent for Arkansas, Delaware, Georgia, New Mexico, North Dakota, South Carolina, and West Virginia. A state may be low by this measure as a result of either very low library expenditures or average or below-average library expenditures with relatively high total expenditures.

Library expenditures by local governments on a per capita basis vary appreciably by size of metropolitan area. Generally the largest SMSAs spend appreciably more per capita on libraries than do the others. As shown in Table 4, all 227 metropolitan areas had an average of $2.90 per capita in 1966-67, but the 24 SMSAs with populations exceeding 1 million averaged $3.36.

Table 4 Expenditures by Local Governments on Public Libraries in SMSAs by Population Size of Metropolitan Area, 1966-67

SMSAs by 1966 Population Size	Number of SMSAs	Total Expenditures (in millions of dollars)	Per Capita Expenditures (in dollars)
1,000,000 or more	24	248.2	3.36
500,000 to 999,999	32	53.9	2.54
300,000 to 499,999	30	30.5	2.41
200,000 to 299,999	40	21.1	1.91
100,000 to 199,999	74	18.5	1.92
50,000 to 99,999	27	5.1	2.72
Totals	227	377.3	2.90

Source: U.S. Bureau of the Census, Census of Governments, 1967, Vol. 5, *Local Governments in Metropolitan Areas* (Washington, D.C., 1969), Table 10.

Average spending per capita then declined with decrease in the size of metropolitan areas to about $1.90 for those with populations of 100,000 to 300,000 and then increased to $2.72 for those of less than 100,000 populations. For expenditures by city governments only, the same relation of per capita expenditures varying directly with size of city appears, without the exception of smaller cities showing unexpectedly high spending.

Within most metropolitan areas, library spending per capita usually varies widely among different jurisdictions. Typically, per capita spending is highest in the central city, although in a few cases per capita expenditures in some suburban jurisdictions with excellent libraries exceed those of the central city. Data from 1966–67 provide examples of variations in per capita expenditures for libraries, as shown in Table 5. These data are on a countywide basis and thus not as specific as if calculated for each separate municipality.

Fees, charges, and fines are other sources of library revenues. Fees may be charged for nonresident users, for book reservations, and for certain research services; fines are levied primarily for overdue or damaged

Table 5 Per Capita Library Expenditures in Three Metropolitan Areas (in dollars)

	New York	San Francisco	Houston
SMSA Average	3.80	4.76	1.42
Central City	4.68	4.88	1.48
Suburban Area #1	0.54 (Suffolk County)	2.56 (Marin County)	0.36 (Liberty County)
Suburban Area #2	1.01 (Nassau County)	5.89 (San Mateo County)	0.95 (Fort Bend County)

Source: U.S. Bureau of the Census, Census of Governments, 1967, Vol. 5, *Local Government in Metropolitan Areas* (Washington, D.C., 1969), Table 12.

books. Limited data indicate that these sources have provided about 5 percent of library revenues during the postwar period. Compared to charges for most other services, library charges have remained relatively constant in proportion to the cost of service.[9]

Gifts for current use and for endowment are still another source of revenue but are relatively small. Although occasionally a large gift or campaign may provide funds for the site for a library or a wing of a building, such gifts are rare and cannot be counted on in a library's budget.

Implication of Trends for Financing Metropolitan Libraries

The metropolitan area offers an excellent opportunity for libraries to cooperate in interlibrary loans, special research collections, exhibits, the operation of binderies, photocopy services, lectures, maps, and other important services. Changes in the population of the central city have made the main library both the major library in the metropolitan area and a research center for business and professional use. Its importance as a research center will increase as research activities grow in the central city.

Many contemporary libraries also offer plays, films, musical performances, consumer education, and discussion groups. Their collections are expanding to include information sources on microfilm, magnetic tapes, disks, punched cards, video tapes, and other media for recording information. These services and facilities add to costs but are necessary improvements.

Branch libraries are frequently located in neighborhoods that have changed their character, as the traditionally most frequent users of the library from the white, middle-income families have moved to the suburbs. Branch libraries in the minority-group or low-income residential neighborhoods are valuable because the residents have relatively few books in their homes, and their access to books is thus primarily through schools and libraries. The libraries must now provide programs contributing to literacy, improved educational levels, a broadening of cultural horizons, and recreation. To achieve these goals, librarians must work effectively with other governmental and private agencies in the metropolitan areas, especially with public schools and recreational and social agencies. Libraries may also have opportunities to relocate or improve their services in areas experiencing urban renewal and housing developments. The location of new branches should be decided on a metropolitan-wide basis. New areas might be served by bookmobiles or other transient library facilities until a permanent library can be started efficiently.

In the rapidly growing suburbs, instead of branch libraries with no users, there are now users but inadequate libraries. The variety and quality of library services are very uneven. In the older suburbs the libraries frequently are strong and well developed, with programs to meet community needs and interests. In the newer areas the problem is how to prevent library services from lagging too far behind new population needs. In those areas, services such as new schools and streets compete with libraries at budget making time and may carry a greater sense of urgency. The libraries need popular and political support to get 2 percent of the budget for themselves. The strong interest of the suburbanites in children and schools strengthens the libraries' case for a place in the budget. Some suburbs may find it most efficient to contract for library services from the county or from an adjacent municipality with a well-developed library system.

County governments, or other governments serving all or a large part of the metropolitan area, can provide library services more efficiently than can the numerous municipalities in the county. It is desirable that any state aid program encourage local communities to coordinate and cooperate—and perhaps even to consolidate—to provide the best services at minimum cost. Any level of government that provides assistance to libraries in metropolitan areas should see to it that library services are at a reasonable minimum throughout the metropolitan area.

Financial incentives should be geared to help those jurisdictions least able, in terms of the local tax base, to maintain library service in their area. New arrangements for providing revenue on a metropolitan-wide basis are under examination in many metropolitan areas. A metropolitan-wide property tax would be a more equitable way of financing metropolitan-wide library services than separate property taxes collected by various library districts. A metropolitan-wide sales tax, income tax, and value-added tax are other alternatives that would produce substantial revenue to relieve the overworked and inequitable property tax.

From the point of view of libraries, it would be desirable to have earmarked taxes on which the libraries would have sole or first claim. From the point of view of good budgeting, however, segregating and earmarking revenues for particular purposes does not lead to the greatest efficiency. The need met by the earmarked tax may change, and the particular function financed by the earmarked tax may be carried out either on a gold-plated basis or on a starvation basis if the need for the service does not change at the same rate as the revenue from the earmarked tax.

Libraries receiving financial support on a metropolitan-wide basis should be expected to make their facilities and services available to all inhabitants of the metropolitan area. An efficient development of library resources in the metropolitan area would require one or more large library systems with a wide range of services. Consolidation of library districts would eliminate competition for funds, duplication of specialized services, and the many technical service operations. One library board could plan the location of facilities and the provision and expansion of services for the entire metropolitan area. The public library system could coordinate efforts effectively with university libraries, private research centers, and public educational institutions.

Title II of the 1966 Demonstration Cities and Metropolitan Development Act requires that libraries be included in metropolitan planning for applications for certain federal loans and grants. Federal legislation and rules, however, do not require a metropolitan library network.

The community orientation of the separate libraries could be continued by encouraging contributions from municipalities, boards of education, and private groups and individuals for the benefit of particular branch or area libraries. Neighborhood advisory boards might assist branch libraries in serving better the interests of the area residents.

In summary, public libraries in metropolitan areas face rising expenditures, expanding pressures for more revenues, diversity of service levels among different jurisdictions within the metropolitan area, and imbalance between needs and resources. Libraries have an advantage in that their budgets are relatively small and are not a decisive factor in major fiscal changes, such as a sharp increase in the property tax rate. Dedicated and effective support from library users can usually justify the library budget, although generally at a level below that recommended by the American Library Association. On the other hand, public libraries do not have the emotional appeal, broad public contact, and visibility of the public schools. Thus large expenditure increases, especially if they must be voted separately, may be difficult to achieve. To deserve and receive support, library services must expand and be responsive to changing clienteles.

The library system in the central city will continue to provide the most important library service to the entire metropolitan area. Reliance on this library system may well increase, regardless of any decline in the population of the central city. Urban libraries should expect to fare well provided they offer efficient and high-quality service in meeting the interests of the changing populations and cooperate on a broad basis with other public and private libraries in the metropolitan areas.

Notes

1. Calculations based on data from U.S. Bureau of the Census, *Local Government Finances in Selected Metropolitan Areas in 1969-70* (Washington, D.C., 1971), Table 3. These data are for 38 of the largest metropolitan areas, which account for half of all local government finances in the United States.

2. U.S. Bureau of the Census *Current Population Reports*, Series P-23, No. 37, "Social and Economic Characteristics of the Population in Metropolitan and Non-metropolitan Areas: 1970 and 1960 (Washington, D.C., 1971).

3. Excellent general discussions of fiscal imbalance are provided in studies of the Advisory Commission on Intergovernmental Relations. See especially *Fiscal Balance in the American Federal System*, Vol. 2, "Metropolitan Fiscal Disparities" (Washington, D.C., 1967); and *Measuring the Fiscal Capacity and Effort of State and Local Areas* (Washington, D.C., 1971).

4. Dick Netzer, *Economics of the Property Tax* (Washington, D.C.: The Brookings Institution, 1966), pp. 116-125.

5. *Economic Report of the President, 1970* (Washington, D.C., 1970), Table C-3. A study of the Cleveland metropolitan area, covering the period 1940-1956, showed that spending for public libraries when adjusted for population growth and inflation had actually declined over this period (from $4.42 to $4.03 in constant dollars per capita), although total spending for libraries increased from $2.2 million in 1940 to $7.0 million in 1956. See also S. Sacks and W. Hellmuth, *Financing Government in a Metropolitan Area: The Cleveland Experience* (New York: The Free Press, 1961), Tables III-10, 11, 12, 13.

6. U.S. Bureau of the Census, Census of Governments, 1967, Vol. 1, *Governmental Organization* (Washington, D.C., 1968), Table 15.

7. U.S. Bureau of the Census, Census of Governments, 1967, Vol. 4, No. 4,

Finances of Municipalities and Township Governments (Washington, D.C., 1969), Table 2.

8. U.S. Bureau of the Census, *Public Employment in 1970* (Washington, D.C., 1971), Tables 3, 8, 9.

9. The National Industrial Conference Board, *Use of Service Changes in Local Government* (New York, 1960), pp. 28–29.

11 The Role and Structure of Metropolitan Libraries

Lowell A. Martin

When considering the public library in the metropolitan area, one thinks first of complex governmental structures and relationships: mainly the suburban political patchwork and the tensions between central city and surrounding area. If one considers cooperative arrangements among public libraries, one promptly becomes enmeshed in political boundaries and taxing jurisdictions. Plans devised to meet such governmental problems are likely to center around some grant for a new metropolitan library structure. The difficulty is that new structures are usually designed to provide the same old service. The functions of the public library—its social role and institutional purposes—in most schemes follow the prevailing city model, which may not be what changing metropolitan areas need.

The social composition of both city and suburban areas is changing. When city libraries appeared a century ago, the metropolitan complex had one population pattern; it had another pattern when suburban libraries were established a half century ago; it has still another pattern today as systems structures are developed for libraries; and it will have a different configuration again before the end of the century. Rather than concentrating on new governmental structures, we would do better to think about what and who the new systems and networks are for. The progression in this paper is from function to structure, with primary concern for clientele.

The Role of the Metropolitan Public Library

The public library, in the metropolitan area as elsewhere, rests upon a series of assumptions: that there is social value in providing the general public with contemporary books and related materials, that commercial channels do not and cannot adequately meet this social need, that the mass media leave significant gaps in information and cultural coverage, that people do not have suitable alternative institutional sources of reading materials, that the cost-benefit ratio of a public utility to serve the purpose is favorable, and that people are self-motivated and will seek out the library. Such assumptions were implicit when the public library appeared in the mid-nineteenth century, and for the most part they continue to be accepted today.

Without venturing into the historical question of whether these assumptions were consistent with the conditions of nineteenth-century America, it is apparent that certain factors underlying them have changed. The public library appeared in a period of print sparsity for any but the most educated and affluent members of society; today there is a glut of printed materials available to the public. The public library appeared in a period of printed communication that the user had to seek out; today film and air wave and sound track carry the thoughts and cries of man in an omnipresent wave, to the point where the individual has to scheme to avoid them. The public library appeared in a period of library scarcity; today libraries proliferate in schools, colleges, business organizations, government offices, cultural agencies, and professional centers. Nowhere is this situation so apparent as in the metropolitan setting.

Some of the new data and materials sources originally were "spin-offs" from the public library. Schools once had no libraries; subsequently collections were maintained in the schools by the public library; next came autonomous school libraries; and now the policy is proposed that school libraries provide all book and related services for children. The businessman, originally unrecognized as a special library client, came to be served by business branches and now relies on special libraries or information centers within commercial and industrial enterprises. Service to government, handled earlier by public libraries, is now rendered by departmental collections in governmental agencies and by municipal and state reference and legislative centers. A galaxy can spin off just so much, and then it begins to lose its central energy.

In the face of the print glut, multimedia pervasion, and agency spin-offs, how has the public library survived? In part by retention of residual publics and in part by slow adjustments to changing conditions.

Public library users are often remnants of publics, many of whose members have become dependent on other sources. Consumers of current popular culture depend upon a remarkable array of magazines, paperbacks, and recordings, forms that play only a modest role in public library collections. In a parallel development, specialists depend upon

scientific and scholarly journals, while such publications in any range
and depth are stocked by only the largest of public libraries. In the
past "professionals" bulked large among public library users, but new
materials and data networks are developing for many such groups; even
the larger public libraries do not seek to build up resources for lawyers,
physicians, engineers, architects, and other professionals. Civic and
cultural "leaders" once constituted a public library clientele; a recent
study in Baltimore of 800 such leaders showed that while they were
more likely to be public library users than members of the total population, they did not depend on the library for the materials directly
used in their leadership capacities. Persons who seek present-day versions
of love and mystery stories find the commercial paperback rack loaded
with such books; the love and mystery sections in most public libraries
are much reduced from what they were several decades ago. Even the
counterculture adherents do not turn to the public library but patronize
bookstores and record shops catering to their interests.

Another category of residual public library users includes the child and
the student. It may seem odd to refer to students, who constitute half
the users of public libraries, as a "residue," but the most clearly documented change in use of public libraries in the past decade has been a
decline in patronage by children of elementary school age. The considerable number of children and young people who continue to turn to the
community agency do so because in some degree school libraries do not
meet their needs. When limitations on school resources are removed,
many more students will cease to use the public library. Students are
not a public that the community library expressly sought, and when
students flocked to public libraries in large numbers after World War II,
some librarians considered them a problem.

Residual publics only partially explain the survival of the public library
in changed times. Over the years the institution itself has adjusted to
new demands. The thrust for extension, for local neighborhood outlets,
is one such adjustment. The idea early took hold of the public library as
delivery system as well as resource; extension in the form of branches
has long preempted a considerable portion of the energy and resources
of city libraries. If the concept of the public library had been limited to
the large central collection, as in various European and Asian countries,

the whole metropolitan library problem would have a different complexion today. But branches were established, not just in distant sections, but in nearby neighborhoods, and then units were established in each suburban town, resulting in the present-day jigsaw metropolitan library service to which these papers are addressed.

The emergence of children's service is another adaptation. Surprisingly little can be found in early testimony on public libraries about the needs of younger children. Yet in recent decades service to youngsters has become one of the distinctive features of the public library. The role of children's service is not simply supplying reading materials that the younger generation wants or demands but rather goes on to (1) opening the experience of reading to children and (2) providing the best of published output for this age level. In pursuit of this mission children's librarians have developed new methods (story hours, for example) and adopted exacting standards for selecting materials. Unlike the official quality standards for adult books, which are sometimes compromised when public pressure is exerted, professed aims and actual performance have usually been in accord in the case of children's services.

The provision of library subject collections grew slowly in the nineteenth century and subsequently was formalized by subject departments in public libraries in the early decades of the present century. In the process the emphasis shifted from the library as repository of what was most in demand to the subject collection reflecting contemporary life. Even city branches and suburban outlets now partake of this trend, resembling small department stores, pale copies of the central units, rather than specialty shops. However, a balanced subject collection may not be the most needed function of smaller library units in the metropolitan region.

Adjustments have also been made in the role of the librarian as personal intermediary between seeker and source. The sequential emergence of the reference librarian, the reader's adviser, the young adult librarian, and most recently the community field worker has been gradual. While some of these intermediaries have become fixtures in library service (the reference librarian, for example), others (the reader's adviser and the young adult librarian) have declined in numbers. Yet one-third of public library users depend on staff members for guidance, a professional function of merit quite separate from the provision and delivery systems provided.

All this is prologue and serves only to set the parameters of the public library today, which is a multipurpose rather than a focused institution. This multiplicity of purpose is the source of both its strength and its weakness, of its flexibility and its ambiguity. The public library has served as a mirror of civilization; it is the institution of record, showing where man has been and where he is now. It has followed demand rather than set goals; it is more reaction oriented than mission oriented. These characteristics have sustained the institution, but concern about its role and function has increased because of the erosion of traditional clientele groups. The remnants of user groups—diversional readers, best seller followers, business and professional inquirers, social commentary readers, cultural respondents—comprise together about 10 percent of the adult population of a metropolitan area. The data indicate that this percentage of nonschool users has not increased in recent decades, despite a steady rise in the educational level of the metropolitan population.

In geographic terms we are dealing with an institution that is moderately convenient: more convenient than bookstores but less convenient than the mails and electronic data channels. The public library is usually too far away for ready access to low-income people of the inner city, whose lives are often confined to small neighborhoods, yet more accessible than it need be to geographically mobile middle-class suburbanites. For most children the library outlet is too distant for easy and safe access (in a recent Philadelphia study 35 percent of the fourth- and sixth-graders claimed that their parents did not permit them to go to the branch library because of distance and traffic arteries). Distance and mobility are additional factors in the public and school library relationship, for approximately three times as many school libraries exist for elementary youngsters in metropolitan areas as branch and suburban public libraries.

Public libraries in metropolitan regions, with their modest subject collections and their general reference librarians, are oriented largely toward a middle range of readers toward which commercial sources are also aimed and which comprises the same clientele for whom other libraries have been formed (that is, school, college, business, and similar libraries). In short, public libraries in metropolitan areas compete for patrons who have various other sources of reading and information and expressional materials while playing down inner-city poor and blue-collar families on the one side and the unaffiliated specialist and cultural sophisticate on the other.

The gulf between the city library and the residents of the urban ghetto has been variously noted and is the subject of a voluminous recent literature. Some public libraries are making efforts to develop an inner-city clientele, but most such efforts are marginal, reflecting no fundamental adjustment in priorities away from the well-supplied middle range and involving no basic change in service programs. What "outreach" is achieved tends to be pulled back when the special resources that support such programs are exhausted.

In contrast with widespread concern about the disadvantaged, the limited relation of the metropolitan public library to increasing numbers of specialists, community and business leaders, government officials, intellectuals, and cultural sophisticates has been less documented. The strongest of the central-city libraries—in Boston, Philadelphia, Detroit, Baltimore, and Los Angeles, for example—have a capacity to serve this clientele, but only a few metropolitan regions have public libraries capable of meeting the needs of this group. What library resources are available to serve the technical and professional needs of the unaffiliated specialist in Hartford, Santa Fe, Orlando, or Duluth? The characteristic of a specialized population today is that it is dispersed, and this dispersal will continue to increase with urban decentralization.

In the past the public library served the partly educated adult, who had relatively few sources of educational materials. Currently the urban public library serves predominantly students, whose school and college libraries are developing the capacity to meet most of their needs. New prospects for public library service are in the several groups mentioned: the unaffiliated specialist, the cultural cosmopolitan, and the under-educated urban slum dweller. The first two groups will grow in size and disperse in location, although within metropolitan areas. The disadvantaged will decrease in numbers, but the decrease will swell the ranks of blue-collar and service workers, who have not been heavy public library users.

The metropolitan public library as a multipurpose agency serving a middle range of reading and educational interests does not have an expanding future. Given an open and multimedia society, the public library in its present orientation is not serving a unique public purpose. Moreover, some of the competing agencies have the edge in responsiveness and convenience. Such a statement should not suggest that the middle range should be abandoned—there are out-of-school and moderately educated adults who regularly use metropolitan libraries—but the future prospects for *increased* use of general subject collections are limited.

The library serving various groups that are off-center in the diversity of American life—made up of persons seeking to find their place in the culture on the one hand or those seeking to extend its boundaries on the other—offers the greater future prospect. The public library has adjusted in the past, from elitist America to utilitarian and mass-culture America. The question now is whether it can do so again for a society highly dependent on complex data for its technological and economic functioning and consciously searching for fresh values in its personal and group life.

The changes in the cultural and governmental milieu in which the public library operates have occurred mostly in metropolitan settings. So far as adjustment has occurred in the institution, it is the city library and the suburban library that have responded. Social, cultural, and political changes that affect public libraries in the years ahead will first be evident in the metropolitan areas. The question is, What will the metropolitan library become in the next decades, and what shape will it assume to carry out functions socially useful and unique?

Structure of the Metropolitan Public Library

The pattern of library service today in the metropolitan area was formed from this background of function fitted to the exigencies of the governmental base in city and suburbs. There was first the central-city library, serving earlier as an informal educational agency for nonschool adults, serving now primarily as a combined student and subject resource, with research strength in a very few of the largest cities. Out from the center in the various sections of the city are branch libraries. The push and pull of the demands of the central unit on the one hand and the branches on the other can be traced in the growth of each city library. Frequently central development has been sacrificed to local convenience.

In function city branches were formerly popular reading centers, stressing diversional materials, best sellers, and utilitarian manuals. Today they are small subject and students' libraries that include a sizable children's section. Two factors brought them into existence: convenience in delivery provision and local identification in service programs. The first has been almost completely achieved and continues to prompt substantial response in middle-level areas of the city. The second aim of local variety and adaptability has been achieved only to a limited extent, with many branches being similar to one another no matter what the differences in neighborhoods.

As suburbs were established beyond the city boundaries, usually each created its own modest library. Exceptions to this pattern include the countywide agency or the occasional combination of city and county units. In the majority of cases local municipal libraries and county libraries both exist in the metropolitan region, in which case the county library is one more piece in the library patchwork. The newest addition is the large township library, located in rapidly growing exurban sections, sometimes with both a central building and branches over a sprawling territory. In the suburbs as in the city the motivating forces in establishing additional library units were convenience of access and local identification. Once established, local libraries soon accumulate an aura of local pride that protects them against amalgamation or consolidation.

As separate small towns grew in America before the metropolitan upsurge, each started its own library; when suburbs sprouted, the pattern was repeated. These many libraries, large and small, central and branch, suburban and exurban, constitute the metropolitan pattern as it exists today and the base from which any restructuring must start.

The nature or purpose of the service provided does not change markedly as one goes from city to suburb and across suburban lines, although capacity differs sharply depending on size and economic level of municipalities. Function has emanated out from the city library; the suburban library seeks to be like its city forerunner. Yet suburban communities can usually afford no better than a partial copy, so that most suburban libraries end up resembling branches of the city library. Functionally they are often ancillary units lacking a formal center. Thus the thrust has been horizontal, spreading a relatively thin layer of service points over the metropolitan landscape. The emerging structure of suburban library systems constitutes an effort to bring strength to an arrangement designed to achieve convenience and localism rather than quality and excellence.

As libraries of all sorts proliferated in the metropolis, a kind of natural web emerged. Each type of library tried to serve its own immediate clientele while attempting to avoid undue overlap or duplication. The new public libraries filled geographic gaps. The school libraries aimed initially to provide curricular and collateral readings, while the public libraries avoided texts. The business libraries sought to acquire working collections while depending on public libraries for wider subject resources. Specialized libraries sought to provide advanced materials in their own fields, leaving the task of providing general resources to the public library. At one time all this could be pictured as a large circle representing the older city public library and a constellation of smaller circles surrounding it, the total more or less fitting together in an informal natural plan.

But the dynamic forces that had given rise to these new agencies continued, and each of these many libraries expanded. The curricular collection of the schools became the media center to serve the total education of the child and teen-ager. The business collection became an information center. The special library built resources with greater depth and scope than those held by the public library. Academic collections, which began as expanded reserve-book rooms, in some cases developed into eminent university libraries with research holdings. As a consequence the large public library was gradually eclipsed and its role made secondary.

The new element in the complex is the formal suburban library system, an umbrella organization over autonomous local public libraries. The system plans, guides, provides, and processes in an effort to counteract the weaknesses of limited collections and isolated staffs. State and federal governments have joined in encouraging and supporting the umbrella organizations. Most of the suburban systems—in New York, New

Jersey, Pennsylvania Illinois, and other states—depend significantly on state money. Federal funds for public libraries, which were devoted primarily to bookmobiles after the rural Library Services Act of 1956, have been shifted in many states to systems plans since the 1964 passage of the Library Services and Construction Act. Metropolitan areas, with their burgeoning populations, have been major recipients of the systems money.

Some of the best of present-day public library service exists in certain of the suburban districts with a systems structure. Both the Westchester and Nassau units outside New York City and also the Suburban and North Suburban units outside Chicago start with a local base of library provision at almost twice the per capita financial level that prevails in the country as a whole. The concentration of population brings substantial support to these systems without imposing the burden of large territory. On the other hand, one has only to move a little farther from the central urban area to the Ramapo-Catskill system, still within the New York metropolitan area, or the DuPage system at the fringe of the Chicago metropolitan area, to find very uneven service. As Lester Stoffel points out in another chapter of this book, a library system is no stronger than its members; cooperative arrangements do not automatically transform poor libraries into good ones.

Note that new systems change neither the functions nor the form of metropolitan library service. The local library remains under its own control, nursing its traditions, justifying its many limitations. The new coordinating structure does not introduce a new level of service, nor does it reach out to broader segments of the population. The system seeks to help each existing library to do a little better in those functions it has been performing. While concrete evidence of improvement is lacking, it is probable that younger and general readers fare better than in metropolitan regions where the umbrella is lacking. But umbrella it is, preserving what is there, seeking to make the institution of yesterday do for today.

Most of the existing systems have not included both central-city and suburban libraries but have been designed for suburban units alone. The result is the development of new federated suburban systems side by side with the older central-city unified system. Relations between the two have been uncertain. The city library watches the suburban systems grow, wondering how much help the older agency should offer the newcomers. If central-city administrators had a clear sense of population trends, they would also be wondering how much help they could obtain in the future from the more populous and wealthier suburban structures. The suburban systems are unsure whether they should seek to duplicate the city library or whether there is some way to draw on its accumulated strength while protecting their new identities. The bureaucratic dance is polite and measured but could have serious overtones. Although a trend may not be likely, in more than one instance city library and metropolitan county library, or city library and suburban library system, will eventually be joined together.

New metropolitan-wide library networks including academic and special libraries as well as large public library systems are being organized in a few places: METRO in the New York City area and MELSA in the Minneapolis area are examples. This is layer upon layer, umbrella above umbrella. Such agencies are new, and their functions and form are not yet clear. Most of them were still being planned in 1971, but their central purpose is evident, that of interinstitutional improvement and utilization of resources outside the middle range of service normally handled by public libraries. In many urban centers, the metropolitan library coordinating agency, rather than the city library, will be the means to meet the needs of an increasingly specialized society.

While these enlarged new systems have been developing, the relation of the central unit of the city library to the metropolitan region has been undergoing significant change. For many decades the city library has influenced library growth in the surrounding area, partly as model, partly with overt leadership, partly by functioning as a second line for materials. As the shift to suburbs accelerated, former city residents continued to use the main library back in the city, thus adding a direct service component to the city-suburban relationship. In instances where registration for home circulation is permitted by the city library, the suburban response has been substantial. The Chicago Public Library carries 70,000 suburban residents on its rolls. In Newark use of central facilities by nonresidents reached 50 percent of total patronage. It is disturbing to watch cities struggling to finance central library services on meager budgets that get no support from suburban users even though the latter are heavy beneficiaries.

This "unofficial" relationship of the central public library to the metropolitan area is being recognized. The New York Public Library is a resource of more than citywide import, and it receives state money. The Chicago Public Library serves as reference and resource center for northern Illinois, the Free Library of Philadelphia for eastern Pennsylvania, the Newark Public Library for northern New Jersey, each with support from state and federal funds. The Enoch Pratt Free Library in Baltimore serves officially as a statewide facility.

The central unit of the city library is becoming a metropolitan library in many places. This trend is likely to continue as states seek to improve library service short of providing duplicate resources. This development can come none too rapidly, for city libraries are increasingly threatened by the crisis in city financing. If a local-state-federal sharing of funding for existing institutions that have a metropolitan role does not move apace, the city library will lose the capacity to play an area-wide role.

The Future of Metropolitan Library Service

Against this background of traditional functions and prevailing structure, what directions are public libraries in metropolitan areas likely to take in the future, and what will be the configuration of their relationships?

In the case of suburban libraries, it is obvious that they cannot individually achieve a range of programs and resources much beyond their present level. The older and larger suburbs near the city boundaries are experiencing many of the problems of the central city, with attendant financial pressures. The suburbs in the traditional sense—upper-income, middle-class, print-oriented—sometimes have distinctive libraries, but most of them are strictly limited in population growth and new revenue sources. The newer, sprawling outer suburbs do have space and may attract industrial tax sources but will probably respond to the demand for public library facilities by duplicating the earlier efforts of the established suburbs.

Branch libraries within cities may show a decline in use earlier than the suburban outlets. General reading of the type that leads to the establishment of the typical branch library with a popular range of subject publications is not a characteristic demand in many sections of the city. This observation is aimed primarily, not at the inner-city ghetto, which does not comprise the bulk of most cities, but rather at the considerable stretches of lower-middle-class neighborhoods. As city budgets come increasingly under pressure and the public library takes. its share of cuts, branch services will be curtailed.

This decline can be anticipated unless branch libraries and suburban libraries develop fresh concepts of community library service. Outreach programs such as those described in Claire Lipsman's essay, now being tried on an experimental basis in the inner city, suggest some directions. However, it is apparent that recent efforts have been inadequate or poorly designed. To this point most library ghetto programs have constituted either minor modifications of existing services or campaigns to encourage people to come in to use unchanged services, rather than a rethinking of the library in relation to persons of limited education and low income. Some of the suburban libraries could move in another direction, away from the body of standard library materials reflecting the prevailing culture to the multiforms of the emerging culture.

Both directions—bringing minorities into the present mainstream and providing a new cultural experience for those disposed to explore beyond established values—assume an aggressive response on the part of the community library that is alien to its traditions. Furthermore, such development may have significance only if priorities are realigned. Without substantial redirection, the community library in the metropolitan region will remain marginal and static.

The public library has in the past assumed different forms and functions as society and clientele groups have changed; it must do so again if it is to survive as a useful public agency. The essential question is whether the metropolitan community library is prepared to serve people as they engage in their search for new cultural goals.

The central unit of the city library presents a different prospect. It has had a metropolitan-wide function for decades, and the importance of this function is increasing. It is, as Conant has suggested, the keystone of a metropolitan library, at least in centers lacking a preeminent combination of university, subject, and research collections. This preeminence has to a degree been recognized by city, metropolitan, county, and state governments alike. Now with a new relationship emerging between the federal government and metropolitan areas, the federal government is becoming increasingly involved. Potentially, federal resources could solve the big-city library financial dilemma, for while both local and state governments are tied to protective, housekeeping, and transport obligations that make a prior claim on the public purse, the federal government has some freedom in reassigning priorities. The rhetoric of federal policy makers concerning improvement in the quality of life may eventually be transformed into action. The new metropolitan library, with roles to play in the informational, educational, and cultural components of the future society, could flourish in the process. One can conjecture as to the future of metropolitan libraries across the country, serving the substantial majority of American people who live in metropolitan districts and maintained financially by the several levels of government.

No one set of functions and no one structure seems either likely or desirable for the emerging metropolitan library. In the few largest centers with the strongest library resources, a formal institutional network in combination with informal interagency utilization by readers is the most probable model, without an organized "metropolitan library" as such. The problem in such well-endowed centers is one of developing equitable utilization policies, and the central unit of the city library can play an important role in developing such policies. The central public library could itself be a resource for advanced university students, say, through the Master's level, thus serving the commuting student and reinforcing the research function of academic institutions that have limited resources. The public library might also serve the research needs of the relatively small group of unaffiliated "amateur scholars" in the general public. The remainder of the energy of public libraries in the very largest cities will inevitably go into neighborhood service.

Most metropolitan centers have some resources of note in agencies other than the public library but fall short of the expanding needs of a technical society. Under these circumstances the central unit of the public library may become a full partner in the multiagency provision of resources and also a channel through which the unaffiliated user may have access to nonpublic collections. In such metropolitan centers—those ranging from a few hundred thousand up to a million people or more—gaps often exist in holdings in traditional subject fields, which the public library should attempt to fill at an advanced level. The central public library also has a responsibility to provide specialized materials that are in local demand but not held by universities, such as regional literature, ethnic and racial collections, documents on urban and governmental affairs, and information on prominent local industry and technology.

The form of the city library as coordinating agency for the metropolitan region is less clear-cut: in some cases the central unit may grow into this role, but it is more likely that a metropolitan-wide library planning agency will come into existence, which will commission the city library for designated services.

In many smaller urban regions the metropolitan public library will become more visible as a separate entity. For lack of other candidates it may become the capstone of library service in its environs. This is no small task, for on the limited population and tax base represented by the metropolitan region of moderate size, it will seek to be the determinant source for academic, technical, social, and cultural endeavor. The smaller metropolitan regions are more numerous than the large ones, and they are often overlooked in plans for library development. It will be interesting to see if they receive proper attention in the face of our preoccupation with megalopolis.

Metropolitan library structure will evolve with discernible speed over the next decade, for man reorganizes relationships more readily than he realigns purposes and adjusts traditions. Suburban library systems will increase in number and expand in activities. City and suburban libraries will seek accommodation, probably achieve parity, and in a few cases progress to coordination. New "METROs" will appear, crossing city-suburban lines and also crossing public-academic-special lines among kinds of libraries. In the process an amalgamation will form of city, suburb, county, state, and federal governments, a far cry from the local village origin of the subscription and proprietary libraries.

And what of function? One view is that the role of the big-city library is outmoded and that the institution will languish. Such a view flies in the face of its record of adjustment, slow as this has been. Innovative, renovative, experimental are not terms one would use in describing the metropolitan public library. But durable, respected, and responsive (in the long run) are terms that do apply. The public library is more of an adaptive than a purposive institution. Like others in our society it is currently being tested to see if it can move toward the America that so many believe is attainable but that so few can describe. The special challenge to the public library is not only whether it can follow change as it has in the past but whether it can be part of a movement that leads our civilization from a revolution aimed at productivity to a revolution aimed at value.

12 Public Library Service to the Urban Disadvantaged

Claire K. Lipsman

The public library is an important element in the complex of educational institutions serving the public. In the past the library, by serving as a means of self-education, played a vital role as a vehicle for not only social and economic mobility but also intellectual development. Today public libraries, together with other educational institutions, face the difficult problems of filling this same role for groups of disadvantaged persons with problems of greater complexity than those of the past.

Public libraries in urban areas are particularly concerned by these problems and the need to find viable solutions. A chief area of concern for those involved in library policy making is the extent to which programs and approaches to this problem should depart from traditional methods and techniques of library operation. According to the traditional view, the major function of libraries is the collection, organization, and dissemination of materials. In pursuing this function, the library views itself as a resource, a repository of information, and concerns itself primarily with the flow of that information. The library meets the needs of users by making available appropriate materials, but it does not assume responsibility for attracting users or for inducing change. A broader view of the library's function interprets the library as an agent of social and individual change. Those who are sensitive to this interpretation are well aware that the disadvantaged do not use the library because of illiteracy, ignorance, apathy, and hostility. To overcome these obstacles, library personnel should seek out and attract people they believe libraries should reach. The responsibility of the library is extended from that of supplying information to that of actively seeking to modify individual behavior and attitudes.

In an effort to promote this broader, active interpretation of the library's role, a number of demonstration programs to serve the disadvantaged have been mounted, most with the assistance of federal funds. Since 1964 approximately $10 million of funds derived under Title I of the Library Services and Construction Act (LSCA) have been expended in support of library services to the disadvantaged; state and local funds have also been employed. Some evaluation efforts have been undertaken, but, in general, information that would lead to more effective allocation of resources has been lacking. Measures of program effectiveness are fragmentary, and few libraries have considered their services in relation to other community resources or needs.

Within this context of inadequate data and criteria for measurement, a study was undertaken in 1969 of public library services to the disadvantaged in selected cities for the U.S. Office of Education. (The study was carried out under OE Contract No. 09-189008-4598 [010].) Field visits were made to fifteen cities with library programs serving the economically disadvantaged. In each city both the services of a library located in a low-income area and the area itself were investigated. The programs studied were selected so as to cover a variety of characteristics in terms of nature of the program, size of the city, ethnic group served, and geographical location of the city.

The Library and Its Constituency

To gain insight into the needs and requirements of library users and potential users, more than 3,000 individuals in fifteen cities, all residents of low-income urban areas living within half a mile of a branch library, were interviewed.

These interviews turned up some obvious findings and some new information. Library usage is a variable associated with income and education: users, in contrast to nonusers, are better educated, more affluent, and more knowledgeable about community affairs and sources of information. Since relatively fewer blacks have attained the levels of education or share other socioeconomic characteristics associated with library use, relatively few black adults patronize libraries. Although the absence of adult users is more conspicuous in the libraries serving black neighborhoods, it appears characteristic to a lesser degree of all libraries located in low-income areas. The libraries retain the youth and student component of library patronage, a source that accounts for a sizable proportion, probably about half, of standard library users, but in general they lack the patronage of nonstudents.

Two-thirds of the library users in ghetto areas are under the age of nineteen; one-third are of elementary school age (twelve and under). The younger ones come more often than the others; 70 percent of the twelve-and-under group come at least once a week. In general, those who do patronize the library come often; more than half come at least once a week, and roughly another 25 percent come at least once a month. The 50–65 percent of frequent library users have probably also been users over a period of some duration. About 60 percent of users have been coming to the library more than two years, and more than half used another library before coming to the present one. Two-thirds of the users have cards.

The most common reasons for coming to the library are related to schoolwork. People also come to read, to take out novels for enjoyment, and to be with friends. Three of these four reasons are associated primarily with youthful patronage. Most of the young children (80 percent) live within six blocks of the library, and most (90 percent) walk. Adult users, who tend to live somewhat farther away, either walk (55–60 percent) or come in a car (30 percent). Hardly anyone uses public transportation to reach the library. In low-income areas 20 percent of library users report family incomes of less than $100 per week, whereas 40 percent of nonusers in the same neighborhoods report incomes this low. Ten percent of library users have finished college as compared to 2 percent of nonusers, and 60 percent of library users are in school, as compared with 30 percent of the U.S. population at large.

Table 1 shows selected characteristics of a subset of the subjects in the survey, namely, adult users and nonusers in two age categories: nineteen to twenty-five years, and twenty-six years and over. Within each of these age groups, differences exist between users and nonusers in terms of characteristics related to educational achievement, that is, school grade completed and current participation in an educational program.

Differences between users and nonusers in the income distribution are statistically significant for the older group, but not for those in the nineteen to twenty-five age bracket. This variance may be due to a finding noted in other studies, that is, that a few years are required for college graduates to overtake nonprofessional workers, since the latter have the benefit of increased work experience. On the other hand, income differences that favor users may also be due to differences in sex distribution: a significantly higher proportion of users are male.

Table 1 Selected Characteristics of Adult Library Users and Nonusers (percent distribution)

	Age 19–25		Age 26 and Over	
	Users (N = 144)	Nonusers (N = 306)	Users (N = 281)	Nonusers (N = 1,340)
Sex				
Male	51	24	37	20
Female	49	76	63	80
Total	100	100	100	100
Race or Ethnic Group				
Black	50	55	41	56
Spanish-speaking	13	8	15	8
Other (not minority)	37	37	44	36
Total	100	100	100	100
School Grade Completed				
1–3	0	1	2	5
4–6	1	3	4	13
7–8	1	6	6	21
9–11	17	31	28	28
Completed high school	38	44	27	23
Some post-high school	28	13	16	7
Completed college	12	1	14	1
Graduate study	3	1	4	1
Total	100	100	100	100
Now Participating in Educational or Vocational Training	24	10	20	3
Not in a program	76	90	80	97
Total	100	100	100	100
Family Weekly Income				
Below $50	8	8	11	17

Table 1 (continued)

	Age 19–25		Age 26 and Over	
	Users (N = 144)	Nonusers (N = 306)	Users (N = 281)	Nonusers (N = 1,340)
$50–99	16	28	16	24
100–149	23	25	25	22
150–200	17	17	20	13
Over $200	23	9	16	6
No response	13	13	12	18
Total	100	100	100	100

Library users are more knowledgeable concerning cultural events, community institutions, and community resources. By contrast, 25 percent of nonusers never heard of their branch or neighborhood library. Of those who have heard of it, only one-third remember having ever visited it. Almost all the nonusers who have heard of the library are not well informed about nonbook materials or activities. Users are more knowledgeable about library materials, and half of them know something about the library's special programs or activities.

Despite the differences between library users and nonusers, there are fundamental preferences common to both, particularly in the area of media and communication. Of all the persons interviewed, 90 percent watch television, and 60 percent watch it daily. More than 80 percent of everyone over the age of twelve usually read the papers, and roughly the same proportion listen to the radio. Despite the fact, however, that virtually everyone is reached by these media, the most common way in which users and nonusers find out about community programs or services is through friends, neighbors, or other members of the family. Only about 10–15 percent find out about these programs through radio, television, or newspapers. People do not fully realize what community programs offer until they hear about them from others.

Users and nonusers were asked to select from a list of library materials and activities those that would be of interest to themselves. The choices made most frequently by both groups were printed materials—books, magazines, and newspapers. Users expressed an almost equally strong interest in information on job training and other community programs or services. The next most popular choice was free entertainment, such as movies, dances, and concerts. Nonusers were generally less interested in any of the items on the list, but about half expressed interest in children's programs and in adult education.

Users and nonusers were also asked to choose subjects of interest from a list that included child care, medical information, legal help, job information, and similar areas related to daily life. Responses to these items are apparently reflections of the sex and age differences between users and nonusers, rather than of differences related to library use. Choices by users were: sports, job information, and racial discrimination. Choices by nonusers were medical information or help, child care, and job information. The interest in employment and related information was pervasive; both users and nonusers had used or visited employment centers more frequently than any other community service or program.

The data do not indicate any clear differences among individuals that can be attributed to variables of racial or ethnic origin. Of all persons interviewed, approximately 60 percent were black, 10 percent Spanish-speaking, and 30 percent white. These proportions were the same for both library users and nonusers. The interviews were conducted in fifteen city neighborhoods, of which eight were predominantly black, two were predominantly white, two were mixed or contiguous black-and-white neighborhoods, and three were predominantly Spanish-speaking. The principal difference among communities was the relative absence of adult users in black neighborhoods. As noted earlier, the variables of income and particularly of education probably account for this difference.

Only 18 percent of library users in white and racially mixed cities reported weekly incomes of less than $100, as compared to 22 percent of users in black cities and 25 percent of users in Spanish-speaking communities. On the average, 15 percent of library users in white and mixed areas were college graduates, as compared to 12 percent in Spanish-speaking areas and only 4 percent in black neighborhoods.

In addition, library users tended to respond idiosyncratically to the library they patronized or the environment in which they were located. In one city where street gangs were a problem, only 6 percent of users came from more than six blocks away. In cities with strong and well-organized poverty agencies, much larger proportions of both users and nonusers had heard of these agencies.

Although researchers were not able to disentangle relationships among socioeconomic, ethnic, and other factors, it is clear that unless these factors are present in such proportion as to produce the patterns of library usage traditionally associated with white middle-class libraries, it is probably necessary for the library to depart substantially from its accustomed role if it is to convert nonusers into users. The middle-class pattern of predominant adult usage—that is, higher percentage holding library cards, higher percentage with stable history of library patronage, predominant interest in borrowing books for enjoyment rather than for aid in school-related subjects, and higher level of educational attainment—is much less typical of black neighborhoods than of other neighborhoods.

In summary, the interviews suggest three major needs in urban disadvantaged areas:

1. The need to respond more fully to the predominantly youthful character of the user population

2. The need to make libraries relevant to the lives of blacks in urban communities

3. The need to respond to prevailing patterns of media preference and modes of communication.

The Library and Other Community Institutions

In the view of the community, the library operates as a local institution delivering services in certain substantive categories. The kinds of services that a library system provides will differ from city to city; however, there is a well-defined spectrum within which libraries customarily operate, a spectrum that includes services in the categories of education, information, culture, and recreation. Obviously, the library is not the only community agency delivering services in these areas. The schools are the primary resource for direct educational services; poverty agencies assume some responsibility for providing information and referral; and both public and private groups may offer cultural and recreational programs or programs intended to motivate interest in learning.

To assess community needs and the availability of resources to meet these needs, representatives of public and private agencies involved in these services in each of the fifteen cities were interviewed. Among those interviewed were: a director of a multipurpose poverty center or agency located in or operating in the selected branch neighborhood; an officer of a public school in the selected branch neighborhood at a level, for example, elementary or secondary, appropriate to the program being studied; a similar representative from a private school serving the neighborhood; and a representative of the city government at the highest policy level at which general familiarity with library programs also existed. These interviews focused on the following areas: perceptions of priority community needs and service areas in which public libraries could contribute effectively; knowledge of library programs and activities; working relationships with the library; and perception of overall library goals.

There was a consensus that the greatest community need was for educational services related to classroom achievement. All institutions rated these services as the top priority, with services for self-education and enhancement of motivation for learning in second and third place, respectively.

Representatives of community institutions, including libraries, were also asked to list all service areas in which they believed that public libraries could contribute effectively. Most respondents agreed that libraries could serve in any of the areas, that is, in education, information dissemination, culture, and recreation. Some, however, expressed doubts about whether specific educational activities, such as teaching or tutoring, were appropriate for libraries. In some cities library trustees expressed doubts about these services; in other cities library staff members suggested that libraries should limit their activities to only the provision of facilities and materials. Only three public schools and three private schools objected to the library's involvement in education. In the area of cultural enrichment, several schools raised questions about library service, particularly the effectiveness of libraries in presentations of black or other ethnic culture. There was also a feeling that the arts—

music, dance, etc.—were more appropriately served elsewhere. Four poverty agencies objected to libraries functioning in an information role. Despite these comments by other community institutions, libraries themselves raised more objections than their institutional peers to their possible effectiveness in the whole range of service areas.

All of the respondents in the twenty-nine schools visited were asked several questions about their schools and their school libraries. Five private schools and four public schools, or 30 percent of the schools, had no libraries at all. Although twenty schools had libraries, only seven of them had a full-time librarian; the rest were open only part-time or used teachers, aides, or parents on a volunteer basis. Although most of the school libraries visited had a number of volumes approaching standards of eight to ten per child, accessibility was limited. Typically, an elementary school child has access to the library only once a week, in a scheduled class period. All elementary libraries but one were open only during school hours, and those secondary school libraries visited were open at most for fifteen to thirty minutes before and after school. Only one school library out of all those visited stayed open until 5 P.M. Thus, the resources of the school libraries, which frequently included records, films and filmstrips, as well as books for school-related work and for pleasure, were virtually unavailable to the student after school or on weekends. The school library as a place in which to work, an after-school study or homework facility, was thus also denied to the student.

In addition to this discontinuity of services and accessibility, there was little integration or coordination of school and public library resources. Of the twenty-nine schools, ten had cooperated with the public library in some sort of joint project other than the standard class visits, but in eight of the ten cases this cooperation was for a one-time activity, such as an art exhibit, the observance of Children's Book Week, or some other limited event. While twenty-three of the schools operated special educational services or programs for disadvantaged students, only five of these had formal support or materials from the public library. Only two schools, both private, reported any joint projects involving materials, although several indicated that in the past they had utilized classroom collections from the public libraries. This practice declined as school libraries were strengthened.

Twenty-two schools indicated that there would be an active interest on the part of the school administration in cooperative projects with the public library, and fourteen schools indicated specifically the kinds of additional resources that they believed the library should acquire. The private schools generally preferred various kinds of audiovisual equipment and materials. Other schools asked for materials on black subjects, easy-to-read materials, and Spanish-language materials. Five schools said they did not know enough about the present holdings of public libraries to comment on additional materials. The standard class visits to libraries and librarian visits to schools served to acquaint the schools and students with library services and programs; nineteen schools felt that students were adequately informed of library programs and services, and the same number stated that the school staff was kept informed of library programs and services.

The existence of these channels for communication, however, did not seem to have facilitated effective coordination. The picture that emerged from this review of school and public library resources was one of wasteful duplication and relatively unused collections of print materials in both the school and the branch libraries, as well as lack of planned working relationships to facilitate priority goals. Even though researchers accepted the practical constraints that might limit joint planning in the area of primary instructional source materials, there remained a vast area of second-level priority needs—for self-education and motivation—in which school and public library interaction could contribute by careful joint planning to reinforce and supplement educational objectives.

The information service function, to the extent that it was provided at all, was largely assumed by the poverty agencies. A number of libraries perceived this service area as one of their functions, but not more than one or two attempted to operate actively as neighborhood information centers. The views expressed by poverty agencies in their relationships with the library were largely noncommittal or negative. In eleven of the fifteen cities some contact and joint activity occurred, but only three of the poverty agencies thought that the cooperative projects had been effective. Most of the agencies said that their staff was kept informed of library activities but indicated that general community awareness of library activities was not satisfactory. All of the poverty agencies expressed an interest in cooperation with the public library on projects, but the prognosis for success of such projects could not be too favorable as long as these agencies were not convinced of the value or outcome of such efforts. On the other hand, the user-nonuser data suggested that the agencies themselves had not mastered the resources and outreach needed to meet community needs for information.

Financial Resources and Their Allocation

Discussion of community resources is not complete without consideration of funding sources. In each city appropriate administrative personnel were asked to state their views as to whether their local municipal administration was interested in expanding financial support of library programs for the disadvantaged. In eight cities the answer was negative; the reasons cited were chiefly lack of funds. Four city sources indicated that they would favor expanded library programs for the disadvantaged, but only if the expansion was achieved by a rearrangement of priorities to divert a larger share of current library budget allocations for this purpose. In only three cities did local officials indicate the likelihood of increased local support for these programs, and these were cities offering a more or less unique political or budgetary situation conducive to expansion of the programs. For the most part, however, the prevailing view of local funding resources must be realistically viewed as negative. Cities face rising social expenditures and shrinking tax revenues, and libraries must compete for these decreasing funds with police and fire departments and other city services.

Thirteen of the fifteen cities visited had received federal financial aid for services to the disadvantaged, eleven from LSCA funds and two from other federal programs. All but one of the programs that had achieved some success in reaching their objectives in service to the disadvantaged had received very substantial support from LSCA, approximating $100,000 per year or more in each city. The support is sizable not so much in absolute dollar terms as in relation to local resources that could be mustered for the same purpose. In one city the demonstration branch enjoyed a budget two to three times that of other branches. It may well be that a relatively large dollar expenditure on program inputs is essential for significant program impact in inner-city areas, in which case local library systems may be obliged to depend even more critically upon federal assistance in this area.

The burgeoning of federally financed social programs in recent years has been followed by the development and refinement of systematic principles and techniques for administering and managing these programs. Most such management approaches utilize the fundamental premises of a planning, programming, and budgeting system (PPBS). Program decisions are made in relation to agreed-on objectives. The decisions are reviewed and revised as information on the results becomes available.

The process of guiding the program by means of planned decision making and subsequent evaluation is new to the administration of library programs for the disadvantaged. As program budgeting becomes a familiar tool in municipal government, however, the program outputs of libraries will be scrutinized critically in relation to the costs. This is especially true when federal programs are the source of support, since these programs require evaluation and accounting for funds.

At the federal level, evaluation is intended to inform and guide policy making, providing answers to questions such as the following: What variables are critical to the success of library programs for the disadvantaged? Which approaches advance what is known about learning and effective education for the disadvantaged? What comparisons can be made between projects on a cost-effectiveness basis?

At the local level, a library system should have feedback on program operations that produces answers not only to general policy questions but also to the management decisions of library programs: Which groups are being reached? How are library services regarded by their recipients? How efficient is the program operation? What new activities should be tried? How do actual program outputs compare with expected outputs? How well does the program succeed in achieving its objectives?

These questions cannot be answered adequately, because existing data-collection practices in library systems are not addressed to this purpose. Data collection continues to be focused on book collection, rather than on patrons or programs. The fifteen library systems were queried as to measures of impact and types of program-related data collection in use. All of the libraries kept records of circulation, and most recorded participation in special events; but few collected any other program-related data on a consistent basis.

In considering what types of data ought to be collected or recorded for evaluative purposes, a schematic model of program relationships and possible measures, such as that shown in Figure 1, was constructed. It was postulated that each of these basic relationships ought to approach an optimum state as follows: Program objectives should be related to individual and community needs, that is, to user requirements; program planning and implementation should carry forward program objectives; program output should reflect the achievement of program objectives and hence the satisfaction of user needs and requirements; and program inputs (costs) should be appropriate to the level of program output.

In the popular sense of the term, evaluation of a social program is considered to be the measurement of the final outcome of a program in terms of its effect on clients. This popular, but limited, concept has created many difficulties, particularly in terms of measuring outcomes of service programs, such as those afforded by the public library. The model set forth provides a way out of this dilemma by suggesting that a library program or project can be evaluated or assessed not only at the end, or point of impact, but at various other points in the planning and implementation process.

This evaluation approach, that is, looking at basic program relationships, was adopted in the study. A greater emphasis was placed upon evaluation of program implementation than upon other aspects of the program process. The emphasis upon program implementation arises in part from the inadequacy of information available for assessment of program objectives, program outputs, and subsequent cost-benefit analysis. It is clear, however, that some rough measure of program results is needed for evaluation purposes. One measure for most of the library programs in the study would have been the change in the number of users. Since virtually all of these programs have as one important objective an increase in the number of library users, numerical increase is a measure that libraries could readily adopt. The reluctance of libraries to count heads can doubtless be ascribed to the inability of some of the special programs of libraries to achieve this objective.

The argument can be made that a program objective can be defined in terms of developing skills, that this objective is as appropriately measured by changes within the individual as by changes in the number of individuals, and that such an internal change is most difficult to mea-

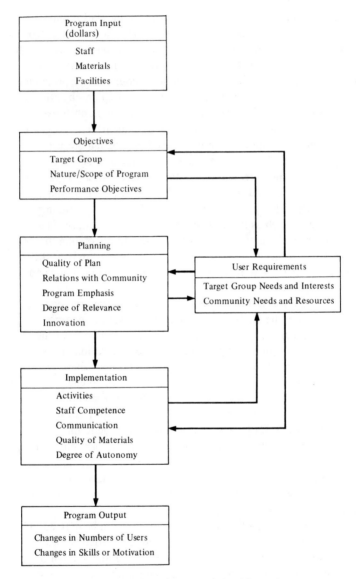

Figure 1 Library program input/output relationships and measures.

sure. Even if substantial gains were to be demonstrated by each individual participating in a library program, however, there would still need to be a sufficient number of users to justify, according to some common standard, the library program inputs. For example, suppose that an annual library program costing $30,000 produces a measurable impact on 50 users. One would still need to consider whether the same impact might be produced by some other method for less than $600 per person, or whether the $600 per person is a feasible expenditure level for this purpose, even if the impact cannot otherwise be produced.

Objectives
One of the troubling aspects of some of the unconventional library programs is that the library personnel themselves have difficulty in defining specific objectives and determining the direction in which the program leads: What do cooking classes or creative dramatics have to do with libraries?

The fundamental nature of libraries as education-oriented institutions, contributing to priority community needs, suggests that their efforts should be focused on both building cognitive skills and meeting affective human needs. Therefore programs should be planned with both of these basic dimensions in mind. Programs designed to enhance cognitive skills may include not only those directly related to reading materials but also functional competencies encompassed in the concepts of individual growth and self-education. Cognitive skills include the ability to acquire and communicate ideas, the ability to reason logically, and personal competence in areas such as physical and mental health, citizenship, family life, and occupational skill. The area of affective needs is equally vast. The findings here suggest that libraries have not thought through the implications of objectives in terms of specific program activities. In both conceptual and pragmatic terms, there are gaps and inconsistencies that need to be addressed.

Program Planning and Implementation
Although the fifteen libraries visited represented a cross section of geographic location, size of city, target group, and type of population, certain major programming elements emerged clearly from the aggregate of individual profiles as those that contributed critically to program success or failure.

Factors contributing to success can be identified as follows: competency and effectiveness of staff, genuine community involvement and support, autonomy in program decision making, high-quality materials, and effectiveness of publicity and promotion. These factors operate powerfully upon program outcomes. Their presence is concomitant with success, and the absence of positive strengths in these factors can lead to program failure.

Staff Effectiveness The constraints of the inner-city environment require much more than the average in program performance; what is not really strong and solid is quickly swept away. The dimensions of staff competency must include not only professional qualifications but also leadership skills, administrative ability, and visibility and status in the community. Although all of these attributes are essential, the distribution of roles and responsibilities can vary. In one successful program for which the staff had been carefully assembled, the director functioned well in an administrative role, having hired one senior staff member to assume responsibility for materials selection and another for community relations. The distribution worked well, and all these functions were expertly performed. In another city the project director selected a team of four to handle materials and community relations jointly.

Community Involvement The degree of community involvement and support is vital to program success; true community involvement is both a political process and an interaction. It is political in the ordinary sense of the term; attracting community support requires the same skills, resources, and continuing effort that would be required for achieving any political aim. The process is the coming together of two or more vested interests, each possessed with some power, some "clout," be it political, social, or economic. Where community involvement is successful, the program developer has understood both the potential and the mechanics for entering into working relationships with other groups to accomplish mutually beneficial aims.

Several of the library programs in the study began with goals related to community involvement: "interpreting the library to the community," "meeting community needs," etc. Most programs characterized by these goals failed. Part of this failure can be attributed to the fact that the libraries did not fully understand the delicacy and difficulty of the task. Successful community support requires interaction, two-way channels of communication between people and/or groups. All too often, libraries expect that community support can be generated by outreach, but outreach is most often understood and implemented by libraries as a one-way flow—from the library outward.

It is true that libraries can and do take their books and other services to locations outside the branch ("into the community"); such activity is praiseworthy, but it is not community involvement and by itself does not generate the kind of community support that is required. Some libraries have also employed outreach workers. If the outreach worker is in the mainstream of the social and political life of the community, is a person of some status in the community, and is knowledgeable about who's who and what's what, he serves as a valuable link between the library and the community. However, several cities have chosen as outreach workers young, white, college-educated females, perhaps with VISTA or Peace Corps experience. Despite the talents, creativity, and sympathy of these young women, the possibilities for effective inter-personal relationships between them and the community are often substantially diminished because they lack adequate personal or profes-sional status. In the absence of that status, black communities would prefer black workers, and Spanish-speaking communities, Spanish-speaking employees.

Autonomy in Program Decision Making Centralization of control is the rule in most library systems, and unfortunately it appears to inhibit programs designed to serve the disadvantaged. The most commonly encountered situation is one in which the program director recommends, and "downtown" decides. The program director is usually able to select activities or materials, but rarely does he have control over such a vital element as staff selection.

Two of the most successful projects in the study were completely different in approach and objectives; one was an exemplary branch operation, and the other a central service selecting and supplying materials to other agencies. Both had in common virtually complete autonomy from the local system, and in both cities this was cited by staff members as a major factor in program success. Conversely, less successful programs suffered from higher- or lower-level sabotage, bureaucratic red tape, and similar organizational obstacles.

Quality of Materials The selection of materials is, or ought to be, what libraries know most about and do best. Most programs whose objectives were directly related to books, reading, and materials in print were successful in assembling and organizing appropriate resources and carrying out their objectives. If these programs failed, the fault was due to inadequate publicity or promotion, rather than to poor materials.

Despite the number of successes, an equal number of projects lacked even a "modest but adequate" collection of materials relevant to blacks, Chicanos, or other minorities. Most projects subscribed to a standard list of periodicals that varied little from city to city and contained few new or special-interest items.

Easy, free-flowing utilization of the most common nonprint materials is still beyond the grasp of virtually all libraries. Only one seemed to be able to screen a short movie as easily and as naturally as selecting a book off the shelf. Easy access is limited by shortages of equipment and by what seems to be a fundamental disinclination towards audiovisual media. Vandalism and theft were occasionally cited as reasons for not stocking or replacing these items. If there were more real interest in expanding to other media, however, more effective ways might be found to maintain the security of the equipment.

Effectiveness of Publicity Publicity is a very important and very much underrated program element. Effective program promotion is an art that requires increasing attention. Most librarians believe, and rightly so, that "word of mouth is the most effective advertising," but they fail to make the comprehensive effort that must go into stimulating and evoking personal communications. For example, in one of the libraries studied a children's project had been operating its activities and turning out flyers and posters and newspaper articles for three years; yet the elementary school principal down the street had never even heard of the project.

Summary and Conclusions

In the last few years numerous institutes, conferences, seminars, monographs, and articles have urged libraries to adopt new and nontraditional approaches in program planning. Libraries have been encouraged to cooperate with other community agencies, to hire staff that can identify with the community, and to move beyond print materials.

There is an urgency, however, in the current scene, which has not been emphasized in previous studies, an urgency that arises from the serious loss of influence and popularity by libraries in low-income areas. Before the spread of paperbacks and television, libraries held a monopoly of a scarce resource, namely, books and other print materials. Secure in this monopoly of the major vehicle for communication and exchange of ideas, libraries did not need to be competitive in their institutional outlook. Recently, the monopoly position has been seriously eroded. Cheap paperbacks are widely available and can be purchased for less than the cost of processing and loan through the public library. The scarce resources in communication are now hardware, audiovisual equipment, and live experiential stimuli. These are the resources that are valued by the educational professionals and also the media that serve as the principal channels of communication for community residents.

In the analysis of program activities that was undertaken in the study, it was these characteristics—use of multimedia, active participation and response by the target group, and prestige attached to the activity—that were associated with successful program outcomes. Some examples illustrate this point. The major and perhaps essential characteristic of a successful program is that it is important to the clientele as well as to the library personnel. Even if the program is designed for children, the activity should have some community status. In some cases the importance may derive from the topic, such as drugs, Vietnam, birth control, and the California grapeworkers' strike. In other cases the status of the activity may derive from the prestige of the adults who are involved in it, such as the teachers, clergy, and doctors in one city who participated in a successful series on sex education for teen-agers.

Another characteristic of successful program activities is direct user participation. Teen-agers participated in selecting films; a teen-age council planned social affairs; young adults learned the art of photography by doing and experimenting; children told stories to the librarian; junior book reviewers advised the librarian on book selections; grade-school children learned to cook in a fully equipped kitchen. In all of these cases the role of the program user was active, rather than passive. He planned, he acted physically, to do or create something. When the activity does involve participants primarily as spectators, they respond best to multi-media stimuli. Presentations involving art, music, dance, and theater are almost universally successful. On the other hand, book talks, lectures, and routine hours of storytelling appear less effective in stimulating audiences to pursue further developmental activities on their own.

The need for more effective integration of public libraries with schools at all levels is strong and clear. If library resources in inner-city areas were coordinated with school resources, there might be enough financial support to provide for services and equipment that neither can now afford. Many respondents expressed a need for closer ties between school and library during school hours. Poverty agencies were particu-larly interested in more services of the type they see as related to formal educational achievement, for example, tutoring, remedial reading, and preschool programs.

The idea of coordinating public libraries with schools is a part of con-temporary planning for new educational and cultural centers, educa-tional parks, and similar innovative educational facilities. Inner-city branches could join with zoos, parks, and museums to offer combined field trips, visual presentations, and reference materials that would present learning as a part of the human experience, a creative sensory approach backed up by independent study or reading projects at any level.

There are also new possibilities for educational activity directed toward adults. Libraries could respond to community needs by including train-ing for those adults who already hold leadership positions in low-income communities. Several poverty agencies, for example, expressed an inter-est in subjects such as organizational development, parliamentary pro-cedures, and topics of political or sociological interest. In general, library involvement in adult education in low-income areas is focused on basic literacy needs and related concerns; consideration of the possi-bilities of meeting more sophisticated needs for technical assistance to community groups might also be valuable. Such activities would make the library useful to "important people" and set up an example that those of lesser public visibility might wish to emulate. The use of innovative equipment, such as closed-circuit television, game-simulation centers, news tickers, and computer terminals, would establish the prestige and popularity of the library with the elite of the local community at the same time that it would offer opportunities for learning not available elsewhere.

It is probable that the urban poor are now better informed than they ever were about the availability of services and assistance from the social sector. Nevertheless, at least half of the library nonusers interviewed in this study were ignorant of information sources in many areas. Libraries could provide useful information specific to the state, city, or neighborhood concerning *opportunities* in employment, higher education, housing, etc.; *procedures* for application or admission to various programs and for the securing of various social services; and *legislation*, including local building codes, tenants' rights, etc.

Collecting and maintaining this type of information would require a considerable manpower effort, since much of the information concerning procedures, for example, rests upon unwritten administrative practices, which may need to be retrieved individually and through personal visits. The information collected must be highly specific, updated frequently, and available under circumstances that provide for dignity and acceptance for the person seeking the information. Even though the information and referral role has been assumed in many cities by the poverty agencies, there is room for more than one source of ready information. Libraries might consider making city hall the focus of their effort and learning everything that any citizen might need or wish to know about dealing with city agencies or departments.

Another way to ensure a program that meets adult needs is to institute some measure of active community control. Several of the libraries visited had organized citizens' advisory groups at one time or another, but none of these lasted very long. Although none of the projects had any active community control, one of the projects visited was about to establish a demonstration branch to be completely administered by a community group. This approach to stimulating adult interest and concern is promising.

The specific activities of inner-city libraries that related to culture were almost universally successful. In several of the cities visited, libraries had offered at one time or another black art, music, dance, and drama, Chicano documentaries and study prints, and live theatrical presentations of puppet shows, folk singers, and similar attractions. Two cities offered ongoing workshops in drama or photography. All of these programs and activities attracted capacity crowds.

The lack of cultural exposure in low-income communities is clear; 65 percent of the nonusers interviewed had never been to a concert, 79 percent had never been to a museum, and 83 percent had never been to an art exhibit. The need here is great, and it is one to which libraries could successfully respond. In the cities visited the major constraints were those of facilities. Adequate accommodations for large audiences are difficult to find in low-income neighborhoods. Nonetheless, cultural activities designed to reflect and develop the heritage, traditions, and history of minority groups are particularly potent in meeting the objectives of urban libraries.

Finally, libraries need to focus upon the collection of information that will be useful as the basis for planning, improving, or modifying their own programs. Information on program functioning might feasibly be collected as it was in this study, that is, through structured interview, observation, and report. This type of information can be collected at regular intervals or as required to support program policy and long-range budgeting.

Program input (cost) data constitute an area in which substantially improved reporting would assist library systems in monitoring their own efforts as well as facilitating cost-effectiveness comparisons among programs. There are several difficulties with existing cost data. The first and the most important one is that relatively few libraries utilize a program-budgeting system. Adequate cost data are available primarily from projects that have been funded entirely by federal sources and for which program sponsors were required to prepare a budget as part of the proposal. Otherwise the cost picture is blurred, even in projects where federal funds represent part of the total cost. Regardless of funding sources, the services or programs for the disadvantaged are not always a distinct entity, either in fact or in the minds of the library fiscal officers; this situation presents many problems in allocating costs.

However, none of these factors need present serious or continuing problems to libraries interested in program evaluation. In the long run, most public libraries will doubtless be required to adopt some form of program budgeting as it gains widespread acceptance at the municipal level. Familiarity with the basic approach should convince libraries of the importance of programmed budgeting both as a planning tool and as a technique helpful in commanding public support for library expenditures in general.

13 The Suburban Library in the Metropolitan Community

Lester L. Stoffel

Nineteen seventy was "the year of the suburb," for in that year the United States passed a major social and political turning point—the nation's suburbs became the largest sector of the population, exceeding for the first time both central cities and all the rest of the country outside metropolitan areas. Evidence of two major population trends now commonly recognized appeared as early as 1900. These were migration from farm to central city and from central city to the outskirts. The automobile intensified the migration. The 1950s have been described by Hauser as "the decade of suburban boom and central-city bust." He predicts that by 1980 there will be 100 million suburbanites as opposed to 70 million central-city residents.[1]

The shopping center and the one-story factory became important parts of the suburban scene following World War II; shopping centers sometimes occupy as much total land area as central business districts. As suburbia has expanded, theaters, churches, restaurants, hotels, art galleries, and social clubs have proliferated in the outer regions of the metropolis. Trucks, automobiles, and expressways have long since released the manufacturer from restricting his selection of sites to central-city locations. White-collar workers can be hired at lower wages in suburban office buildings with parking facilities. Suburban industrial parks offer attractions to many types of industries. During the 1950s transportation advantages once enjoyed by central cities were reduced; in some industries the multistory building became obsolete; and geographical decentralization came into fashion, a forecast of substantial change in the economic functions of central areas.

Central cities were until the 1960s outnumbered by rural areas. With the one-man, one-vote principle enunciated by Supreme Court decisions of the 1960s, mayors of big cities envisioned the imminent salvation of the cities. Urbanists foresaw the shifting of state power, concern, and funds by increasing of city representation in Congress and state legisla-

An earlier version of this paper appeared in "The Public Library in the Urban Setting," ed. Leon Carnovsky, *Library Quarterly* **38** (January 1968): 1–108.

tures. Although the rural grip has been loosened, the suburbs are the major beneficiaries, and suburban attitudes toward the city are often apathetic and even hostile.

What is the suburb? It is the place where the average upwardly mobile, middle-class American lives; where the predominating life-style revolves around parental aspirations for children; where conformity and homogeneity reign; where the opinion leader is caught in a "hotbed of participation"; and where "the organization man" lives. Suburbanites are commuters who usually own homes with access to open space and room for children to play. The suburb is the compromise of modern metropolitan living with the rural small-town life of the past.

There are also, of course, industrial suburbs, slum suburbs, race-track suburbs, and honky-tonk suburbs, the latter consisting of nightclubs, amusement parks, and used-car lots. Aging suburbs border major cities and have become indistinguishable from them.

Suburbs are political entities, provincial and, in the larger metropolitan view, antiquated. In their determination to be independent of the city, suburbanites foster an alienation between themselves and city dwellers. "The justification of suburban legal independence rests on the classic belief in grassroots democracy, our long-standing conviction that small political units represent the purest expression of popular rule, that the government closest to home is best. The defense of suburban autonomy is that no voter is a faceless member in a political rally, but an individual citizen who knows his elected officials, can judge their performance personally and hold them accountable."[2]

It is easy to conceive of the metropolis with one government as a natural result of modern technology. But the suburbanite who is determined to remain independent of the city is a factor of considerable importance in the future of local governmental arrangements.

Because of the suburbanite's conviction that the *small* organization provides the best management of public affairs, suburbia comprises hundreds of local governments serving as a refuge for those who want to partake of the advantages of the city while living apart from it and ignoring its problems. Each suburban government maintains its independence, enacting ordinances, holding elections, zoning land, granting building permits, fixing speed limits, providing health, welfare, and public library services, and raising taxes. In many localities fire departments are operated by volunteers. Some suburban police forces are poorly equipped; others are quite professional. One suburb's water supply may be adequate for summer lawn watering, while another requires strict rationing. Within this framework, the suburbanite is said to be breeding a whole generation that will never have known the city at all.

Within this general profile of suburbia, what is the role of the suburban public library? Let us take, for example, the Suburban Library System of Illinois, which embraces a community of autonomous public libraries in the Chicago area. This system serves a population of approximately 1,300,000, of which 300,000 have no local public library service. The average population served by a member library is about 17,000. Of 57 member libraries, 18 serve less than 10,000 people. The largest library in the system serves about 62,000; the smallest, 757. In ten years there will be at least 88 member libraries, unless larger units are established to serve multiple suburbs.

The book collections of these libraries include about 1,500,000 volumes, ranging from a few hundred to 140,000 volumes. The largest library adds about 10,000 volumes a year. Not only are these book collections inadequate to meet the demand of the population, but extensive duplication of titles among the member libraries also indicates a lack of depth of resources within the system. A recent study indicated that a given title held by one member library of the Suburban Library System will also be found in as many as twenty other member libraries. The same study revealed a 15 percent probability that any library in the system would have a title published from 1963 to 1967.[3]

Only 11 of the 57 libraries are headed by graduate librarians. Most libraries are open 54 hours per week. Since only 16 libraries are members of a regional book-processing center, theoretically employees in 41 libraries could be duplicating book orders to be cataloged, classified, and simultaneously processed.

The Suburban Library System is only one of several library networks established since 1966 in the Illinois portion of the Chicago Standard Metropolitan Statistical Area. The North Suburban Library System, the DuPage Library System, and portions of two others duplicate, in many ways, the characteristics of the Suburban Library System, which includes only the western and southern Chicago suburbs.

Since the 1800s the Chicago suburbs have held independent referenda to establish libraries, elect library boards, levy taxes for operation, hire administrators, erect buildings, purchase books and supplies, report, account, and audit separate expenditures of funds—all of this activity, for the most part, resulting in library service that fails to reach minimum standards.

There is increasing recognition that local governmental units are not equipped to deal effectively with area-wide problems. Area-wide planning, though still not popular among suburbanites, is becoming a necessity. Government consolidation is not developing at a rapid rate, however, and it is doubtful that suburbia will readily abandon its firmly held desire for independent local government. The most promising solution appears to be the creation of special units to handle specific problems such as sanitation, water supply, and library service. However, unless the current attitudes of suburbanites toward the central city change, even this solution may not be feasible. Witness efforts of Saint Louis, Missouri, to establish a metropolitan area-wide cultural district to support the city zoo and art museum and the suburban science museum. The county museum is paid for by private funds, while the city facilities are supported by city property owners. When the bill came up for a vote in the state legislature, 15 of the 26 suburban legislators either opposed it or lacked sufficient interest to be present. The bill was defeated.

The organization of networks of library systems, in New York and elsewhere, is evidence that some public libraries acknowledge their interdependence and are willing to join in cooperative endeavors. The systems being created by densely populated and growing suburban communities show promise of becoming the most effective of these special units. The movement to the suburbs has engendered sophisticated new demands that the suburban library is not equipped to meet. One recourse is to join with neighbors in the same predicament. The suburban librarian who believes cooperative federation is the answer is deluding himself, however, for the main reference and research resource remains the large-city library. Suburban public libraries will always be dependent on the central city for subject collections in depth. Although the total number of volumes held by suburban libraries may exceed that of the city library, duplication in their collections may result in a smaller number of titles than are held by most large-city libraries.

Cooperation between large-city libraries and others in the metropolitan area exists to a degree. According to Jack Ramsey, chief librarian of the public library in Glendale, California, the Los Angeles Public Library "is a restrained colossus which is not only a leader among public libraries in the nation, but also is one which has aided the development of independent libraries within its immediate scope of influence." The New York Public Library's Circulation Department has adopted a policy of permitting any resident of New York State to use his library card when visiting the city or issuing a New York Public Library card to allow regular use of the library. Suburban use of the large-city library for reference and other purposes has been going on for years and is growing with the increased student use of public libraries.

The Cleveland Public Library and the Cuyahoga County Public Library have been leaders in a metropolitan area study and in the development of a uniform salary scale for the area libraries. These two libraries have begun a "silent merger" working toward joint processing of library materials and a joint audiovisual program.

The Enoch Pratt Free Library in Baltimore is engaged in two cooperative programs—County Services and Metropolitan Maryland Library Service. County Services, established by written contract in 1960, combines into one service system all of the state's county libraries. Metropolitan Maryland Library Service, begun in January 1965, is a cooperative program involving the seven metropolitan area counties and the city of Baltimore and is entirely supported by federal Library Services and Construction Act funds. Not all the participants sign a contract, but each files an annual application for funds with the state's Division of Library Development and Services. The Enoch Pratt Free Library receives compensation for its part in the reciprocal borrowing program as well as an annual payment of $50,000 to be used in strengthening its reference collections and capabilities. The Metropolitan Maryland Library Service program serves as an excellent example of a cooperative program between the large-city library and suburban areas. The cooperation was made possible because the administrators of some of the libraries had held regular meetings since 1961 to define and discuss mutual problems and to work out solutions. A climate of acceptance of metropolitan service resulted from the mutual respect and trust established by these meetings.

Reciprocal borrowing privileges were first limited to adult books and were extended to include children's books. Daily truck delivery to send and return books and films to and from the Pratt Library expedited the use of materials. During the first year of operation, a two-week study of use patterns was made. Over 80 percent of the books borrowed by nonresidents were provided by Pratt. The problems encountered did not require changes in services or regulations. In fact, reciprocal borrowing was expanded to include all types of libraries within the state. The Metropolitan Maryland Library Service program is complemented by the County Services Program, linked by teletype. Book reviews prepared by Pratt Library staff are transmitted to all county libraries, and ambiguous interlibrary loan requests are clarified through this communication system.

The Chicago Public Library, as one of Illinois's four designated Research and Reference Centers, carries on a heavy interlibrary loan program with the suburban library systems. The service includes delivery to peripheral Chicago branch libraries where the materials are picked up by the requesting systems. In return, Chicago receives an annual grant from state funds.

In spite of these and other examples of cooperation, the degree of cooperation between the resource center and the suburbs is still minimal when measured against the need of the suburbs.

What is the suburban librarian's attitude toward the large-city library? In an effort to sample the viewpoint from the suburban libraries, letters were written in 1967 to 30 suburban librarians. Replies were received from 20. They were asked whether, in their opinion, the large-city library was fulfilling its responsibilities; how the proximity of the city library affected their libraries' policies; and, finally, what they saw as the future relationship between the suburban libraries and the large-city library.

With very few exceptions, these suburban librarians recognized their dependence on the city library and acknowledged the effect of the proximity of its collection on their book selection policies. One exception stated: "Policies that govern my library are not in any way influenced by the proximity of the metropolitan library. We are developing our own resources as though this library were the only resource available to the community. This, of course, is only to insure the highest ideals; in practice we borrow heavily from the State Library."

On the other hand, most replies reflected dependence on the city library: "While it is tempting to take the large city library for granted, its very existence makes the suburban librarian's job easier. It is not necessary to stock expensive and infrequently used materials. He can concentrate on the more popular and put more money in a circulating collection than would otherwise be possible."

Most suburban librarians acknowledged the cooperative efforts already in existence. "Our principal call is for interloan of books. We have had excellent cooperation." "Children's librarian meetings have been open to suburban librarians for years." One librarian was grateful for being able to attend the city library's book discussion meetings and to seek the advice of its subject specialists.

The suburban librarians also strongly voiced the opinion that the city library was *not* fulfilling its responsibilities as they saw them from the suburbs. The problems as seen from the suburbs naturally varied among metropolitan areas. While one metropolitan library was praised for excellent cooperation in interloan of materials, another was accused of "the lack of cooperation on the basic idea of exchange of materials," which the suburban librarian called "the shame of our metropolitan area." One suburban librarian (not a Maryland resident) did not think "any of the metropolitan public libraries, except for Enoch Pratt, are fulfilling their professional library responsibilities to the metropolitan area." A few larger libraries were subjected to severe criticism. An example from one suburb should be enough: "Before the large city library can play any positive role in relation to suburban libraries, it must itself become a progressive modern institution, with an enlightened book selection policy, truly superior resources, and a determination to meet the needs of its patrons."

In general the suburban librarians did not ignore their own responsibilities. One, in criticizing the metropolitan library, summed up by writing: "Who's to blame—ours collectively!" Another shared the blame between suburb and large city equally: "Often suburban librarians are too involved in a jealous, competitive or a resentful, snubbed attitude towards the big city library and are unable to look for help towards a more cooperative relationship. Big city libraries are just as much to blame. Most of them have very great shortcomings. The librarians tend to be defensive. They do not feel in a position to lead and they don't want to be asked to."

Leadership was the characteristic most frequently stated as lacking in big-city librarians. Could this be a change in attitude? Did the suburban librarian of ten or twenty years ago look to the large-city library for leadership? One correspondent pointed out attempts on the part of the city library to offer leadership in the 1940s and 1950s. The attempts had not been welcome even at that time.

The suburban librarian now seeks leadership from the metropolitan library in several ways. He wants the city library to be "a cultural force commanding the respect of the citizenry at large," "a good example," "a model for suburban library boards." He wants the large library to build better materials collections and share them by serving the patron through the suburban library. Interloan was described variously as a "moral obligation" and a "professional responsibility." He admits inter-loan of books in a metropolitan situation is largely a one-way matter. All the respondent suburban librarians agreed that the metropolitan library should be reimbursed for the cost of sharing, but there was justifiable concern whether anyone, including the city librarian, knew what the costs actually were. State and federal funds were the only sources of funds mentioned to meet the costs.

Next to the desire for leadership from the city library, the suburban librarians most frequently mentioned the need for communication. "It is important that both the suburban librarian and the director of the central library be willing to communicate with each other, to sit down and talk things over and not be inaccessible one to the other."

A study of New York State library systems draws attention to some of the problems facing the large-city libraries:

For the most part, one sees these city libraries hard pressed to maintain traditional services at a sound level in the face of limited funds, rising costs, unstable community conditions, the increasing scope of reader interests and of material being published and the rising demands of a high school and college group that lacks adequate resources within their own institutions. Fresh approaches and new programs, whether for the underprivileged or for a growing cultural elite or for the business community, are few and far between.[4]

Except for the fact that many problems are similar, though on a much larger scale, to those facing suburban libraries, it is doubtful that suburban librarians are aware of the pervasiveness of such problems in the library operations of large cities. Size may conceivably be confused, in the minds of some, with affluence.

There is evidence, however, of an attempt by suburban librarians to understand the problems of the large-city library. In the survey mentioned, two believed their city libraries had so many problems that they probably "are not interested in acquiring any more . . . by extending service." One perceptive suburban librarian wrote: "I think the questions involved are rather difficult for either the city or suburban librarian to answer, if neither has had experience in both libraries. Not all the problems of the city library are known to the suburban library and vice versa."

The suburban librarians saw hope for better relationships with the large-city library in the future. "Cooperation will have to become the by-word." A metropolitan area-wide borrower's card, an efficient and practical communication system, union lists, book catalogs, daily delivery, centralized processing, advice of big-city library specialists, the pioneer work of the large-city library in projects, and sharing experience and knowledge were among those cooperative possibilities mentioned. Financing such projects by state rather than federal funds seemed more likely to the suburban librarian.

The study of New York State library systems previously referred to indicates interlibrary loan to be the most successful device for extending physical accessibility of materials. In the northern part of the state alone, interlibrary loans increased 200 percent in seven years. Very few libraries (other than strong central libraries) drew more than 10 percent of their users from beyond a ten-mile radius. Lack of staff skills, inadequate bibliographic tools, and the long interval between request and receipt are problems of interlibrary loan that have so far defied solution.

The New York study indicates that getting the reader the materials he needs is the problem that has received the least attention. Lowell A. Martin and Roberta Bowler in their 1965 study of California public library service indicate the problem of mounting demand on the few strong collections and suggest the chaneling of requests through systems headquarters before forwarding them to the city library.[5] Francis R. St. John, while admitting an accurate determination has been impossible, suggests that the cost of an interlibrary loan may range from $7.50 to $10.00.

Obviously, the interlibrary loan problem is only one of many that affect service to residents of metropolitan areas. The publication explosion continues, student use of libraries without regard to political boundaries increases, the educational level of the population rises, technology accelerates in development, the population grows and migrates beyond the service limits of the city library. These pressures are forcing the library profession to seek a coordinated approach to service. Richard Meier looks forward "to a day, perhaps a decade or so hence, when it would be economical to construct a documentation system for a metropolis that is as physically integrated as the banking system is now becoming."[6]

There have been a number of recent developments and proposals for a coordinated approach to metropolitan area library problems. The Metropolitan Library Service Agency (MELSA), in the Minneapolis–Saint Paul metropolitan area, is a governmental unit serving all public libraries, including the smaller ones, but created only by the larger public library systems of the area. Under the control of a lay board, with an advisory committee of librarians, this agency does whatever its member libraries want, including complete reciprocity in borrowing, interlibrary loan, television and radio commercials. Other possibilities include joint book selection with subject specialization, central reference service, research and experimentation, central ordering, cataloging and processing, data processing, and daily delivery. MELSA includes six counties and the city libraries of Minneapolis and Saint Paul. The financing of MELSA is through service charges and state and federal grants.

Martin and Bowler propose Reader Subject Center Libraries for California "wherever 200,000 or more people live within driving distance (one half hour) in metropolitan areas." Nelson Associates recommends for New York "for cataloging and acquisitions, one center . . . to meet all the public library needs of the state, including those of New York City."

Although existing regions may not have the opportunity to plan library service before the metropolitan area is developed, the experience of Columbia, Maryland, after it has developed its plan for joint village, school, and public libraries and established a nonprofit corporation to administer public communication and information services, may point the way toward solutions.

The formation of cooperative suburban library systems is making suburban librarians and boards increasingly aware of their interdependence with the city library. The creation of federated suburban systems is developing leadership and the ability of suburbia to speak through a few representative leaders. A dialogue between the suburban library and the historic reference library is now possible.

On the other hand, the large-city library with its users migrating to the suburbs and its eroding tax base will find it increasingly necessary to take part in the dialogue. The need for concentrated federal and state financial support of the historic resource center is now at hand. Suburban backing of adequate support will be required. The suburbs and the city have a vital part to play in library service of the future. The suburban systems will not be strong enough to stand alone. The large-city library is no longer strong enough to do without the help of the suburban systems. In recognizing their interdependence, both the city and suburban libraries can work together more effectively.

State libraries are beginning to recognize the need for coordinated effort in metropolitan area service. Lowell Martin suggests a statewide library structure of five related levels of service and interlibrary use of resources, along with a recommendation to abolish the limitations on use imposed by governmental jurisdictions. Included in the New York, Illinois, Pennsylvania, and Massachusetts system organizations are attempts to solve some of these problems on a statewide basis. It is apparent that the problems of metropolitan areas deserve top priority at the present stage of public library development.

To provide a beginning to a coordinated approach, the administrator of each large-city library should provide the leadership that the suburban librarians now seek. Regularly scheduled meetings called by the large-city library with representatives of the suburban libraries (system heads where they exist) would establish communications and improve understanding of mutual problems. Together they could form a powerful lobbying group and convince state governments of the seriousness of metropolitan area library problems.

Federal, state, or foundation funds should be sought to finance a research and development staff to work with the coordinating group. Although many state plans for use of Library Services and Construction Act funds include funds for studies and research, there is little evidence that they are being used on metropolitan area problems. Ralph W. Conant has suggested that highly competent research and management teams be established by groups of cooperating libraries. Among the functions of these teams would be the proposing of network library systems, intergovernmental agreements, and other arrangements among autonomous libraries across jurisdictional and functional lines. Another possibility is that each large-city library could concentrate its research on a different set of metropolitan library problems and share the findings with due regard for area differences.

The suburban librarian's view of the large-city library differs as much as the level of suburban library service. Suburbia has librarians who have thought little about the relationship as well as some who understand the problems of the large-city library. Suburban librarians are themselves facing problems that, in their view, require the assistance of their large neighbor. Suburban librarians are now ready to get on with the job of working with the big-city librarian toward realistically solving the problems of coordinated service.

Greenaway admits that "much of the state leadership exists in the local library, yet too often the city library is too independent and not sufficiently cooperative in solving statewide problems."[7] On the other hand, are suburban libraries any less independent or more cooperative in dealing with metropolitan library problems? Are suburban librarians prepared to face up to the consequences of erosion of financial support of the city library? With the political power swinging to suburbia, are suburban librarians and trustees ready to join with the city librarian and trustees to find the solutions to the maintenance of the largest library resource of the metropolitan area? Lowell Martin summed up the interdependence of city and suburban libraries well:

Utilization of an existing large city library as the nucleus of a metropolitan level of service can proceed on the basis of one of two assumptions. One is that such an agency already has considerable strength and should share it with those who lack a similar facility, either by free provision or with token payments. For all its appeal to the natural instincts of librarians to open and extend service, this approach does not provide a sound, long-term basis for library development in metropolitan centers, for our cities face problems of virtual survival that are straining their financial capacity to the utmost. Another approach is to recognize that the region has an asset in the large central library that has been built up over the years, that access to this resource saves the surrounding areas substantial outlays, and an equitable distribution of costs should, therefore, be found—not by draining off the limited financial base of the large city library, but by contributing to and reinforcing that base in the interest of the city and suburb and metropolitan region alike.[8]

Public library systems have established methods of providing central reference, interlibrary loan, audiovisual programs, and delivery services. From the suburban resident's point of view, the creation of cooperative library systems has brought him the best of both worlds. His local library is providing services not possible before the advent of such cooperative systems. He finds it easier to secure needed materials even when his local library doesn't own them. At the same time, his local library has retained its autonomy, satisfying the suburbanite's strong attachment to local control. In fact, he sees the neighboring big-city school system searching for ways to decentralize to provide a neighborhood voice in school operations, while in his suburban refuge he enjoys a school system and public library of manageable size over which, if he is so inclined, he can exercise some influence.

If the suburbanite is to be able to satisfy his sophisticated needs in all their variety, the cooperative systems will not be the final solution. Formal working relationships with all types of libraries in entire metropolitan areas—including the large central-city public library—will be needed. Beyond these area relationships lies the goal of a national library network to enable the nation's library resources to be used by any individual who has need of them.

Notes

1. Philip M. Hauser and Martin Taitel, "Population Trends–Prologue to Library Development," *Library Trends* **10** (July 1961): 20.

2. Robert C. Wood, *Suburbia, Its People and Their Politics* (Boston: Houghton Mifflin Co., 1959), p. 12.

3. Eugene S. Schwartz and Henry I. Saxe, *A Bibliographic Bank for Resource Sharing in Library Systems: A Feasibility Study* (Chicago: I.I.T. Research Institute, 1969).

4. State Education Department Division of Evaluation, *Emerging Library Systems, the 1963-66 Evaluation of the New York State Public Library Systems* (Albany: University of the State of New York, 1967), pp. x–6.

5. Lowell A. Martin and Roberta Bowler, *Public Library Service Equal to the Challenge of California: A Report to the State Librarian* (Sacramento, California: California State Library, 1965).

6. Richard L. Meier, "The Library: An Instrument for Metropolitan Communications," in *The Public Library and the City: Symposium on Library Functions in the Changing Metropolis, Dedham, Mass., 1963*, ed. Ralph W. Conant (Cambridge, Mass.: M.I.T. Press, 1965), p. 86.

7. Emerson Greenaway, "The Effect of Urbanization on Metropolitan Libraries," in *Problems of Library Services in Metropolitan Areas*, report of a seminar directed by Dorothy Bendix (Philadelphia: Drexel Press, 1966), p. 17.

8. Lowell A. Martin, *Library Response to Urban Change: A Study of the Chicago Public Library* (Chicago: American Library Association, 1969), p. 253.

14 The Vantage Point of an Urban Planner

Norman Elkin

It is increasingly difficult to plan community institutions with singleness of purpose. The pace and pervasiveness of social change and the unevenness with which social change affects different segments of society compel community institutions to serve many apparently contradictory ends simultaneously. The differential impact of change creates many subconstituencies whose needs are so disparate from each other that a community institution, to remain viable, must literally be "all things to all men." As a consequence, institutions are confronted with the task of differentiating their services and adapting their styles of service to satisfy the diverse needs of all the groups that collectively make up their constituency.

This paper is addressed to several particular dimensions of social change as they affect the planning and service orientation of community institutions like the public library system. The first part examines the implications of population mobility, while the second part examines the implications of *im*mobility. The last part considers one aspect of the competition between public and private values.

The Implications of Population Mobility

The personal mobility of the Automobile Age has made it possible for people to cover routinely great distances for such everyday chores as going to work and shopping, for recreation and play, and even for social visiting. As a consequence, centrality of location is losing its power to order the distribution of land uses and community institutions. We are witnessing the phenomenon of dislocation of location. From one perspective we can see the urban community emerging as an amorphous regional agglomeration in which any number of locations are as likely to be as accessible as any other number of locations. It is becoming as easy for the urban dweller to get to a factory, church, office, doctor, school, stadium, museum, or library on the perimeter of a metropolitan region as it is (or once was?) to reach such facilities in the "heart" of the city. New expressway systems have made large-scale urban developments feasible in areas heretofore considered inaccessible. To document the magnitude of this reorientation of spatial development, one need only point to the fact that 90 percent of all new industrial jobs are in suburban areas, mainly on the perimeter of regional expressway "loops" that bypass central cities.

The equalization of accessibility and the concomitant diminution of locational advantage of any one part of the urban region are simultaneously freeing institutions from the constraints of location and freeing the public from dependence on nearby or centrally located institutions. Individual institutions no longer enjoy a hegemony over constituencies because of the accessibility factor. To the extent that a progressive distribution of national income makes possible the exercise of private choice in transportation, institutions will find themselves competing for the favor and patronage of constituencies.

Population mobility is also altering the configuration of population distribution as families and individuals seek environments within metropolitan areas that suit their life-styles and economic status. As a result, the old pyramid of population, with density peaking near the city center, leveling in the "middle neighborhoods," and sloping sharply down toward the periphery of the city and the suburban belt, is dissipating rapidly as the inner city thins out and the suburban belt increases both in gross population and in density. This is creating an urban community evenly spread across a metropolitan region at middle-level densities. One of the implications for the public library is that there may no longer be a need for a main downtown library, that is, a "mother library" supporting, guiding, and overseeing an urban library system. (The same premise applies to medical, educational, and other cultural and public service institutions.) On the other hand, there will be a need for major institutional facilities in the middle and outer reaches of the metropolitan community, perhaps of the same scale as there once was for such facilities downtown. Whether or not these outlying, or "regional," facilities are as large as the old central institutions, it is almost certain that the day of the "mini" branch facility is gone. The typical regional facility of the future will be considerably larger; in fact, it is likely that all future libraries—central and branch—will be optimum middle-sized operations somewhere between the old central "giant" and the small branch facility.

Once the public accepts the need for major institutions in noncentral areas, there will be a companion need to structure service systems on an *independent regional*, rather than on a municipally controlled, basis. Thus it is conceivable that a metropolitan area will one day have four or five *independent* regional library systems. Such systems not only will exist side by side, territorially, but might even overlap and compete. Such situations might lead to reform and innovation; and the general public will benefit. It will become harder as time goes by to accept the old form of institutional dominance, whether it is the oversized downtown library or the undersized suburban library, although their advocates will continue to argue for them because their symbolic status values as reminders of the past will be defended long after their functional values have disappeared.

A root problem for the library in responding to demographic change is that the library is a political creature, a publicly supported institution with no independent financing except for occasional grants from private universities and foundations. The dilemma is that the political community (that is, the city, village, town, county) that supports the library is farther and farther removed geographically from the demographic or "natural" urban community. Thus, for the library to respond to the demographic changes in the metropolitan community, it must go against the grain of the political jurisdictions that divide the metropolitan community. For example, Chicago is a metropolitan community of approximately 7,000,000 persons. Of these people, 3,300,000 live in the central city, and 3,700,000 live in 200 suburban cities and villages with an average population of 18,500. It is nigh impossible to rationally structure a library system on this jurisdictional basis.

Constructive responses to this condition have surfaced in Illinois through such counterjurisdictional devices as the Suburban Library Service, which is a "common-market" approach to regionalization of resources in heavily populated metropolitan areas, and the multicounty Library District in the more sparsely populated areas of the state. In this regard, the library in Illinois is perhaps more responsive than many other public institutions to demographic change and rising public service expectations. The incompatibility between service needs and the fragmented structure of government in metropolitan areas, a condition that affects public services in all parts of the country, is one reason for the

current national interest in modernizing and restructuring city government, which may yet result in some form of regional or metropolitan
government. The alternative will be subregional public agencies that
bypass established jurisdictions in order to furnish public services that
are in high demand and low supply. Transportation, water supply, and
pollution control rank high on the list. So do hospital and library planning.

Implications of Immobility

While the need for regionalization of library systems stems essentially
from the dispersal of a highly mobile population over the suburban
and exurban hinterland, the *immobility* of large segments of society
creates a contrary need for highly localized community institutions. The
immobile generally embrace not only the poor but also the aged, the
infirm, the handicapped, the illiterate, and other socially and economically disadvantaged groups. This immobility poses a dilemma for
all community planners and all community institutions, a dilemma often
expressed in terms of centralization versus decentralization.

The choice between centralization and decentralization is more apparent than real because an institution, to remain viable, must serve *both*
regional and local needs. The question is how many resources and what
kinds of services to provide at each level. To answer this question libraries and other established community institutions must first reverse their
traditional notion that local or "branch" facilities are to provide a
uniform minimum base service to local constituencies, while central or
main facilities are to provide *depth and specialization* for a more selective universe of users. The conditions that account for the immobility of
large segments of the urban population are of such a character that local
(decentralized) facilities increasingly require special personnel, special
programs, and special "delivery systems" to function even reasonably
well. While the specialization needed at the local level is a different kind
than most community institutions are used to providing, or even prepared to provide, it is essential that the required specialization be provided if the institution is to maintain a viable posture in the inner city.
This may involve the recruitment of new personnel whose orientation
is toward the new specializations. Thus, the professional librarian, like

many other professionals, may have to broaden the definition of his profession in order to integrate such personnel into the overall library system. Pursued diligently, a program to serve the relatively immobile populations would result in a major redistribution of expenditures, with a smaller share allocated to conventional programs and facilities and a larger share earmarked for new local programs and facilities.

The Social Value of Privacy

All institutions, the public library included, serve many purposes, some of them only remotely related to the avowed purpose of the institution. The planner therefore looks at community institutions, whether school, library, hospital, park, or shopping center, with a critical eye, wondering how many purposes any given institution can perform above and beyond its avowed purpose. Can it reorder land uses? Can it enrich the quality of urban street life? Can it contribute to the prosperity of the citizens? Can its presence contribute to a sense of security? Single-minded concentration by institutional functionaries on avowed institutional purposes is myopic and lends credence to critics who claim that urban institutions are insensitive to humanistic values. After all, what does it *mean*, for example, when a park expert says, "People don't use big parks anymore"? It simply means that *his* criterion of *use* is the number of people who attend the park at different hours of the day or different weeks of the year. Yet people who enjoy looking out over the park from their windows, though they never set foot in the park, *are* using the park as much as spectators at a movie use or consume a film. The thousands of urban dwellers who inhale better air by virtue of the oxygen-producing capability of the park's plant life, even though they may never play soccer in the park, *are* using the park.

Turning to the library, how does one weigh the relative merits of a library that circulates a million volumes a year against another that gives spiritual refreshment to 100,000 persons by offering a retreat from the workaday world in the sanctuary of its reading room? Which one is making a greater contribution to the social good? The answer depends on whose criteria of use are being applied and for what purposes. Libraries are vulnerable if they do not systematically measure *usage* in terms that are relevant to cultural development and social good. However, there is little evidence that they do. The library has to be more than the "keeper of the books," and its contribution to the general culture has to be defined in broader terms than volume circulation.

There is a need to understand the broad spectrum of social usage and to create as many avenues for their satisfaction as resources allow. The library is only one public in.   ·tion among many competing for land, accessibility, and public funds. Yet, the future of the library is tied to the future of all public service institutions. Collectively, they are engaged in a broad contest over how national resources are to be divided between public and private values. Some social critics contend that the public standard of living (as measured by the quality of roads, schools, libraries, and hospitals) is being undermined by a national obsession with the production and consumption of "private" goods and services.

To achieve a favorable division of resources, it may be necessary for public service institutions to meet some of the basic wants that underlie the public's preoccupation with private values. One of those wants is a popular desire to expand the area of *personal privacy*.

The industrial revolution, with its factory cities, tenements and row-houses, congested neighborhoods, and crowded streetcars and its intrusion of noise and smoke into everyday life, deprived people of privacy. The great strides in housing made during the last twenty years have been advances in privacy: the reduction in overcrowding, a more favorable ratio of shelter space to population generally, and the progressive elimination of the practice of sharing "private" (that is, kitchen and bath) facilities. The expansion of the housing supply has been seized upon by young married couples as an opportunity to move into quarters separate from their parents and in-laws. The mode of living in which several generations of the family occupied the same house has all but vanished among white families and is being steadily reduced among black families. Furthermore, the number of persons living alone (single adults, widows and widowers, divorced persons, the elderly, etc.) is increasing at a substantially greater rate than are households generally.

Fewer and fewer new homes are being built in America with less than two bathrooms, or without a family room, den, or recreation room. These may sound like Madison Avenue-induced "wants," but the reality is that space that provides *privacy* is at a premium. Surveys reveal that large proportions of the public, at all ages, simply do not have places in their own homes where they can be alone and *read quietly* if they desire or rooms where they can visit with friends.

  The option of privacy affects many institutions but is particularly important for those institutions concerned with education, literacy, and intellectual pursuits in general. Society needs sanctuaries of privacy for the purposes of meditation and study, spiritual refreshment, and escape from the din. At various times and in various ways the cathedral, the university, and the park have all served these purposes. So has the library. In the years to come, if there is to be a reasonable balance of accounts between the investment of national resources into the public standard of living and the private standard of living, public institutions such as the library will have to make a contribution to privacy, especially among the deprived of the inner cities, or the pendulum will swing even further toward private consumption to the jeopardy of public institutions. The library may need to view itself as a home away from home, an all-purpose community institution where people can compensate for some of the shortcomings in other parts of their environment. The library has been called "the people's university." Perhaps, to merit that accolade today, it must first be "the neighborhood's university."

IV Critical Issues

15 The Education of Librarians

D. J. Foskett

Those of us who are concerned with the education of librarians are
constantly being reminded that our students of today will be in positions of authority in the twenty-first century; we are urged to throw
overboard all that we have learned by study and experience and turn our
attention instead to the new technological marvels that are rendering
our methods, and ourselves as well, obsolete. Nowhere, however, can
one find a systematic analysis of what is likely to happen that justifies
this exhortation. It is highly significant, for example, that in his notori-
ous *Libraries of the Future*,[1] J. C. R. Licklider envisages libraries as
being completely replaced by "procognitive systems." Licklider is not a
librarian and provides no evidence to show that he knows what goes on
in libraries. He is, on the other hand, a computer expert; yet he seems
unable to envisage any correspondingly dramatic turn of events in
computer technology, and the procognitive system of the year 2000 is
no more than a description of what is technically possible today. This is
not, of course, the first time that a technologist has written a book to
prove that the book has no further use. Edison, in 1913, thought that it
would soon be replaced by the motion picture; yet today, when libraries
are flourishing as never before, the motion picture industry lurches from
crisis to crisis, while in the library "resource center," the film takes its
proper place as an instrument of education beside the book.

The fact is that this kind of pragmatic approach is simply not enough;
anyone can sit down and describe what could be done with a given technology. Henry Ford's vision of everyone owning a private motorcar may
result, in the end, in the abolition of private motorcars. A much more
fruitful approach is that of the analyst, the philosopher. In the field of
management, for example, the introduction of program, planning, and
budgeting systems has already revolutionized the conduct of large-scale
enterprises, because it forces managers to think analytically—to identify
their objectives and to plot ways of achieving them in relation to available resources. For a profession, the identification of objectives must
precede the description of the technology required; the reverse approach,

in which the technology is allowed to dictate the objectives, has led to a trail of disasters without parallel in the history of library and information services. One rarely reads of these things in our literature; but, as we all know, the literature is not the only way in which information circulates. The "chat at the bar" may well be more revealing, voluntarily or involuntarily, than the printed word, especially when the latter is composed, as it so often is, in a mood of unjustified euphoria.

Obviously, this does not mean that we ought to spurn the advantages of the new technology. What it does mean is that the students of today must be so prepared, in their professional education, that they are able to bring to bear an understanding not just of what the technology can do but of what it ought to be required to do. While it is of the first importance that librarians should appreciate the capabilities of computers, it is no less important that computer specialists should, in their turn, pay heed to the opinions of librarians, who in this discussion are likely to have a far deeper understanding of the real needs of library users. The profession may, and should, change its view on the nature and scope of its activities from time to time; as a profession, it should be alert to the significance of new ideas and be ready, indeed anxious, to incorporate them into its education program. But, as a profession, it has also the duty to preserve its integrity, not for its own sake, but because the integrity of a profession is the highest form of safeguard for those whom the profession serves. If we believe in the social value of library science, it is for us to demonstrate and maintain the unity of professional activities and standards amid the diversity of readers' needs. It may seem a far cry from the small-town branch library to the great corporation's information storage and retrieval system, yet fundamentally these serve the same social purpose: they help to achieve the transfer of organized thought from one mind to another, through the medium of what Jesse Shera calls "graphic records."[2] Shera's concept of "social epistemology," in fact, offers what is perhaps the best attempt so far to provide a general philosophical basis for library and information science.

The education of librarians must be designed as education for a profession, and although I cannot here analyze this statement in depth, I will try to clarify what I mean in general terms. What characterizes a profession, above all, is that it does not exist for its own sake. A profession comes into being when a group of individuals, recognizing the existence of a genuine social need, join together to find means of meeting that need through the elaboration of certain techniques. The need is primary; a professional person does not seek to create a want, nor could the service he offers be provided just as well by a different group. The social need for a library service is far removed from the creations of Madison Avenue and can hardly be met by accountants or dentists, valuable though their services are, any more than a librarian, qua librarian, is himself a dentist, or chemist, or teacher.

A professional does not, moreover, promote his own wares. His group has its objectives and techniques, to be sure; but what he does with them is determined by the group consensus, and not by his own personal interest. At times he may find that he has to sacrifice his interest in the cause of the profession, and he does this without question. This is not because the profession has itself an intrinsic value above the value of its members. It is, rather, that the profession, as a corporate body, guarantees the competence and the motivation of its members and thereby acts to safeguard the interests of those who benefit by the service. In our case, there are readers, users of information, people who, for one reason or another, wish or need to know what someone else has had to say and embodied in a graphic record.

There are three major factors to be considered in a discussion of education for a profession—apart from many others that are minor from the strictly educational standpoint, such as the availability of the necessary funds. They may be briefly summarized thus:

1. The needs of the student
2. The needs of the employer
3. The needs of the profession .

The student, who has probably begun his course with a minimum of practical experience, needs above all a thorough grounding in all those areas of professional activity in which he will be required to operate and, in due course, to make decisions. Since he intends to be a "professional," it is likely that he will reach a post that will accord him a certain amount of managerial responsibility fairly soon after the completion of his initial training. He must therefore receive from his teachers a convincing account of what things are done in the name of professional activity, why they are done in a particular manner, and what principles of organization underlie their implementation. This means that he must receive a *reasonable* account; it is not sufficient for him merely to be told that such and such is the case and required to memorize these facts. He has to assimilate a whole structure of rational discourse into his own understanding, in order to reach a satisfactory level of professional judgment as well as competence. This is particularly true in the present age, when library and information services are going through a period of rapid transition, and the methods in use even five years ago may well be entirely obsolete by the time that the new student reaches his first position of authority. Indeed, it is part of the very nature of a library school that it prepares for tomorrow rather than describes what happens today.

The needs of the employer, on the other hand, actually conflict with these requirements to some extent. It is clear that the employer would be very pleased to receive from library schools young would-be professionals who are mentally alert and vigorous, full of knowledge about the very latest advances in techniques, and at the same time malleable and amenable to the practical instruction of those who have been in the system for some time and are already in positions of authority. But the employer wants more than this: he wants to recruit from the schools new employees who can be immediately posted to a particular job, already having the ability to do that job, requiring very little practical instruction from the employer, and thus causing a minimum of "wasted" time. These two requirements are in conflict with each other, of course, and the arguments for both sides are set out in more or less detail from time to time in the professional literature.

The needs of the profession determine the basic requirements of the other two categories. The management of a library and information service is not an end in itself, however much we may like to think it is. This category might well have been called instead "the needs of users," a perfectly accurate description in principle, in order to emphasize that the needs of the profession do, in fact, derive from the needs of users. The requirements of the profession, as we have already seen, are that it should, as a corporate body—a professional association—have a full awareness of what its corporate role should be in relation to the various institutions of society. It should have the social responsibility for ensuring that its members are thoroughly motivated by the desire to provide for these various institutions services at the highest level of professional competence; that is, it should be the guardian of the professional conscience. It follows that it should also have the responsibility of maintaining professional standards of performance; that is, as a corporate body, it should keep a continuous watch on the development of practical methods for implementing professional aims. The identification and public discussion of these aims is also a matter for professional educators, and we have the right to expect the younger members of the profession to bring a critical eye to current formulation of aims; and we must accept the possible need to modify them in the light of changing circumstances and beliefs.

An institution setting up an initial course, therefore, has a responsibility not only to the student who is being taught and the employer who is the cash customer for the product but also to a generalized body of professionally accepted knowledge and wisdom. To the extent that this body is generalized, it has to be theoretical, and we now have to ask ourselves, Is there such a generalized body of knowledge to be imparted to students in library schools? If there is not, should there be? If there is, what are its components?

One cannot answer any of these questions with a mere "yes" or "no." My own view, baldly stated, is that the task of the school is to inculcate an attitude of mind rather than produce a walking encyclopedia of factual information, however up-to-date; that is, the student must be given a professional awareness, a conceptual framework through which he can bring professional judgment to bear upon the practical problems that he will meet when he works in a library. I do not think it is the role of the schools to develop practical skills to a high pitch of excellence, since I believe that this can only be done in an actual working situation, and I have elaborated these arguments in my article "The Social and Intellectual Challenge of the Library Service."[3] My reason for taking this stand is that, since professional activities are devoted to the service of social ends and are not ends in themselves, to learn about professional activities is not merely to be instructed in certain practices that have come into common use. The young entrant's scrutiny of professional practices is not that of the young apprentice learning how to handle his tools, though it contains an element of this; it is rather an "academic" exploration of the type of product that society requires first of all. This should result in a keener understanding of the function of the tools and of their appropriateness for that function. If this attitude of mind is developed in the student, he will be highly motivated toward acquiring excellence in practical skill and will set about his work, when he comes into employment, with that eagerness and sense of devotion that characterizes the professional mind. This sort of attitude can hardly be inculcated in a school that concentrates on the "how-to-do-it" approach, teaching practical skills without the true professional foundation studies. Experience shows all too clearly that a student from such a school may well go to work in a library that does not use those methods at all. The range of methods used in a large city library is, in any case, so wide that no library school could be sure of teaching practical skill in all of them.

If one accepts this line of argument, the answer to the first question is that we not only should, but must, have a body of generalized theoretical knowledge that a student can learn and use both to interpret the practical situations of his work and to formulate his own role for himself—his duties and responsibilities—in the light of a professional consensus. Such an intellectual approach cannot but foster the desire to perform well and will thus lead to the attainment of a standard of excellence in those practical skills that are called for by the job at hand, whereas the mere instruction in practical skills, however devotedly and expertly carried out during initial training, may well lead to frustration or even consternation when the newly fledged professional finds that what he has just learned has to be almost immediately unlearned.

The ultimate inefficiency of teaching only practical skills is underlined by the rapidity with which the library and information service scene is actually undergoing change. It is surely vital that those who are going to be in charge of affairs in ten or twenty years' time must at this stage be analyzing problems on the basis of a sound theoretical foundation, rather than tackling them in a purely pragmatic or "bull-at-a-gate" fashion. For want of such an analytical approach, the application of computers in libraries has produced all these disasters; after twenty years, we are only now reaching a point where there are systems with genuine bibliographical value. Yet the literature is full of accounts of this, that, or the other system that purports, like the "procognitive system," to show the one and only right course for the future. It is therefore in the immediate interest of both the student and the profession that the initial course should comprise this theoretical foundation; it is, furthermore, in the not-too-long-term interests of employers, also, though it will inevitably mean that they will have to spend more time on their induction courses when newcomers arrive. On the other hand, they will receive a bonus in that these newcomers will be sharper in their understanding of what their roles are to be.

Now, it is one thing to agree on the necessity for establishing a theoretical corpus on which to build a course of study; it is quite another to agree on its content. I start here from the belief that a genuinely new discipline is coming into being, sometimes called "Informatics" (though I hold no particular brief for this term, which has other connotations in some parts of Europe), which is based not merely on the improvement of traditional library techniques but also on a wider range of study, and which is relevant to the whole process of the communication of knowledge and information.[4] These are not the same things, but libraries and the acquisition, arrangement, and dissemination of written records are central to this process.

The traditional role of the librarian since antiquity has been that of a curator. The original libraries held records of one sort or another, of information like astronomical and meteorological data, as in Egypt, and of the sayings and opinions of priests and wise men, as in the various sacred books. The function of the curator was not merely to look after the documents in the physical sense, to see that they did not get damaged, but also to guard them in the sense of preventing access for anyone but the privileged elite. The curator made it possible for civilization to advance more rapidly by substituting reliance on recorded and cumulated knowledge for reliance on oral and limited, prejudiced communication. The traditional techniques of librarianship were developed as a system for identification, recognition, and retrieval of individual documents for the sake of their information and are closely analogous to the functions of the human memory. The human mind observes, commits to storage, and recollects when necessary; it classifies, indexes, and retrieves. And, as J. S. Bruner says regarding the need to go beyond the mere enumeration of instances and to understand fundamentals, "Perhaps the most basic thing that can be said about human memory after a century of intensive research is that unless detail is placed into a structured pattern it is rapidly forgotten."[5] The most recent valuable research on the psychological aspects of memory, by Jean Piaget in Geneva, or J. P. Guilford in California, for example, has been based on the observation and identification of the ways in which these structured patterns have been built up. They are, as one would expect, very similar to the theories developed by S. R. Ranganathan, J. E. Farradane, B. C. Vickery, and the British Classification Research Group, who have always insisted that the value of classification for librarians is in retrieval and reference services, and not just in the arrangement of physical objects on shelves, useful though this is.

The techniques of the curator were designed to parallel or make a model of this kind of "structure of intellect," as Guilford calls it.[6] This required first of all systems for the identification and description of objects, which led to the study of cataloging and bibliography in all its forms; then came the arrangement of these objects—documents—in a sequence that could be recognized by each subject specialist as corresponding to the way in which he thought about his subject. Finally, the store itself had to be organized and staffed. These were the main elements of education for librarians for many years. The problems of users were not thought to be a necessary part of the curriculum; in scholarly libraries the librarians themselves were scholars and knew the problems at first hand. In the public libraries that were founded in the nineteenth century, however, there was a new and important element, namely, the uplifting or "moral" effect of good literature and its consequent value for society. Andrew Carnegie was a strong protagonist of this view.

The lengthy controversies that have raged over recent years about the content of library school curricula testify to both the problems that have arisen and our failure to solve them. There have been two vital factors: first, the differentiation of specialist knowledge through the increase in research and discovery, made visible by the growth of publication; and second, the invention of new machines for data processing, which make it possible to handle these publications more cheaply and expeditiously than with traditional manual methods. There are now many more writers, many more subjects about which much more is known, many more libraries to store and retrieve the documents, and many more users of the information they contain. These factors have combined to produce a qualitative change in the role expected of the librarian. He has to act in a more positive way vis-à-vis his charges, and not remain a curator (particularly in the "guardian" sense). The new techniques and the new forms of secondary publication such as indexes, abstracts, and surveys may be developments of traditional forms, but combined with new forms of social organization of users and of their relations to the flow of information, they make it necessary for us to rethink our educational programs not simply in the light of understanding the mechanisms of technique but in relation to new social situations —the real needs of users in our contemporary civilization. Few would deny that this need has reached a point of crisis; few would deny, moreover, that this results, particularly in the modern city, very largely from failures of communication among different social groups. Librarians have a special responsibility in such a situation.

The situation today calls for a dynamic approach to the use of library materials, the cultivation of "information officer" attitudes among public library staff. In the first place, libraries must free themselves from limitation to print and exploit all the media of communication, as is now being done so well in school "resource centers," such as those developed through the Knapp School Library project and the British Schools Council Resource Center project at the University of London Institute of Education, which began at the end of 1970. The creative use of these media could certainly help to bridge the gap between those groups whose culture is largely literate and disadvantaged groups—in urban slum areas, for example—whose cultures are very often based on oral communication rather than reading and who, for that very reason, find themselves out of harmony with the complexities of modern urban life. In Italy, for example, the Telescuola program for eradicating rural adult illiteracy has been hearteningly successful.

The new British Open University provides another fine example of what can be done to bring all levels of education right into the home, by means of radio and television programs geared to a formal academic curriculum; and such "external degree" systems will provide a formidable challenge to the public library. There can surely be no doubt that the prospect of groups of Matthew Arnold's "true disciples of culture" —people who read with purpose—offers an opportunity not to be missed. On the one hand, the students will need information services even more than those at residential universities; on the other hand, the tutors will welcome the chance of having academically alert colleagues around the corner from their students. This development of information service in the public library means more than the usual readers' advisory service. It means close and continuous association with all groups of readers, coming to grips with their problems in their own terms, not merely answering questions, responding to stimuli. It means knowing what each reader is interested in, approaching specialist literature with his objectives in view, so that his developing needs can be anticipated and he can feel secure in the knowledge that the library personnel understand his needs and know how to bring their professional skills to bear in order to meet them.

The solution does not lie in the wholesale application of computers to every possible process, however, even though the computer has acted as the catalyst in changing the librarian's role. Many of those who write about computers in information service seem to imagine that every transaction in a library resolves itself into a question and answer situation, that libraries have only to supply discrete pieces of data. Information has been reified into a commodity, and all the enthusiasm and skill devoted to production drives goes into its manufacture. The single research worker, recording and publishing his results when he considers his project complete, has been replaced by the research team, whose program is continuous and whose publications form a record, not of a finished work, but of every step, no matter how trivial, along a never-ending road. J. M. Ziman, whose concept of science as public knowledge[7] involves libraries as an integral part of the scientific process, has also emphasized that this does not mean that every little thought has to be stored: the specialist literature is in danger of becoming clogged with work of no value to anyone, and we are actually guilty of using expensive machinery to process vast quantities of rubbish in order to prove what vast quantities we can process. Equally futilely, much of the so-called research in mechanized documentation, supported in some cases by reputable universities and government grants, is based on "models" that are so remote from real life as to make the results unusable except in similarly remote circumstances. Moreover, when the production process is based solely on the least effort for the producer, as it usually is, the interests of the user suffer; for while a "simple" input operation may indeed make it possible to use unskilled clerical labor at input, the output is likely to prove just as "simple," that is, it will be so primitive in use that it will either give unsatisfactory results or demand an exorbitant effort on the user's part. But since no user will waste his time if he can help it, many of the bibliographical marvels produced by this philosophy lie moldering on library shelves.

The purpose of libraries is, not to provide work for computers, but to effect communication, and this includes communication of values as well as of facts, of insight as well as of information. It is difficult to make a quantitative assessment of this service, because one can rarely point to a visible saving against which to balance the librarian's effort. Nevertheless, we know that users put a value on library services not only because it can provide useful information but also because it ensures access to those productions of the human mind that cannot themselves be measured in economic terms, either, but which add, in Whitehead's phrase, a quality to life beyond the mere fact of life. What Shakespeare has to tell us in *Hamlet* is not the facts of the case, which were historically inaccurate, but what it feels like to be a sensitive human being caught in an agony of indecision—what it means to suffer as Hamlet, or Gertrude, or Ophelia suffered.

We need to view our educational process in a much wider manner, not, as in the past, to concentrate on the inward-looking examination of the details of what goes on in libraries. We can learn a great deal from general systems theory, the point of which is to view every item, every technique, every process, as being part of some whole, or entity, which has its own individuality, but which is at the same time part of a still larger whole, or system. All library and information service ought to be viewed in this way; we have to turn our eyes outward, to consider what goes on in libraries as part of a whole in relation to the larger wholes of which we are part. We can consider our stock, for example, in relation to the whole body of information and knowledge: information may be regarded as the data given to us by our senses as we grapple with the environment; information processed by a human mind becomes knowledge, and all knowledge in this sense is unique to an individual; knowledge transformed by experience ripens into wisdom, which, because experience can be communicated and shared through insight, can become part of the common possession of humanity.

We can consider ourselves in relation to the documents we have to work with. Because our horizons are widened, we do not have to throw away the study and development of techniques of publication, acquisition, recording, and retrieving. We must go further than this, of course, and consider ourselves and our techniques in relation to library users, so we need far more sociological studies of the ways in which people find and use information. Most of the studies of how scientists acquire information are not flattering to libraries: the table is usually headed by "chats at the bar," the truth of which we can confirm from our own experience. Yet such an eminent scientist as Ziman can say that "a laboratory without a library is like a decorticated cat: the motor activities continue to function, but lack co-ordination of memory and purpose."

We also have to consider users themselves as members of systems: biological systems in relation to their families, spatial systems in relation to their communities, professional in relation to their work, recreational in relation to their play, and so on. Each person is a member of several different kinds of groups and is likely to have different library and information needs arising from these several group memberships. Now it is not too difficult for the university librarian, or the special librarian, or the information scientist to identify these particular needs, since their users form readily identifiable groups, and they become members of these groups precisely in order to pursue publicly recognized objectives. In this sense, then, it is easy to devise an appropriate curriculum for professional education to suit those environments. This is not the case with the public library. "The right book for the right reader at the right time" is an honorable slogan, no doubt, but it does not say much in practical terms. Certainly the public library has the duty to serve local industry and the students and faculty of local universities; if they require the public service, as taxpayers they are entitled to it. But they do not claim this right because they are industrialists or academics, because of their membership of those groups. Indeed, one could say that they claim it in spite of their being such.

Is it possible, then, to identify any library need that may be said to be characteristic of public library users, as such? Do they not constitute too diverse a collection of people, sharing only the one common feature that they all live in the same area? If we choose to regard libraries as obsolescent and see our future in procognitive systems, the answer to these questions will be that this diversity is such that no single system can cope with it, that each member will have to link himself up with some procognitive system; it will not matter if no system exists in the neighborhood, because he will not be visiting any store but receiving all his information on his own television screen or on-line access point. Put thus baldly, the theory shows up its weakness. It regards human beings in a totally mechanistic behaviorist way and neglects completely the essential human need that is met by reading as opposed to merely consulting stores of data.

What links us together as members of a local community is that we are people, not information processors. We are human members of a human social group, and what distinctively characterizes the human being is that he has a mind that is capable not only of information processing but also of creatively transforming sensory and other data so that they are assimilated into his memory structure and contribute to the growth and development of his self, his personality. This creation and re-creation of the personality is bound to assume a far higher importance in the future, provided that we are wise enough to develop the civilized use of the leisure that modern technology offers us. We need, and will continue to need, the facility of reading because we need to ponder, to consider, to reflect upon what great men have said about the human condition. We do not simply ask questions of Shakespeare, Goethe, and Balzac; we approach their work in a spirit of inquiry, to be sure, but what we derive from them is not answers to questions. They give us a view of man that is both subtler and more far-ranging than our own, therefore helping us to a greater mastery of ourselves and our environment and enabling us to live our lives more successfully—not in their terms, but in our own. This insight into the nature of humanity, of course, characterizes all the arts, and it is no accident that in many towns in the United Kingdom the libraries, museums, and art galleries come under the same authority and are situated near one another.

A library, in short, provides information, education, recreation; and in respect to the last, it should provide a genuine opportunity for the individual to re-create himself—to refresh and restore the human spirit. This is rather more than merely adding a few facts to the sum of what he knows already and is no luxury even in terms of economic well-being, for the mind of the creative scientist or technologist achieves distinction through its human qualities, just as much as the mind of the artist. Users of libraries should now be able to expect the same dynamism from librarians in the cause of education and recreation that has already been developed in the service of information handling. For public librarians, it means that they must cultivate the same kind of close and continuous association with all their readers as is preeminently displayed in the industrial information service. They must act as educators in the true sense, by providing means for the refinement of the mind, that sharpening of the understanding that will enable information to be processed into knowledge, and knowledge transformed into wisdom. This will not be easy, especially as more and more people come to live in cities or their suburbs and, for most people, the possibility increases that that part of their lives spent in work will be more and more subject to automation, and they themselves will be reduced to the status of machine minders. But librarians must take the opportunity offered by this situation, if the quality of life is to be maintained; and if we can bring to the literature of the humanities the positive attitude that has been so successful with the literature of science and technology, we could even contribute to improving that quality.

The general framework of the curriculum of library schools should therefore be based on these lines:

The Universe of Knowledge: the study of the forms of knowledge, the structure of subjects, and their interrelationships

Production and Publication of Knowledge: the research process; formal systems of publishing, social and technical facets of the book trade; primary and secondary classes of documents

Acquisition and Arrangement of Materials: sources of documents and information about documents; classification and indexing, information retrieval systems

247 THE EDUCATION OF LIBRARIANS

Dissemination and Use of Knowledge: current awareness services; psychology and sociology of users and user groups
Library and Information Service Technology: the use (not the manufacture) of all types of hardware; the basic sciences (for example, logic, mathematics), in detail sufficient only to acquire an understanding of how these devices may be used efficiently
Planning and Management: techniques necessary to implement technological devices, including general systems theory, PPBS, statistical and other techniques of scientific management, deployed in the context of the library profession
Comparative Librarianship: the study of national and international systems; comparative methodology applied to all facets of library operation.
It is evident that this outline ranges very widely indeed, and it would be realizable in practice only at the cost of eliminating much of the pettifogging detail that now clogs up most courses and makes them so dreary for students and teachers. I suggest that in return it offers the chance to *educate* our young people, to inculcate in them an awareness not only of their professional duty but also of the excitement and inspiration that they will derive from the knowledge that that duty, well performed, plays a vital role in the service of our fellow human beings.

Notes
1. J. C. R. Licklider, *Libraries of the Future* (Cambridge, Mass.: MIT Press, 1965).

2. J. M. Shera, *Libraries and the Organization of Knowledge* (London: Crosby, Lockwood, 1965).

3. D. J. Foskett, "The Social and Intellectual Challenge of the Library Service," *Library Association Record* 70, no. 12 (December 1968): 305–309.

4. D. J. Foskett, "Progress in Documentation: 'Informatics,'" *Journal of Documentation* 26, no. 4 (December 1970): 340–369.

5. J. S. Bruner, *The Process of Education* (New York: Vintage Books, 1960), p. 24.

6. J. P. Guilford, *Intelligence, Creativity and Their Educational Implications* (San Diego, California: R. R. Knapp, 1968).

7. J. M. Ziman, *Public Knowledge: The Social Dimension of Science* (Cambridge, England: Cambridge University Press, 1968).

16 The Role of Technology in the Future of Libraries

John Tebbel

So much has already been written about the new technology and its various applications to the printed word that it would take a library of respectable size to house this literature. The human retriever who attempts to extract the relevant information from it and give it some kind of perspective has one advantage over the mechanical system that conceivably might do the job for him. He can attempt to separate fantasy from fact, illusion from reality. Humanists are encouraged to realize that no machine yet invented or conceived can make that kind of evaluation.

Having made it, however, one must accept the probability of human error. One man's fantasy is another man's fact, and the enthusiasts of the technological revolution are inclined to reject out of hand any intimation that profound change is not just around the corner. Yet it is difficult for an observer with no ax to grind, surveying the vast store of information on the subject, to believe that the changes will be as profound, rapid, or complete as so many people appear to believe. McLuhan's theory that the linear world was about to be engulfed and replaced by electronics is coming to be seen as the pretentious nonsense it always was. The theory and the professor himself have experienced a meteoric rise and an equally meteoric fall. Certainly, technology will produce great changes, but what it is theoretically capable of doing and what it may actually do are quite possibly two different things.

It is, for instance, more than a little ironic to talk about automated libraries and the nationwide conversion of them into giant information storage and retrieval centers when thousands of libraries are having difficulty simply staying in existence. When a great institution like the New York Public Library is forced to cut its services to the bone, it is idle to talk about the blessings of technology. The technologists argue that the long-range benefits of their systems will save immense sums of money in the operation of libraries, and they are correct; but all of these systems are so expensive that no library in the country is presently able to convert to them in any large-scale way. The systems will not be less expensive until they can be produced in sufficient quantity to bring the prices down, and there will be no purpose in producing that quantity until the market is large enough to accommodate it.

Consequently, the long-range objectives come down to how the shorter-range goals are going to be achieved—that is, how libraries will be financed in the future, at a time when both communities and universities, their source of support, are unable or unwilling to maintain present standards, much less expand them. Until this fundamental problem is solved, the theories of technology are not likely to be tested in practical terms except in small-scale efforts.

We must assume, however, that the problem *will* be solved, since it is inconceivable that society, in spite of all its failings, would simply let its storehouses of knowledge wither away. In the wings, then, are a variety of devices waiting to come on stage. Some of them are capable of utterly transforming existing practices. Others are simply refinements of what we already possess. The new problem will be how and where to apply these devices, because obviously the small-town and the big-city or university libraries are not going to have the same requirements. As David Foskett wisely observes in the preceding chapter, the question is not simply one of librarians learning to understand technology; it also includes the need for technologists to understand the problems and requirements of libraries.

If the history of technology tells us anything, it is that established systems are not immediately replaced by new ones but coexist for indefinite periods of time. Books were threatened with extinction in the eyes of the prophets first by the bicycle craze in the 1890s, then successively by the automobile, the motion picture, radio, and television. Yet they all prosper today, and even the bicycle is having a kind of renaissance. Consequently, it is not difficult to forecast that the library of the future will have (as indeed many do today) a wide range of ways to serve its customers, from traditional books to several kinds of electronic devices—audio, visual, and audiovisual.

From the standpoint of the library, rather than of its users, no doubt the most significant change is one already in process, the use of microfilm and microfiche as a means of storage. As professionals in the field know, this is probably the fastest-growing area in communications technology. It is now a $500 million industry and can be expected to reach $1.25 billion by 1975. Its dramatic rise can be accounted for by the introduction of automated retrieval devices and the invention of equipment combining microfilm's storage capacity with higher computer output speeds. Until now, business and industry have been the chief recipients of these benefits, but libraries and the home reader can be expected to share in them increasingly.

Technology enthusiasts readily suggest that libraries could solve their perennial space problems by putting everything on their shelves into microfilm or microfiche and employing batteries of table readers to provide access for their patrons. Already, of course, microfilm has been a major help in storing newspapers and periodicals, and now comes microfiche, with its ability through ultrafiche to get as many as 3,200 pages on one microfiche-size film card. More than a thousand pages of information can be filmed in a little more than one-and-a-half square inches; and as for 16-millimeter roll film, a hundred feet of it will hold up to 3,000 standard letter-size documents. Color microfiche has just arrived, offering high-fidelity reproduction.

The implications of the Encyclopaedia Britannica's publication on microfiche of 20,000 volumes of its Library of American Civilization and similar projects under way by National Cash Register are not lost on either libraries or their informed users, nor are the possibilities inherent in microfilm cassettes overlooked. Obviously, a library's stock can be reduced to microfilm and microfiche, thus solving the storage problem that has driven so many librarians out of their minds, particularly those who have budgets that permit little or no expansion. But first of all, there is the expense of the reduction, which is considerable, and second, there is the much more formidable problem of providing the library's users with access to the stock. Librarians who are already using the readers that have become available are well aware of the problems they raise. Some are mechanically awkward to use. Often they break down, and the difficulty of having them serviced is even worse than that incurred in getting any other kind of appliance repaired. Business once boasted the American system was built on service; today few companies can so much as spell it, let alone practice it.

The new devices, in production and on the drawing boards, will solve some of these difficulties. Definition of the images is much better in these machines, and sophisticated machinery has sharply speeded up retrieval time, although a sophisticated machine raises larger repair problems when it breaks down. There remains the problem of servicing these machines in large numbers, since their number will be proportionate to the amount of material stored in such forms. One can visualize a future library in which the stacks are reduced to a fraction of their present size, but the reading rooms of such a library will have to be greatly enlarged and, no doubt, divided into carrels. Considering what havoc library users can wreak on an object as simple as a book, it is not hard to imagine the breakage and vandalism inherent in these viewers and their often fragile film.

Since it is so easy and cheap to duplicate microfiche cards, we can expect that readers will be checking them out instead of books, since several volumes are provided at a time on a single card. They can be read at home, with either a lap reader, already available for less than a hundred dollars, or a slim reader-projector, small and light enough to slip into a briefcase, which can employ lap, table, wall, or ceiling as a viewing area. There is a snake in this Eden, however. Inexpensive fiche copiers will make it possible for the patron to copy for his own shelves what he checks out of the library, and it would be quite possible for him to compile in a short time a formidable library of his own. What happens to library use then? What, in fact, happens to the author's royalties, already diminished by library use, not to mention the publisher's profit? What is right for the reader is not necessarily right for the remainder of the book business. Traffic on this street must flow both ways, or it will stop flowing entirely.

Micrographics is only one aspect of the technological revolution with which libraries will have to deal. The ubiquitous computer is another. Lowell A. Martin divides computer use into two broad categories: its use for bibliographical control—documentation, reproduction, and distribution; and its use as an information retriever.[1] The first use, Martin believes, is already being established and in ten years will be widely utilized by libraries to rebuild bibliographic systems for identifying and locating resources. He envisions regional cataloging centers, using a national record of publications compiled on tape, from which will come individual library catalogs and bibliographies for individual readers.

For the reader, computers are already able to provide a giant step forward through facsimile transmission, utilizing their other function as an information retriever. When the machinery is installed—another large "if," considering library budgets—a reader can go to a branch of a state library system anywhere and obtain from a central source, probably in the state capital, a facsimile copy of any article from a magazine or other stored document—even, presumably, a microfiche card. Thus the library acts out its traditional role as a link between reader and stored printed matter, only using different means to do it.

Computers offer the localized services just described, but also, as Martin points out, they have the capability of creating huge information banks, in which the process will not be transferring printed matter to the reader through duplication but rather creating a collection of information for the individual user—"instant publishing or individual custom-made publishing," as he calls it. Again, the obstacle is not technology but money. The capital investment required is presently far above the ability of any library to supply. The impetus for this development will have to come from government or well-heeled, special-interest organizations.

Of these two uses, the computer as bibliographic controller is the more immediate and feasible. The prospects were explored by the Yale Library Research Department in a year-long study of how the library might use computers to organize its 8 million catalog cards. According to Ben-Ami Lipetz, head of the department, the study demonstrated that while computer methods might someday replace card catalogs in large libraries, it was most unlikely that any single computer program could be devised that would replace human ability to find specific books or documents. It was conceivable, however, Lipetz noted, that new computer methods might make it possible to consider data from several viewpoints at once, in the way human users do now, but it was nevertheless doubtful that they would ever equal human ability to compensate for inadequacies in the information. One could scarcely expect impressive retrieval information from automated catalogs, he concluded, if these catalogs contained only information that had been copied directly from input documents, without benefit of annotation and association.

In brief, the Yale study asserts the belief that human searchers through present catalogs are usually successful and probably more successful than machines would be. When they are not, it is because the books were not cataloged properly, or the user didn't know how to use the tools available.

Accessibility, of course, is always the key word, and most specialists agree with Joseph Becker, president, Becker & Hayes, Inc., that the primary result of marrying computers to electronic communications, as far as libraries are concerned, will be to transform them into active transmitters and distributors of information, making future knowledge "incomparably accessible." This will be done, he believes, in four ways: applying the computer to the performance of internal library functions; using new techniques of information retrieval; making possible communication with multimedia files; and creating library networks.[2]

The computer has proved its usefulness in library housekeeping. Book ordering, accounting, and the clerical processing of records by computer are already available to those libraries that can afford it. A few libraries have been able to take the logical next step and use their computers as businesses do, to compare cost and effectiveness, to produce data on such problems as quality and rate of service. Library automation, in this sense, is growing as rapidly as budgets will allow.

What remains to be determined are how far libraries can be mechanized, for what useful purposes, and how library networks can be organized on a regional, national, or international basis. Communications theorists have long been fascinated by the possibilities of making books available to readers at home in some kind of printout form or by showing them page by page on a screen, through central banks of information tapped by cable. It has been proposed that the entire Library of Congress be put on film and/or microfiche, as a first step toward making it accessible by means of these home machines.

The machinery for making this happy dream possible exists, at least in prototype form. There are two major conceptions of how it might work. One envisages the book (or newspaper or magainze, for that matter) flipping over slowly on a television screen, the speed controlled by the user, who presumably would have to know what he was looking for and where to look for it. Coming to a page he wished to examine at leisure, he would set the machine for hold and switch to a slave machine that would give him a printout of the page. Another method would be to have the book transmitted through a home viewer, probably a lap model like the one already available for microfiche, which would be connected to a cable system, much like the telephone is today. In either case, the user would have to possess a directory of information centers and a master index to material available so that he could dial whatever he wanted.

These proposals presuppose three conditions, only one of which is presently fulfilled. First, the home machinery would be needed, and that could easily be made available in the present state of the science. The second condition would be a transmission system employing either cable or satellite transmission using laser beams. Both of these are technically possible, and, in fact, we are on the way, probably within this decade, to the home information and entertainment console that is connected by cable or satellite to the audiovisual resources of the world. The third condition is the equipment in the information bank to complete the chain and put the information on the air or cable. Here the technology is less advanced, in spite of some optimistic claims, but no one doubts that it can be worked out. Looming over all these possibilities is the formidable expense involved. It is not something that can be done piecemeal. It will have to be done in a large, comprehensive way by an agency, governmental or business or both, with extraordinary resources.

There are some who believe that the problems involved in cable- or satellite-connected information centers will not be solved before these systems are overtaken by the video cassette, whose possibilities are so staggering that those who have invested a great deal of money in it, including many of the leading organizations in the communications industry, find themselves carried away by the prospects and optimistic to a degree that some observers think is excessive. Here again technology is not the problem. It is possible now to put both information and entertainment, in color if desired and including a mixture of motion pictures and stills, or either, on film contained in a cassette no larger than the ones presently used for music. This cassette can be placed in a projector no larger than a home machine and viewed either on a small screen in the device itself or projected on a wall or a home movie screen. Only a failure to arrive at standardization—there are several video cassette systems available—prevents the spectacular growth of this industry, just as a similar lack is holding up the microfiche and microfilm industries. When this difficulty is resolved, as it surely will be, a whole new era in home entertainment will have arrived, comparable to the introduction of the long-playing record or the arrival of television itself.

Books can also be packaged as video cassettes and circulated through libraries or bought from a bookstore. Whether it will prove desirable to circulate them in this way remains a question. If mass production of cassettes makes low prices possible, that would be one advantage. If it is the kind of book that makes a mixture of text and pictures, both motion and still, desirable, that would be another distinct advantage, and one can easily imagine a whole new kind of book being produced using this mixture of techniques. But in the case of many books—novels, for example—would there be any particular advantage in taking out a cassette from a library instead of a bound book? Even if it could be viewed at home on a machine one could hold in the lap or take to bed, the advantages, if any, are not self-evident.

Of all the developments in communications technology applicable to libraries, it appears that those having to do with the mechanization of library procedures may be the most important in the near future, since they will lead to significant changes in both administration and practice. Gerard Salton, professor of computer science at Cornell University, is one expert who takes this view. He sees the mechanization process taking six directions: the treatment of business operations; processing of document acquisitions; content processing; generation and maintenance of many types of lists and records; control of circulation records; and handling of reference and research work.

"In the end," Professor Salton concludes his analysis, "one may expect that the trends toward the mechanization of library operations on the one hand, and toward cooperative arrangements and network operations on the other hand, will proceed together at an accelerating pace. The budget pressures will inevitably force the sharing of resources, which in turn will impose the standardization that is required for an economically viable implementation of mechanized library operations. At the same time, the introduction of mechanized procedures creates more favorable conditions for further standardization and for the creation of successful library networks."[3]

While the impact of the computer is growing in library operation and new technology begins to emerge with the possibilities for change outlined by Salton, another machine has already made deep inroads into old patterns and is beginning to raise some serious and highly complicated problems. No one is certain how far the copying machine will go beyond the considerable place it now occupies, but its potential appears limited only by the complications of copyright. Some idea of the threat it poses to publishing is contained in this anecdote by Herbert S. Bailey, Jr., director of the Princeton University Press: "A scholar recently told me that he had canceled all his subscriptions to scholarly journals. They were taking up too much shelf space, and he found that it is easier and cheaper to scan the tables of contents in the library and get photocopies of only those articles that interest him. He is building a personal reference library in the form of copies of articles in file drawers. Of course, this scholar is not paying for the articles, he is paying only for the copying; and if all scholars followed his practice, there would be no scholarly journals."[4]

Copying in the library is commonplace, and it is now possible to copy by remote control. It will be only a matter of time, in the opinion of some experts, before all major libraries, and perhaps even bookstores, will be connected by wire, and books or articles inserted in a machine in any one of them will be reproduced at any point desired along the network. Theoretically, a library would need only one copy of a book. General circulation would disappear, because it would be cheaper to provide the user with his own copy. The original book would never leave the library.

Although this appears to be a cheaper and easier method of book distribution than any we have considered here, there are serious flaws in the idea. The major one is the whole question of copyright and the obvious implications for writers, none of which had yet been resolved by the Congress in mid-1971. But there is also the problem of who would produce the one book required for copying. Certainly not the publishing business as we know it today. And who would write the book? Certainly not an author whose work could be copied endlessly without recompense. It will not be easy to solve these problems, because it is difficult to control copying once it is instituted. The flagrant violation of copyright is even now reaching major proprotions, in spite of the effort by publishers to halt it through altering their copyright notices.

Bailey forecast in 1966 that combining the computer with remote copying technology would render some types of publications, like scholarly journals, symposia, and certain reference works, obsolete, since it would be necessary to publish only the indexes and perhaps summaries or digests with them. This process is, in fact, under way in various fields, but progress is slow. Money again is the problem.

However, there are other obstacles besides money in the path of technology. One is the display of warning signals that the new world may not be as brave as advertised. From as far away as Makarere University in Kampala, Uganda, the assistant librarian, Sanford Berman, warns that developing technology may be creating an "untouchable elite" within his profession, "a coalition of technocrats and bureaucrats dedicated—even if somewhat unwittingly—to making themselves indispensable by virtue of their ability to manipulate and expand the 'new technology' plus the more complicated administrative-budgetary apparatus associated with it. If many colleagues share this suspicion, it might be well to profoundly reassess our fundamental attitudes and priorities before things get totally out of hand."[5]

Berman raises the question of whether the supermechanization of libraries might discourage some current and potential users who want only the kind of access they are accustomed to having. He worries, too, about the effect of automation on employment and the possibility that the increasing emphasis on technology will impose an inflexibility on some of the libraries' operations. In trying to determine priorities and attitudes, he suggests, we may have "reached a philosophical, if not also spiritual, watershed. Which way do we go? Which side are we on?"

There is unquestionably a real danger that technology may be employed where it is not really needed. Ellsworth Mason reports making an evaluation visit to a small college with a collection of 175,000 volumes and a peak daily circulation of 700 that was automating its circulation records —"an action," says Mason, "tantamount to renting a Boeing 747 to deliver a bonbon across town."[6] Mason, director of library services at Hofstra University, is frankly antitechnology, and specifically anticomputer, where libraries are concerned. After studying problems in ten major research libraries on a fellowship from the Council on Library Resources, he is convinced "that the high costs of computerization make it unfeasible for library operations and that it will become increasingly expensive in the future. The computer feeds on libraries. We actually devote large amounts of talent and massive amounts of money (perhaps $25 million a year in academic libraries alone) to *diminish* collections and *reduce* services, exactly at a time when libraries are starved for both, by channeling money into extravagant computerization projects which have little or no library benefits. . . ."

Another library information specialist who views automation with a cold eye is Daniel Melcher, former president of the R. R. Bowker Company. On the subject of central data banks, he wonders "what proportion of library patrons are going to value this kind of speed enough to be willing to pay its cost. I get the impression that the fellow who is vaguely resolved to take out a copy of *War and Peace*, if he can ever find one on the shelf, is getting lumped in with the surgeon who has a patient hanging between life and death and needs quick information from the National Library of Medicine."[7] While he has no doubt that the promised electronic miracles are technologically possible, Melcher has "the gravest doubts about how soon they are going to be really practical or desirable except in very special circumstances. In a very high proportion of current library inquiries, even our old-fashioned library methods provide fast and satisfactory answers. Of the remainder, some would probably go unsatisfied in any case, and the residue might well survive modest delays rather than warrant involvement of heavy hardware."

Humanists in general take a skeptical approach to technology, but since they are all users of libraries and want to see them improved, some have taken a more generous view than one might expect. One of these is Peter Simmons, a former information systems research analyst and supervisor of MARC production in the Information Systems Office of the Library of Congress. Simmons warns that the transition from punched cards in a clerical operation to automating a total information retrieval system cannot be made overnight, but the changes that are being made, he believes, are increasingly imaginative in library operations. At the Library of Congress, the MARC (an acronym derived from Machine Readable Catalog) Project is one of two major automation programs. This project is an attempt to produce and distribute catalog records in machine-readable form as a prime source of bibliographic data. The other project is a study of the Library's central bibliographic system, including acquisitions, cataloging, circulation control, and reference activities relevant to the central catalog, with a view toward discovering how automation can best be applied to the whole complex. Simmons thinks that "there can be no doubt that bibliographic records will be accessible in the libraries of the future by means which are not now practical."[8]

Since this prediction was made, there has been a general trend in the United States government toward automating its enormous store of records. At the National Microfilm Association's annual convention in 1971, the Navy announced that thirteen of the eighteen firms that had submitted technical proposals for its major catalog microprinting contract had been asked to submit formal price bids. By the end of this century, it is estimated, only 50 percent of our records, government or otherwise, will be on paper.

It is clear, then, that technology is going to play an important, if as yet undetermined, role in the library of the future, in spite of the caution and the outright opposition attending its advance. Cost will limit that advance in all but the largest libraries, and even in them the limitations will be determined by the fluctuating state of the national economy. The machinery exists to automate libraries almost completely, and it is entirely feasible to construct great information banks and to interconnect libraries as well as to connect users with knowledge sources. The imponderables include not only the astronomical costs of so profound a change but also their acceptance by the people they are intended to serve. No one knows just how much technology people want or need in this field or how much they are willing to accept. No one knows, for example, how many people simply want to hold a book in their hands, as they have for centuries, and carry it around with them if they like. Is anyone going to take a microfiche lap reader into the bathroom, for example, or onto a bus? And other mechanisms are even less flexible. It is possible that technological progress will founder on the rock of human nature. All anyone can be certain of today is that there will be change in the future, as there always has been. How soon, how much, and what it will consist of are subjects for speculation.

Notes

1. Lowell A. Martin, "The Changes Ahead," *Library Journal* (June 15, 1971): 2054-2058.

2. Joseph Becker, "Electronic Innovations in the Library," *Electronic Age* (Winter 1967-1968): 23-26.

3. Gerard Salton, "On the Development of Libraries and Information Centers," *Library Journal* (October 15, 1970): 3433-3442.

4. Herbert S. Bailey, Jr., "Book Publishers and the New Technologies," *Saturday Review* (June 11, 1966): 41-43.

5. Sanford Berman, "Let It All Hang Out," *Library Journal* (June 15, 1971): 2054-2058.

6. Ellsworth Mason, "The Great Gas Bubble Prick't; or, Computers Revealed—by a Gentleman of Quality," *College and Research Libraries* (May 1971): 183-196.

7. Daniel Melcher, "Automation: Rosy Prospects and Cold Facts," *Library Journal* (March 15, 1968): 1105-1109.

8. Peter Simmons, "Automation in American Libraries," *Computers and the Humanities* (January 1968): 101-113.

17 Libraries and Telecommunications

John W. Bystrom

Libraries are not yet very demanding of telecommunications. They could remain so. The concepts of role, constituency, and service and the practices that develop from them may demand only modest increases in telecommunications traffic.

The amount of coordination and cooperation that develops among libraries will be one of the key factors in creating greater demand for telecommunications services. A greater need for telecommunications will result with the achievement of one of the goals of a national library plan: a nationwide system of service that can be responsive to the legitimate demands from a user of one type of library through use of the resources of another library.

Yet a nationwide system can operate even if the demand on telecommunications transmission is small. Increased demand will depend on the adoption of certain types of terminal equipment not now in use and on equal treatment for nonprint materials. Demand will also be increased by a serious effort on the part of libraries to reach the general public by electronic means. For purposes of discussion, networks may be divided into those serving relationships among institutions and those serving relationships between institution and client. There has been much interest in the former. As for the latter, technology to serve researchers has center stage, and applications to meet general needs are largely untouched. If telecommunications networks are ever used to deliver knowledge to the general public, there will be an entirely new level of demand for transmission services.

Will new nationwide telecommunications network facilities be developed for library use? Probably they will not, without a forceful, mission-oriented national program. If one lists some of the questions of library policy that make the future of telecommunications networks for librar-

An earlier version of this paper was presented at the Conference on Interlibrary Communications and Information Networks, sponsored by the American Library Association, September 28–October 2, 1970, and subsequently appeared in *Interlibrary Communications and Information Networks*, pp. 27–43.

ies uncertain, the size and complexity of the network development problem becomes evident:

1. The role of the library in storing and delivering materials in nonprint forms
2. The rate and degree to which automation will be adopted
3. The relationship of libraries to independent bibliographic, material handling, and archival efforts of the disciplines
4. The development and acceptance of national standards of procedure
5. The extent of new public financial support
6. The effectiveness of new tools and their availability in forms and at costs that will assure use in institutions and homes
7. The resolution of outside constraining factors, such as the copyright question
8. The relative utilization by libraries of "off-the-shelf" versus "on-the-line" media delivery systems
9. The role of private industry in the information field
10. The degree to which libraries show themselves able and willing to attack the geographical and social barriers to expanded service.

While these uncertainties make the nature of library traffic and future requirements for communications difficult to predict, there are similar uncertainties about the capacities of telecommunications to respond. The telecommunications industry is highly volatile, with change effecting change. Library networking will have to conform largely to available transmission facilities, and network growth will depend in large part on the extent to which new telecommunications facilities are constructed for general use. The traffic that libraries have to offer probably is not sufficient in itself to warrant large-scale independent telecommunications systems—in contrast to educational television (ETV) broadcasting, for example.

The technology on which telecommunications networking is based has produced a series of major innovations. Federal policy, which determines the pace and direction of development, has been a battleground. In the course of these struggles there have been actions designed to shape communications policy in support of education. Attention has focused on noncommercial television broadcasting, but libraries have not seen the need to play an active role.

The capacity of the nation's transmission system for optimum library services is dependent on a number of unpredictable factors:

1. Federal support policies: the extent to which, for any of a number of different reasons, telecommunications networking is supported by comprehensive federal intervention

2. Enlightened use of the spectrum: the extent to which library and information systems will be represented and recognized as valued users of the nation's spectrum-supported telecommunications

3. Growth of transmission and switching capacity: the extent to which private capital is turned into new plant and broad-band and digital capacities are increased, satellites applied effectively, etc.

4. Cost reductions: the extent to which economies of scale and design are passed on—and perhaps even diverted—to library and information systems users

5. User sophistication: the extent to which research and development activities, training programs, and pilot projects are mounted within information and library enterprises

6. Effective marketing: the extent to which industry produces services and equipment that meet library requirements at acceptable costs.

The circumstances necessary for sound application to libraries of telecommunications networks are dependent on conditions determined by a wide range of political, social, industrial, and professional decisions, as well as by technological development. Libraries do not constitute an independent, tightly bound system. They are constrained by their sponsoring organizations; they are also dependent on the publishing industry and on abstracting and indexing services from outside. A major influence on the future will be the extent to which libraries adopt a dynamic posture in order to succeed better in their mission and work aggressively to modify the telecommunications environment created by the policies and practices outside their operations.

Despite the magnitude of network development, there is a point at which all activities meet. That is the doorstep of government—federal, state, and local. The federal government has a variety of accepted functions that influence the availability and acceptability of telecommunication services: It is a regulator of interstate telecommunications services through control of the radio spectrum; it is a user of communications that it both leases and owns; it is a promoter of advancement in science and technology and is therefore concerned with the flow of information necessary to that advancement; in the national interest it supports essential work that cannot be accomplished in the free market, such as the space program, the subsidy of ETV, etc.; and it supports research and development activities in telecommunications.

Add to these the federal government's involvement in libraries: It operates library services for the federal agencies; it promotes development of libraries and information systems through grants and contracts; and it provides leadership in the development of library policy through planning grants and efforts such as the National Advisory Commission on Libraries appointed by President Johnson.

State governments regulate telecommunications within the state, own and operate telecommunications systems in many instances, and lease services in every instance. They perform a leadership function for both public and private libraries, in terms of regulation, and have responsibility for the educational system in the state.

Local governments exercise powers as franchisers of public utilities, which now include telecommunications systems by cable, and are operators of libraries and schools.

All three levels are deeply involved in making decisions that affect the growth of telecommunications networks, decisions that, when projected into the future, can be seen to have a direct influence on the basic character of library operations.

Federal Telecommunications Policy: National Coordination of Information System Development

Three major national citizen advisory groups have recommended national development centers to facilitate the application of systems technology to the more effective dissemination of knowledge. The first of these, the President's Task Force on Communications Policy, initiated in August 1967, was struck by "the lack of interdisciplinary research into questions of communication policy" and recommended in its report the establishment within government of a "central source of technical and systems advice and assistance in telecommunications." It proposed "greater multi-disciplinary capability within the Executive Branch" to integrate the variety of policies and interests in communication and to initiate "experimental operations" where needed.[1]

The National Advisory Commission on Libraries, the second of these advisory groups, in one of five major recommendations proposed a "National Commission on Libraries and Information Science as a continuing Federal planning agency," a proposal that became law in 1970. Another of the commission's recommendations was the "establishment of a Federal Institute of Library and Information Science" with the Department of Health, Education, and Welfare. A principal task was to be "the system engineering and technical direction involved in the design and implementation of an integrated national library and information system." Beyond that it was to be concerned with the "changing needs of information users and the effectiveness of libraries and information systems in meeting those needs."[2]

The latter recommendation was viewed with enthusiasm in a report, completed in August 1969, by the third group, the Committee on Instructional Technology. In addition to endorsing the Federal Institute of Library and Information Science, the committee proposed a National Institute of Instructional Technology, which was to be a constituent of a National Institute of Education. (Also suggested in the report was a Library of Educational Resources "to assist school and college libraries to transform themselves into comprehensive learning centers; and stimulate interconnections among specialized libraries, data banks, schools, and colleges for comprehensive and efficient access to instructional materials and educational management data.")[3]

The committee's major recommendation received additional support when President Nixon proposed to Congress on March 3, 1970, the creation of a National Institute of Education "as a focus for educational research and experimentation." While this was comparable to the committee's recommendations, it was also similar to a proposal made in October 1968, during the presidential campaign, when he called for the creation of a National Institute for the Educational Future. The president made no mention of an Institute for Libraries.

The three reports are history. What influence they will exert on the new Office of Telecommunication Policy and the National Commission on Libraries and Information Science is to be seen. They stand as evidence of the importance attached to the establishment of a working center for information systems development.

The Communication Satellite The communication satellite provides opportunities for the advancement of education throughout the world by separating the factor of distance from the cost of transmission. Much of the attention at the federal level directed to the use of telecommunications in education has been based on federal interests in space and in the technological innovations of the space programs. However, in 1967 President Johnson made several speeches that focused attention on the use of telecommunications technology for libraries and information systems. At the Conference on World Education at Williamsburg, Virginia, on October 8, 1967, he pictured outstanding library facilities being made available any place in the world through the development of existing technology.[4] At the signing of the Public Broadcasting Act on November 7, 1967, he looked beyond a broadcasting system to "a great network for knowledge" that would employ "every means of sending and storing information that the individual can use." He pictured an "Electric Knowledge Bank" comparable in value to the Federal Reserve Bank.[5]

In the meantime a President's Task Force on Communications Policy, a subcabinet made up of representatives from major departments, recommended a demonstration satellite program to develop information. Television broadcasting networks were emphasized as potential users, and the importance of a wide range of purposes was also stressed. In this context the Biomedical Communications Network proposed by the National Library of Medicine was noted.

Policy guidance from the new administration came on January 23, 1970, when the White House recommended to the Federal Communications Commission that essentially no limit be placed on applicants for domestic satellite authorizations. Thus distributions of high-speed data required by a national library and information network received attention equal to that given the network needs of television broadcasting.

The first use of satellite relay for routine exchange of library materials and for regular college instruction was made by the University of Hawaii, using NASA's ATS-1 to interconnect campuses on separate islands within the state. International exchange by satellite among Pacific Basin universities is under development. Plans for future uses include a contract between NASA and India that will allow use of ATS–F, now under construction, for a large-scale demonstration extending at least one year.

Educational Television Networks In shaping aspirations for library telecommunications networks, one must consider the fact that it has taken fifteen years of determined effort to achieve a "real time" or "live" ETV network without direct federal participation and support. Like the library, the ETV broadcast station lacks a market economy on which to base development. The alternative to the marketplace in the United States is the taxpayer or a foundation.

The problem for the ETV network was the high cost. Although the federal government seemed the only source of support, its control over programs was feared. The Carnegie Commission estimated the cost of national interconnection of state networks at $9 million annually for leased services from a common carrier. For an operator-owned carrier, a capital cost of $30 million and an annual cost of $6 million would be required. The Carnegie Commission recommended free or low-cost rates for ETV interconnection. A provision to encourage the Federal Communications Commission to allow such rates was included in the Public Broadcasting Act.

A second alternative was that contained in the Ford Foundation offer of August 1966, which proposed to establish a private satellite corporation to be subsidized by the Ford Foundation. It would lease interconnection services to the three commercial networks and provide channels for an ETV broadcast network. Channels were also to be made available to elementary, secondary, and higher education. In addition, $31 million was to be provided for ETV broadcast programs from the difference in network operating costs and the amount to be charged the three commercial networks. The originator of the idea of free interconnection for ETV was the American Broadcasting Company, which had petitioned the Federal Communications Commission for authority to operate a satellite for interconnection of their affiliated stations and had promised free interconnection service and some dollar subsidy to the ETV network. The Ford proposal was in the form of comments to the Federal Communications Commission in response to the ABC request.

The search for ETV resources has produced a Corporation for Public

Broadcasting, a statutory authority to undergird negotiations for low transmission rates; this authority embodies a dynamic idea that still may be used by a government serious about recasting national priorities. While ETV networks and library networks are far from analogous, the contributions to public policy made by one may be helpful to development of the other.

Rate Reductions A principal deterrent to ETV networking is the cost of interconnections. In the implementation of library telecommunications networks the problem eventually becomes the same—raising funds and reducing costs.

Efforts at the federal level to secure rate benefits have taken three forms. Free or reduced rates for education have been advocated with limited success. Through the rate-making process the government is in a position to provide special benefits to educational users in the public interest. The effect is to subsidize a high-priority function. Costs of transmissions are shifted from favored users to nonfavored users, just as post office book rates pass the burden to the general taxpayer or other users. Claims for educational advantages have been made on the basis of fair return to the taxpayer for profit-producing benefits provided private industry.

A second form of rate benefit is that negotiated by the government as an administrator. Bulk rates made possible through large traffic volume have served to greatly reduce unit costs.

Third, the government operates or leases systems. Military, space research, transportation, law enforcement, and other recognized federal functions use government-operated or leased-dedicated systems. There have been no dedicated systems in education, a responsibility primarily of the states. It is worth considering, however, that since the establishment of the Library of Congress, the federal government has performed library and information functions. Furthermore, information transfer may be accomplished in support of many purposes, including those in which the federal role is primary.

First, let us consider the opportunities existing for reduced rates. The policy of the Federal Communications Commission in connection with common-carrier charges in interstate commerce has been equal rates for equal service to all comers. The Public Broadcasting Act of 1967 sought to modify this policy. The Federal Communications Commission was authorized to approve free or low-cost interconnection of noncommercial education television stations. A provision authorizing the Federal Communications Commission to approve free or low-cost interconnection of institutions of higher education was later included in the Higher Education Act of 1968.

Second, as a major user of telecommunications, the federal government enjoys rate advantages that could be used under some circumstances for library networks. For example, state governments have been eligible in most instances for Federal Telpak arrangements. Yet only twelve states have utilized Federal Telpak rates, averaging forty cents per voice channel mile per month. In some instances where federal rate advantages could be very helpful, however, they cannot be used. Demonstrations supported by federal grants involving networks, for example, are not eligible. This limitation has proved a major deterrent to the funding of experiments involving telecommunication applications.

Third, if we are serious about networking, we need to review the possibilities of utilizing the federal government's telecommunications services and systems. There is, of course, the FTS system, the basic government long-distance telephone system. Of special interest to libraries in their present state of readiness is the Advanced Record System developed by the General Services Administration and operated under contract with Western Union. The ARS was designed to interconnect not only conventional teleprinter (narrow-band) subscriber stations but also all known varieties of high-speed terminal devices requiring broad-band transmission facilities. The system is capable of forwarding traffic to Western Union's TELEX and the Bell system TWX, of exchange traffic with AUTODIN of the Department of Defense, and of refile to the Western Union Public Message System. The various federal rate and systems advantages might be captured under a plan by which one or all of the national libraries served as agents for a network of constituent or affiliated libraries.

Certainly a comprehensive approach to networking will involve concern for costs as well as appropriations. Good housekeepers will demand a careful study of the existing rate advantages for libraries. Statesmen will

provide some assistance to those who are seeking to open up the telecommunications systems of the country for educational use.

Scientific and Technological Information It has been generally accepted
that under the American system of distribution of powers the promotion
of libraries is grouped with authority for education and is reserved to
the states, with the exception of library functions that are an extension
of some recognized federal function. Until recent years any federal
interest in information had been based on some accepted federal power.
Science and technology have benefited from the link with defense and
industry.

  In 1962 the Committee on Scientific and Technical Information
(COSATI) was organized within the Federal Council for Science and
Technology. Made up of representatives from federal information organizations, it has focused on improvements in handling scientific and technical information in the government and in developing information
systems to store and circulate scientific and technical information to
practitioners.

  The interest of the Office of Science and Technology encouraged a
series of reports to advance solutions. Among the most influential of
these studies was the Baker Report (1958) on "Improving the Availability of Scientific and Technical Information in the United States,"
which made recommendations for stimulating nationwide activities
in publication, data centers, unpublished research information, storage
and retrieval, and mechanical translation.

  Three later reports received much attention within government circles.
The Crawford Report (1962) on "Scientific and Technological Communication in the Government" recommended improvements in scientific information, a plan for orderly transition to the new systems,
and solutions to problems associated with restrictions on the flow of
information; the Weinberg Report (1963) on "Science, Government and
Information" discussed problems of the information transfer chain and
information systems and made suggestions for action by the scientific
and technical community and by government agencies; and the report
of the Systems Development Corporation (1965) on "National Docu-

ment Handling Systems in Science and Technology" provided guidelines
for coordination and nonduplicative development of federal information activities.

The problem brought on by the rapid increase in amounts of information has been under attack from both the U.S. Office of Education and
the National Science Foundation. Grant awards of the two agencies
reveal a strong interest in efforts to retrieve and make available reports
of the products of research. The importance attached to networking has
increased with the rise of the computer and the recognition that the
decentralized system under development for the retrieval of information
was difficult to query.

The U.S. Office of Education also has been involved in broadening
information retrieval activity. The Educational Research Information
Center (ERIC) was expanded in 1964 to comprise nineteen regional
centers, including one on library and information sciences.

An example of the involvement of the disciplines in information retrieval is the Council of Social Science Data Archives. There are approximately twenty-five member organizations in the council, each active in
gathering data. Computer development and telecommunications are
among the council's major concerns.

A problem that has become apparent is the need for access by the
scientist on the university campus where the library is not linked to
appropriate computerized information systems. Both the National
Science Foundation and USOE have shown concern for the problem.
It has appeared to some that any science information network would
have to be linked eventually to a university library network if it were to
perform effectively. A number of proposals for funding have sought to
test the extent to which a discipline-centered information service could
be used by a broader public when made available through a general
library.

The future of networks for science and technology cannot be foreseen. The time is not far away when the technical potential will exist
for networking at reasonable cost, and pressures created by investments
in the collection and storing of data will be greater. A national plan is
needed that will be accepted generally as the one to best serve both
individual needs and the national interest.

The State and Telecommunications Network Development

State telecommunications networks are growing in variety. They assist many kinds of public activities, including education, law enforcement, forest protection, highway safety, public health, and aid to disaster areas.

What benefits can libraries obtain from these state telecommunications activities? Telecommunications can be essential to the operation of a state library plan where there is differentiation of function or sharing of materials. A state telecommunications network can be the key to plans for extending services to the less populated areas and for expanding functions as might be required by the concept of a community information center.

The state information network has been viewed in two ways. As a primary system for the state or region it has its own identity and is responsive to both institutional and private demands from within the state. It has also been viewed as a node or regional center of a national system, retransmitting to local points. State telecommunications operations are by now sufficiently well established in many states to warrant consideration in planning of library networks and information systems.

Efforts are being made in some states to develop statewide telecommunications management, with a backbone network for all kinds of administrative purposes. Over the last five years there has been a movement to create central state telecommunication authorities sometimes headed by appointed commissions. The state of Nebraska is a leading example; Illinois, Iowa, Massachusetts, and California have also participated in this trend.

A review of a number of statewide telecommunications plans reveals little input from libraries. Libraries with their TELEX and telephone have seen little to gain immediately from the state networks. Often state planning has depended for funding on the Office of Civil Defense; for this reason emergency communication has been a prime objective. However, there are basic pressures that may encourage libraries to use state telecommunication systems when they exist. Joint use of communication systems by many agencies is more effective and less costly.

The state ETV network also represents a resource. State ETV systems may eventually serve as the basis for the development of educational telecommunications networks in some states. A possible course of

development is to have two major state networks, an administrative
network and an educational network, each administered separately. In
other states the ETV network and the state administrative network
may be developed together. An Illinois study concluded that under
some circumstances this development would be more economical.

A third type of development is the linking of particular classes of
institutions. The interconnection of health and educational operations
for purposes of sharing services and materials continues to move forward.

Educational computer networks involving interstate interconnections
as well as intrastate links are expanding very rapidly. Teletypewriter
networks for library systems are, of course, becoming commonplace.

There is also a steady growth in interconnections linking industrial
plants and offices to university centers. These telecommunications
interconnections will grow, undoubtedly, as new health and educational
institutions are opened to serve an expanding and more demanding
population. Benefits to libraries will be judged ad hoc by local management with professional associations playing an important role in the
sharing of experience. Any national strategy for library network development must take into account the strong likelihood that in a substantial
number of states the linkage of what is now a few health or educational
centers will eventually result in a comprehensive statewide educational
network service.

On the basis of the limited state experience thus far it is possible to
project future directions. Special-purpose telecommunications networks
will be activated within the state for a variety of objectives depending
on social appeal, local leadership, and federal participation; the pressures
for more sophisticated uses and for economy of operations will result in
a grouping of needs and central planning facilities, either owned or
leased; in most cases libraries will not operate complete systems, but
they will work with state telecommunications entities; and the communication needs of libraries will be small initially. The availability of
network capability, however, will be an incentive for thinking in terms
of a statewide system and will also encourage expanded nonprint services. New methods will result in extended services to the general public,
to researchers, and to government and industry.

Libraries can benefit by observing some of the limitations encountered by growing state telecommunications systems. First, development varies greatly from state to state. Any effort that seeks to develop a national network on the basis of linking existing state networks has an uncertain future. Second, network development takes time. The successful development of the Nebraska central telecommunications system extended over five years. Third, no one has yet determined how national network standards can be gracefully yet rigorously imposed on independent state operations. Private common-carrier history suggests the difficulty of maintaining transmission standards without strong central control. Experiences in the development of a national law enforcement network as well as civil defense networks deserve attention. Fourth, state telecommunications developments have tended to support purposes for which federal assistance and leadership are available. Therefore, when state telecommunications networks for libraries are viewed as part of a national system, it seems evident that only strong federal incentives and a firmly directed program can produce the uniformity necessary to units in a federal network.

Yet there is a basis in present development for pilot demonstrations of statewide information networks. In selected states there is the capacity for statewide relay of the signals as part of a prototype national system. Where national library network plans benefit from high social priorities, as could be the case with a National Medical Communication System, a prototype national service could supply information over interstate links to some states, to be retransmitted over statewide systems to points of need. In some states the telecommunications potential exists for projects such as EDUCOM, conducted by the Interuniversity Communications Council, in which a statewide network of colleges and universities is linked with national libraries.

Furthermore, there are telecommunications resources in a few states to allow for state pilot projects in extending public library services. Libraries must be prepared to exploit opportunities as they develop. State telecommunications development thus far reflects the principle that networks are shaped by the functional demands of the users. Libraries should be able to speak with sufficient authority about their needs to influence the structure of telecommunications systems.

There is also the question of how statewide telecommunications will be used to bring better service to more users. Is state library organization and planning sufficiently strong and coherent to create a purpose for state library networks? David Weber and Frederick Lynden point to only three states—Hawaii, New York, and Pennsylvania—with strong library systems involving centralization of key functions.[6]

Beyond interlibrary loans, centralized reference, and copy transmission, all on a relatively small scale, there are few uses for state telecommunications networks that would not be disputed by working librarians on practical grounds. Experience to date does not provide a persuasive basis for risky attempts at massive restructuring of old institutions currently performing functions that the public understands. A carefully programmed effort needs to be considered to encourage conceptualization and testing in libraries of new practical methods for distributing information to the public by means of telecommunications.

Municipalities and the Cable System

High-capacity cable systems have passed out of the state of technological innovation and are about to be introduced into operating urban society. We are in a period of political and economic innovation. The future position of libraries and information systems in relation to these telecommunications services, along with man's future access to information, are being determined today.

The "wired city" concept has appeared in the context of an extension of existing community antenna television service (CATV), which conceals its importance for information systems and libraries, and a distinction should be drawn between two kinds of systems. The CATV system typically has twelve channels for one-way delivery of television programs to home television receivers. It is both a transmission system and a program service and lacks the versatility expected of the future urban cable transmission system. It is tied in purpose to the delivery of commercial television programs; other uses are incidental to that purpose.

The hypothetical "wired city" system has many purposes, most of them potential. The concept represents an effort to exploit fully the increased coaxial cable capacity that technology has made available. Cable systems using present technology have the potential capability of about thirty television channels. It has been stated as practical to extend

the range to fifty channels. The Electronic Industry Association visu-
alizes a dual communication system in our cities involving fifty channels
with two-way facilities, limited switching, and capability for communication by sound, pictures, data, and facsimile. The opportunity this
would open up for information transfer is obvious.

The limited application of high-capacity cable telecommunications
systems to large centers of population is a matter of cost. The President's
Task Force on Communication Policy concluded that application of
cable telecommunications to the nation as a whole was financially out
of the question. It has been estimated that capital outlay for systems
serving New York City alone would exceed one billion dollars.

The probability that urban areas will be served by broad-band, versatile
cable transmission systems puts before libraries basic questions of institutional character and function. In adapting to this telecommunications
development, libraries could become different institutions.

Most of the new tools for the home, such as facsimile recorders, high-
speed coders, and stored television displays, require the high-capacity
cable systems to be available sometime in the future. The growth of
urban cable service is now heavily dependent on the decision-making
processes of municipal government within conditions set by the Federal
Communications Commission. These decisions and the requirements for
raising investment capital are shaping networks that have the potential
of linking libraries and information centers to the home and place of
business. The access to such systems that libraries will enjoy will be
determined largely by government regulatory action. Thus, it is important that libraries are capable of bringing to focus their future requirements at those moments when government regulatory policies and
practices are set.

Issues that seem of concern to libraries are these: increased number of
channels, two-way capacity, terms of the franchise, free use by favored
public users, methods of financing, and delay in decision to allow for
long-range studies of potential utilization. The Federal Communications
Commission plans to require that the new system be designed to accommodate two-way communications for those subscribers who want them.

What is the role of libraries at this time in the face of these unresolved
issues? The limited use made by libraries of the existing 2,300 CATV

systems raises questions as to future library participation in a high-capacity, two-way cable system.

Today's CATV operator has a positive incentive to offer a variety of programs and, unlike the broadcaster, has sufficient channels to seek to appeal to minority tastes. Where can one get the programs to fill twelve or twenty channels? There is an existing opportunity for a public library program service. Academic meetings such as the general proceedings of the annual convention of the American Association for the Advancement of Science have been programmed on public broadcasting stations; uncopyrighted government and archival films can be displayed; children's story hours and other regular parts of the library service can be distributed; even the Library of Congress's recorded books for the blind might be offered.

Despite existing opportunities, the uses of CATV systems by libraries have been small. There is the question of how such programming fits into library objectives and functions. But also the question of readiness is raised. How well prepared are libraries to take advantage of the service extension opportunities provided by cable systems?

With the emergence of the "wired city," libraries have two directions of action to consider. One is to determine what uses, if any, the old institution will make of the new. This direction will require planned study and pilot demonstrations. The second line of policy is the mounting of strategic and tactical responses to help assure cable systems that will perform effectively in serving library and other information retrieval functions.

The broad position on which the case for libraries rests has been well stated by Sidney Dean: "A metropolis without open communication channels and media cannot function as a market economy, a free society, or a self-governing polity."[7]

It would be fortunate if the future use of urban cable services could be fully thought out today. A national library strategy could be helpful at a time when decisions are being made that will determine the specifications and the purposes for which the new systems will be used. There is little concrete experience, however, on which to base estimates of future library use. In fact, no assurance can be given that libraries will use the cable systems at all.

Nevertheless, it is possible at this stage to determine the qualities of a cable system that open up communication and allow a place for libraries and other as yet undeveloped information systems. Specifications that best serve libraries can be reasoned from the technical and economic character of the system. For example, libraries cannot engage in economic competition for channels against profit-making industry. Library use will depend on regulatory concessions made to libraries as favored users. Concessions will come most easily if the channels are large in number and readily accessible. Also, systems that provide for two-way, rather than one-way, communication are necessary to information exchange. Systems that are capable of interconnection with other systems and are suited to all kinds of terminal equipment are better than systems that are not. Characteristics desirable for free and rapid transfer of information can determine a national library posture.

At the same time, a clear and convincing picture of the use to which libraries and information services will put the new cable systems is needed. Innovations necessary to the exploitation of future telecommunications capability require the involvement of library management. Predictions must eventually face the rigors of application, with the tests of cost, public acceptance, and operating feasibility. Pilot projects may be needed that would utilize the most advanced of the existing cable systems.

The movement of events is such that public policy toward urban cable systems is likely to be determined, however, before the results of studies and pilot projects come in. The economic base for the new industry will be laid and capital raised on the basis of market methods already formulated. Libraries will stand with hat in hand alongside other educational users who lack the financial bargaining power of an industry in search of markets. The system will be so firmly rooted as to be all but unchangeable.

Politics and economics will determine development of cable systems and may foreclose the future. The plan and the manner in which the library position is advocated deserve immediate attention. Restrictions on active participation in political decision making, real and customary, need to be faced and methods for surmounting them found.

The future is also dependent on innovation in utilization. This is a primary responsibility of the librarian, but one he cannot meet effectively without the assistance of many disciplines. Development requires both a prepared case and a social mechanism to bring argument to bear upon the centers of decision.

Some Proposals for Today and the Near Future

The widely dispersed library and information activities of the country are not organized to develop a comprehensive national network system involving telecommunications and automation. The central mechanisms required to control essential conditions are lacking. Despite the advances of the last few years, there remains a need for coordination of common purposes that will require a number of years to evolve. The National Commission on Libraries and Information Science will provide a focal point for leadership. However, the use of a presidentially appointed commission to operate a network system is out of the question.

Librarians are without a central approach to research and without a plan for national network development. There have been proposals for pieces of a system but no broader framework. Moreover, there is uneasiness as to the effect that implementation of a part will have on efforts to deal with the whole. Specifically, if the needs of the academic elite are served, will it set back efforts to meet the information needs of the general public?

There has been almost no effort to grapple with the problem of financing. Financing involves not only the costs of telecommunications network operations but also the increased cost of library operations resulting from improved access to materials. As yet, no library strategy for the development and use of statewide telecommunication systems and urban cable systems or for international exchange by satellite exists.

A number of actions are proposed with two purposes in mind: first, to develop a capacity for central planning and operation without interfering with the essential independence of separate institutions and without subordinating libraries to a line organization and, second, to respond to the rapid changes in telecommunications in a way that is advantageous to information network growth.

A Public Corporation In the 1930s the government used the corporation to open up the supply of financial capital; in the 1960s it used the corporation to open up communication. On three separate occasions the corporation has been established to facilitate application of new communications technology to the needs of society: Communication Satellite Corporation, authorized in 1962; Corporation for Public Broadcasting, authorized in 1967; and a private corporation to take over the U.S. Post Office Department, approved in 1970. Why not establish next an Information Transfer Corporation?

The basic questions are these: Will network functions be managed inside or outside the federal government? Will networks be created by a variety of ad hoc arrangements or be the product of central management and design?

The primary function of the corporation would be to arrange for the storage and transfer of information. It would serve as a method for channeling public funds into information development. Supported by federal appropriations, it would be able to make payments to institutions for the storage of information used and to copyright holders for the use of information. Its primary relationships would be with libraries and information storage agencies. Although it would not become involved in statewide distribution or urban cable systems, it could, because of its central position, assure the compatibility of telecommunications systems. The corporation could provide for high unit efficiency, for it would negotiate bulk rates with private industry for telecommunications and computer services. The major objective would be to increase equal opportunity for information by facilitating the work of libraries.

In its action creating corporations the federal government has each time recognized the importance to society of open channels for communication. The Corporation for Public Broadcasting increased the number of broadcast program choices. The public corporation has been used to avoid the restrictive practices of government administration.

An information transfer corporation would also escape the constraints that are imposed on government operations. I refer to the fiscal and personnel practices, statutory and policy limitations, and time-consuming review. It could operate outside the United States with the freedom of any industrial corporation. It would be a force in providing visibility and identity to libraries, not as parts of some host institution, but as independent activities determined to preserve and extend the individual right to information.

Because it can collect demand, the corporation becomes a management tool by which library telecommunications requirements can be determined. New uses can be studied and predicted. Industry receives the information needed to warrant investment in response. The corporation is a means by which technological innovations can be introduced into library services. Furthermore, a corporation makes it possible to plan and mount a general system. It provides central control and the vital power to enforce system standards. This may be accomplished by little more than a contract with a common carrier. But a corporation also has the capability to utilize alternatives: to operate a totally owned system using government spectrum space, lease a specially designed service from a communications company, use a federally operated communications service through a national library facility, and so on. It can join with other major entities, such as the Corporation for Public Broadcasting, in joint use of services.

The information transfer corporation will not be possible for perhaps five years. We have to learn more about costs and benefits, and foundation support will be necessary for the study. Conceptualization, professional acceptance, and congressional action all require time. I refer to the experience of the Corporation for Public Broadcasting: A year was spent in developing the interest of the government and the profession; the Carnegie Commission required something over a year and Congress something less. The first appropriation came well over four years after the campaign began. I think in the case of an information transfer corporation, the process would take even longer.

The time to treat a national network with the seriousness a corporation implies has not yet arrived. A telecommunications network will not operate until such time as a standard record has been developed and received acceptance along with a universal language for an automated bibliographical control system. The Library of Congress looks to sometime in 1972 or later for this product. Nevertheless, the ETV experience indicates that if we are interested in an operating national telecommunications network for libraries during this decade, it is not too early to begin organized study of ways and means.

Research Institute Without some form of national institute, libraries lack the mechanism to coordinate the detailed technical planning, research, and demonstration that the National Advisory Commission on Libraries recommended as essential to the development of a national library system. The need for an institute is well recognized, and since a public one cannot be expected in the immediate future, a private one should be organized to carry out the purposes. Establishment of an Institute for Libraries and Information Systems would provide a problem-solving base for continuing communication among the many interested groups that must eventually be a part of a national information system development.

Action Center Issues that ultimately affect the cost of telecommunications and the access to libraries are determined by municipal agencies, state commissions, the Federal Communications Commission, General Services Administration, Interdepartmental Radio Advisory Committee, and the Congress of the United States. As potential users of state networks, urban cable systems, and satellite interconnections, libraries have basic interests in decisions made by these agencies. A laissez-faire approach with occasional appeals for united action cannot be effective over such a broad and complex front. While one can properly advise that the local library director lead the fight for public channel concessions at a cable franchise hearing, to base national development entirely on the separate actions of hundreds of independent institutions is not likely to assure full exploitation of opportunities or a uniformly high level of access to new telecommunication systems.

Basic application patterns for the new transmission technologies will be set over the next five years and most often in response to the "squeaky wheel." In bringing to bear the requirements of libraries for telecommunications, no behavior originating within government can substitute for strong, organized citizen action outside government.

A National Action Center should be organized to create a telecommunications environment favorable to the growth of information networks. As a private entity it could move at all levels of government and have a general maneuverability that government agencies lack. It would be designed for effectiveness in adversary relationships and would be a source of information and support to local libraries.

Finance Study There is agreement that an increased proportion of funding for libraries must come from Washington. In the past decade the federal programs for libraries followed the general pattern for the new health and education programs. Categorical programs for construction, research and development, professional improvement, and services were broken down by classes, institutions, and populations to be served. No steady-state network system is possible under an extension of existing funding patterns.

Is a national library system based on networking possible without federal financing to support the performance of that mission? Ideally, the pattern of funding for a national system should promote the achievement of primary objectives. The Carnegie Commission on Educational Television recommended a plan that reinforced their principal concern, insulation from political influence. One form of library funding might be geared properly to encourage the collection and circulation of materials demanded by users.

A federal funding program for the support of circulation could not be developed without a much clearer picture of operating costs. There are enormous difficulties in cost accounting. Nevertheless, something approaching a market situation might be made workable. A federally supported fund for reimbursement of national circulation is suggested here. Libraries would draw payments from the fund based upon the interlibrary loans made. The reimbursement schedule would allow a "profit" over actual operating costs. Libraries with large collections would thereby gain resources needed for continued growth. Interlibrary loans would no longer be a burden on the major institutions. The decisions of users would determine growth.

A serious approach to networking cannot neglect the subject of financing. Such a study involves the whole of the library and information service enterprise. Reliance on the present federal patterns of block and formula grants or committee-approved special grants is not conducive to system growth and operation. It is not realistic to expect rapid interlibrary loans, improved reference service, and the direct distribution of some kinds of materials without great changes in the flow of materials and in the cost structure for the libraries involved. The findings of the study should include recommendations for federal financing designed to increase information opportunities for the user.

Maintaining Momentum "A program of action" prepared for the
National Advisory Commission and included in *Libraries at Large*
(Chapter VII) advises, as an approach to future technological development, a process of identifying and supporting selected "high impact"
activities. Such activities should include:
1. Urban networks: What, if any, will be the effect of the wired city on
libraries? A multidisciplinary study group with representation from
urban libraries might examine the implications for libraries of cable
systems and suggest feasible applications. The opportunity would be
provided for conceptual meshing of urban library policies and operations with the technological potential of the wired-city system.
2. Statewide networks: The planning of library services using statewide
telecommunications networks should be funded in selected states.
Superior effects would merit further funding for the preparation of
detailed plans. If warranted, and if the necessary technical and organizational conditions existed within the state, the funding of a few demonstration projects might result.
3. National prototype projects: The three national libraries should
receive the active support of the profession in efforts to mount national
network demonstrations.
4. Satellite strategy: Libraries should actively participate in all efforts to
extend the principle of free or low-cost education.
5. National network forecast: Several national network models have
been prepared that would serve particular information objectives.

Networks and the Federal Role: A Personal View
The sad truth is that there are many unresolved problems standing in
the way of a national system of library telecommunications networks.
Although a number of important efforts, such as those of the National
Task Force on Automation and Other Cooperative Services, are clearing
away the problems relating to messages, the status of telecommunications development—statewide networks, urban cable systems, national
prototype projects—provides no assurance that the normal progression
of events will accommodate the future needs of libraries. The impression is quite the contrary. Nor does the commendable growth in sharing
among libraries documented elsewhere give us assurance that, lacking

greater direction, these separate cooperative programs will inevitably evolve into a well-integrated and equitable national library network. A new level of activity is needed, broader in scope, more coherent in plan, and with much greater involvement by the public and private forces in the field.

Development of library use of telecommunications networks can be viewed in two phases: creation of the essential conditions, involving an array of actions over the next five years; and initiation and expansion of a steady-state national system sometime thereafter. The earlier phase would use existing federal resources augmented by foundation aid and encompass programs of public action to shape government policy so as to permit educational application of telecommunication and the development and authorization of a steady-state plan. The later phase would require an entirely new level of federal financial support and new operating and management mechanisms.

A principal question in the course of future development is the nature of the role to be assumed by the federal government. A second major question concerns the nature and goals of private organized effort. Only with private organized action outside government can the environment created by government practices, such as regulation of cable systems, be successfully modified to allow for optimum library network development. Organized private action will be required, also, if developmental and financial roles of government are to be expanded.

In considering national library and information networking, we can easily underestimate the problem. The present library system is representative of an earlier era of more or less autonomous units serving clusters of people, with relationships between units tending to be personal as much as institutional. Now we are considering marrying this highly autonomous library system to library telecommunications networks that require a great amount of integrative behavior with consistency and conformity by participants. In the process the problems also change from those determined locally, or within the institution, to problems that require national solutions and national mechanisms to implement those solutions.

As far as libraries are concerned, telecommunications networking is not simply one more technical advance. A functioning network heralds the entry of the library into the industrial age. A national network requires central planning and control of the elements needed to assure function of an apparatus that is a national instrument and yet made up of parts that continue to reflect local needs. We will observe a process that has been repeated many times during the industrialization of the nation—the application of technology to hand methods, resulting in increased availability of services. It is also a process in which the small unit often fails or is merged with the larger unit.

The term "network" can signify many forms and degrees of cooperation. To achieve the major goals of the National Advisory Commission, one can envisage a national library network system made up of regional or state library network systems. Essentially, all locations are provided with access to information on total national and international holdings and access within prescribed limits to the materials contained in the total holding. Telecommunications in this national library system are used routinely for cooperation in acquisitions, technical processing, organizing and maintaining library collections, as well as in sharing resources to meet service demands and in providing access to the total national store. It is a system that uses state or regional telecommunications networks for rapid response and urban cable systems for convenience to the client.

A working telecommunications network demands more than a will to cooperate among entities. Sufficient control over the future is required to provide adequate financial resources, enlightened regulation, sound technology, operational competence, and effective articulation of user needs and habits. A national library system will be able to plan cooperative action and exercise the control needed to apply the plans and measure results; these powers are nonexistent in today's laissez-faire system.

The greatest obstacle in the way of system development is the library's fear that its autonomy will be lost. The library has a number of protections, anchored as it is to a host institution, dependent on local funding, public and private, and protected under state and local statutes. Yet the effect of a national service on local autonomy is a question that cannot be set aside. How can we construct and gain operational effectiveness for a coherent set of national objectives and practices while at the same time preserving as much as possible the ability of individual library units and small systems to adapt to the special needs of their community?

It is said that since libraries do not determine content as in the case of television there need be little concern over government influence. Yet libraries do determine access to information. Access can be influenced indirectly by apathetic administration, adherence to old processes, failure to understand the needs of the users, and it can also be influenced directly by funding priorities. For different reasons the question of federal control is as real for libraries as it is for the mass media.

If the federal government were to manage a national library network, there would be, it seems to me, some danger that the system would respond best to knowledge requirements growing out of the directions and purposes of established bureaucracy. The federal government is not only a source of finance but also an interested party. It includes within its house a great many information users and library institutions. Can any of these honestly speak for the varied needs of the general citizen? The special functions of government—economic development, social control, scientific growth—will receive emphasis, while the general needs of man for knowledge to control himself, his environment, his society, and his nation will face a subtle neglect. Will the needs of science and technology, for which the federal government provides large resources, be emphasized over the humanities and the arts, for which the federal government provides only the smallest token of assistance?

The power of the federal government must be offset by solid increases in organized power and initiative outside government. Increase in power outside government is desirable for a second reason. It is usually over-looked that a national library network would not be supported by a market economy out of which steam for development can come. Libraries have been told to imitate the network practices of industry. Unlike industry, there are no profits for libraries to be generated with expanded networks. If anything, networks may produce losses when used to increase circulation of materials, unless they are linking units of a single central system.

What source is to supply the steam? In the absence of a market economy, the only power available for advancement of a national pattern of networking is the national government. How is the federal power to be evoked? We have observed examples of presidential leadership, foundation leadership, and pressure from science and industry, each seeking to link federal powers to development of a network. What will constitute a sufficiently powerful motivating force to support such leadership? Nothing less, I suggest, than the combined forces of those who would benefit—industry, government, the information-using disciplines, and the citizen, joined by the private foundations and the library professional—all sharing in a campaign of program planning and persuasion.

There is a good reason for the national administration to turn a friendly hand to the improvement of libraries and information services. With recent appointments there are within the executive office of the president unusually strong abilities in the area of telecommunications. The administration, furthermore, has rather successfully challenged the highly centralized character of our mass media. It has been met with the charge that its attack, far from representing a concern for the citizen's access to all kinds of opinion, is exclusively concerned with its own public exposure. There could be no such confusion in the promotion of libraries as the communication medium that provides full and free access to the opinions of the world.

Notes

1. *Report of the President's Task Force on Communications Policy* (Washington, D.C.: Government Printing Office, 1967), Chapter IX.

2. National Advisory Commission on Libraries, *Libraries at Large: Tradition, Innovation, and the National Interest*, eds. Douglas M. Knight and E. Shepley Nourse (New York and London: Bowker, 1969), p. 518.

3. U.S. Congress, House Committee on Education and Labor, *To Improve Education:* A report to the President and the Congress of the United States by the Committee on Instructional Technology (Washington, D.C.: Government Printing Office, 1970), p. 45.

4. Lyndon B. Johnson, in *Public Papers of the Presidents 1967* (Washington, D.C.: Government Printing Office, 1968).

5. Ibid.

6. David C. Weber and Frederick C. Lynden, *Survey of Interlibrary Cooperation*, Conference on Interlibrary Communications and Information Networks, Warrenton, Virginia, September 1970 (mimeo).

7. Sidney Dean, "Hitches in the Cable," *Nation* (July 20, 1970): 45.

18 The Changing Capacities of Print and the Varying Utilities of Libraries

Kathleen Molz

We move today in a "world without walls." The phrase is borrowed from the French critic and author André Malraux, who externalized so brilliantly in his "museum without walls" the effect of modern photography and facsimile reproduction in the field of the fine arts. Today, because of the vastness of the art publishing industry, every man becomes his own curator, selecting for his home or his office the foremost of those treasures that were once the sole prerogative of the museum and gallery visitor. The phrase has been extended so that we now speak of "schools without walls" or "universities without walls," and perhaps it is time to delineate that "world without walls" in which we live.

Modern technology and contemporary transportation have placed us in this world, and of it, even beyond it—into outer space and on other planets. There is nothing particularly new about innovation, exploration, and discovery; what the modern communications media have done for us, however, is to make us witnesses to that discovery and exploration. Technology, through some 225 million television sets in a hundred nations of the world, permits us to sit in our living rooms and watch mankind walking on the moon and soon after to see the news clips showing us exactly how the Pope reacted to the same event. Technology permits us not only *instantaneous* awareness of natural calamity or historic happening but also *simultaneous* awareness, making of mankind one gigantic family in its perception of news and one very small and humbled household in its reaction to it. From this example, one might wonder if the truly great event occasioned by the moonshot was the landing itself or our permissive hobnobbing with the papacy—both occurrences are significant and unique to the twentieth century. "The whole world is watching," call out the youth of Chicago, and we watch them apprising us of the fact itself.

In this changing configuration of communications media, the place of print is being drastically altered. Let us consider, for example, the situation of the average American in the 1860s. The act of writing and

its subsequent transfer to print reigned supreme: the social activism of
the period was reflected in a significant novel that triggered behavioral
patterns in a war of two factions; the reportage of that war was the
matter of the noted pictorial weeklies; its subsequent analysis through
untold histories and commentaries was based upon its massive documentation—the lists of the war dead, the government reports dealing
with the disabled and maimed, journals and memoirs, letters from
parents to sons away from home, the speeches of politicians, the literature of emancipation and abolition. The period remains unexcelled in
the transfer of human witness—the transfer of every sight and sound
from the cannonball at Sumter through the cries of Andersonville to the
silent burden of the slow-winding train from Washington to Springfield—
into written document and printed record and, ultimately, into history.
It was during such a period, a period of the unrivaled achievement of
print in communicating the present and preserving the past, that the
American public library was founded.

Compare the print-dominated scene of the America of 1860 or 1870
or even 1880 with the communications realities of our present-day
society, with its recordings of famous voices, its documentaries of social
problems, its news photos, its films, even its coinage of the phrase "oral
history," and the difference, however much we seem to acknowledge it,
is almost overwhelming. Such a contrast begs two questions: What
relevance does that institution so singularly nourished by many of us,
the library, now have? And, perhaps more significantly, what relevance
has the medium of print in a multimedia world?

This latter question I shall take up first, and I should like to deal with
three prevailing attitudes, or postures, (not necessarily consonant with
one another) concerning the medium of print and the act of reading
that seem characteristic of our present culture.

The first attitude is posited on the theory that print has lost its primacy
as the medium for the relay of news and for the analyses of affairs and
has become instead the medium, not of public communication, but
rather of introspection, the medium best guaranteed to gain for the
reader privacy in this noisy, multimedia society. The second postulates
that reading, at least serious reading, was and remains an elitist avocation, demanding leisure and education, an avocation that is gradually

declining in a society of semiliterates. And the third, certainly the most vocal and emphatic, identifies reading and print orientation with basic education and entry into a society in which the obligations of citizenship, the choice of occupation, and the increase of income are all in part determined by the mastery of words. In brief, the first of these attitudes deals with reading as a part of mass communication, the second with reading as art and high culture, and the third with reading as skill.

A massive amount of documentation would seem to validate the first of these postures. Not only have the theorists of mass communication attested to the rapid spread of audiovisual, in contrast to printed, devices, but the medium of print itself is also evincing changes. The mass circulating weeklies are still being published, yet their pages dwindle as their advertisers seek other and more popular means of displaying their wares. The daily newspaper, once the central source of national and international news, now liberally covers local affairs in a proliferation of "feature" pages, and the local press more and more picks up the nationally syndicated column of commentary and editorial assessment. Even *Time* magazine, ironically in view of its name, has succumbed to the posture that print is the conveyor of opinion and evaluation; thus, it now includes an "essay" of analysis on some national topic and for the first time in its history ascribes views to individuals by permitting the discreet use of initials in small type to inform us who is saying what about whom. And, finally, the academic community has been subjected to this changing attitude about print. Compare, for example, the biographies of Huey Long and John Keats, both published within the last few years and both notable prizewinners. The footnotes in the biography of Keats identify edition, memoir, letter, archive; the footnotes in the biography of Huey Long often refer to radio address, confidential communication, memoir in Oral History Project, and interview.

Print then, at least in terms of the popular press and to some degree of the academic press, is no longer a first source of public information; it is a source, rather, of informed opinion, this latter still a powerful force, for print not only has the capacity to review itself but also carries the authoritarian weight to review media unlike itself, and all of us look to print for our reviews of film, television, and recording. If print has lost its primacy as the chief agent of news about events, it has retained a role, perhaps even more important, of adjudicator of public opinion and taste, and it is obvious from any bibliography on the subject of mass communications that the theorists of the subject use print, and books, and ultimately reading, to expound their ideas.

The second postulate that reading, at least serious reading, is suffering a decline has been put forward by a number of aestheticians and critics, perhaps most notably George Steiner, whose essay on "The Retreat from the Word" appeared almost a decade ago in the *Kenyon Review*. Recently, Steiner contributed the lead article to the *Times Literary Supplement* on the "future of the book," and because his ideas have many implications for librarians, at least some of them should be detailed here. Steiner contends that the classical age of the book declined toward the close of the nineteenth century, for in his view reading demands a climate of privacy and leisure as well as an awareness of the literature of the past, an awareness that can be achieved only through privileged education. Steiner also believes that reading and the literate tradition have been "eroded" by the sense of impermanence, a sense of mortality characteristic of modern art forms that celebrate the ephemeral and transcendent. He writes,

Certain aspects of this suspicion of transcendence are graphically present in the paperback book. The private library, with its leather spines and shadows, is all but obsolete; the hard-cover tome, the work in more than one volume, the collected oeuvre, may become so. The paperback revolution has obvious economic and sociological sources, related to ever-increasing printing costs and the image of a new mass audience. . . . But it also corresponds to deeper, internal changes in the status of literacy. The paperback is decidely ephemeral; it does not make for a library in the old sense. The book, as Montesquieu and Mallarmé understood it, had a stability of format to which the current paperback lays no claim. The threefold matrix of literary creation, of reading and of time defeated or transcended, found its expressive guise in the bound printed work privately held, hedged with quiet. Today, the pact with and against time, with and against the authority of the individual ego, operative in the classic act of writing and reading, is wholly under review.[1]

In contrast to this assignment of reading as an elitist and private phenomenon is the third of the attitudes to which I referred: reading as skill. Traditionally, at least in this country, this third attitude dates back to the "three Rs" concept of the public schools. It is typified in the well-known engraving of Lincoln as a child reading beside the fireplace in the log cabin; it is reflected today in the recommendations of black psychologist Kenneth Clark, who calls for a moratorium on the teaching of all subjects in the public schools with the exception of reading and math; it is apparent to all those who witness the persistent argumentation over the theories of the teaching of reading evident in Jeanne Chall's classic study, *Learning to Read: The Great Debate*; and it is climaxed in our day by the enunciation of a national "right to read" effort, which has for the first time received a presidential endorsement. Here reading is regarded as the keystone in the educational arch, the proverbial key to unlock the storehouse of learning.

These three attitudes, or postures, then—reflecting, first, the decline of print as a primary source of public information; second, the decline of serious reading as a characteristic of lay culture; and last, the renaissance of the populist and egalitarian belief that reading is and must be the bottom rung of the educational ladder—cast their own unique shadows on the current and future course of the nation's libraries.

As has already been noted, the public library was founded during a period of print dominance. In essence, the printed word embraced during the nineteenth century all three major capacities of any mode of communication: print was then the source of news and general information; it was the chief means for the exchange of serious ideas; and last, it was the economical and therefore the primary mechanism of the schooling experience. Emily Dickinson has expressed this power of the printed word perfectly:

There is no Frigate like a Book
To take us Lands away
Nor any Coursers like a Page
Of prancing Poetry—
This Traverse may the poorest take
Without oppress of Toll—
How frugal is the Chariot
That bears the Human soul.[2]

In this exquisite poem, now unfortunately so often relegated to children's anthologies, the poet has conveyed all three capacities: it was print that then transported the reader to new continents and to new experiences; it was print that allowed even the poorest person access to the literate experience; and finally, it was print, even within the confines of its frugality, that permitted the initiate admittance into the recesses of high culture. Reading was, then, indeed communication, skill, and art.

By the same token, it was the library, housing the current newspapers and periodicals, that functioned as a respectable source of information. It was the library, assembling the great retrospective collections of past writers of eminence, that served as the purveyor of the cultural and historic record. And it was the library, disseminating and circulating its materials to the ordinary household, that became the chief instrumentality for the free distribution of books in a democratic society. If the analogy can be drawn between the capacities of print and the functions of libraries, it can be said that print as a means of public communication refers to the general reference and informational function of libraries; print as the point of entry into high culture and serious scholarship relates to the library's role in acquisitions and collection building; and print as the instrument of equalized educational opportunity is closely attuned to the library's circulation and dissemination practices.

The question of print's sole utility in a multimedia world has been touched on; now it is time to examine the viability of this single instrumentality, the library, to maintain an efficient and satisfactory service in a society that no longer views print as its sole means of communication. I write this, not to suggest that libraries are no longer useful in modern society, but only to indicate that libraries will be forced to face new issues as they adapt to a multimedia world.

The library as a major source of public information will change. Generalized public information may, indeed, be of use to the student, but in an age geared to the data needs of the specialist, such information may be found wanting. Portents of the new discipline-oriented specialization in information transfer already exist in the network sponsored by the National Library of Medicine, in the proposed data aggregation of the National Agricultural Library with its land-grant college affiliates, and in the burgeoning lists of special collections and specific information demands for a whole host of topics, ranging from law to banking to industry.

Lowell Martin has suggested that one of the shortcomings of public libraries in handling general reference questions is "a concept of resources limited to the book or at most the book and the magazine rather than to the full range of communication media."[3] His point is well taken; the librarian who relies upon the latest edition of the *World Almanac* for data about the U.S. Secretary of Interior, Premier of France, or King of Jordan may find himself hopelessly obsolete in his iteration of anachronistic data. Poignant among the examples of a librarian's dependency on print is William Manchester's minor footnote to the assassination of President John F. Kennedy: "A petty functionary at the Library of Congress, clinging to a pet prejudice of librarians, refused to believe a word until it had been confirmed by the *New York Times*."[4]

The wresting away of the traditionally trained librarian from this symbolic dependency on the printed word is not a simple matter; education for the novice together with retraining for the initiated must cultivate in librarians a respect for sophisticated means of communication other than print. Otherwise, the general reference function of future libraries will be oriented totally toward bibliography: the checking of sources, identification of titles and authors, and verifications of imprints and signatures, primarily for the term paper writer and the dissertation candidate.

Even though the costs will be great and alterations slow, reference inquiries in libraries will ultimately be influenced by the whole range of communications media that libraries will assemble as well as the gamut of devices now under development that will permit the transfer of information with great speed and facility. Nascent experiments with telecommunications networking, telefacsimile transmission, and computerization of data presage a period in which questioners will receive their answers by means other than the traditional printed source. Indeed, the multimedia learning environment already evident in certain exemplary school libraries and media centers portends an adult agency with a variety of formats for educational materials designed to help the self-learner as well as to retrain the adult as employee in the changing technological society.

The utility of print and of libraries in providing an entry into high culture will not, on the contrary, be greatly challenged. Until the twentieth century, the written record had been man's chief means to interpret past cultures and civilizations. It is true that other arts—dance, music, architecture, painting, sculpture, and graphics—have contributed to contemporary understanding of the past, yet our comprehension of these contributions has been largely a matter of interpretation and analysis. This scholarship, morever, has been conveyed to us through the written record in either manuscript or print form. Put another way, Schliemann rediscovered Troy because of Homer; Shakespeare celebrated Cleopatra because of Plutarch; and Freudian psychology identified the Oedipus complex because of Sophocles.

Libraries that have housed these records, whether they are in research institutes, universities, or even large municipalities, will continue to maintain that atmosphere of quiet and that climate of leisure, signalized by George Steiner, as proper conduits to the pursuit of serious reading and scholarship. With their massive collections and their commitment to elaborate housing arrangements, the great research libraries will continue their work of classification and codification to make manifest the work of yesterday to the denizens of today. Computers may indeed assist such libraries in record keeping and circulation flow, but they are misapplied, in terms of information retrieval, to the files of centuries-old records in the entire tissue of a civilization, running a historical gamut from hieroglyph to computer-set type.

These last few paragraphs may appear to some as contradictory or incongruent. The distinction should be made clear: Questions based on contemporary data will be rendered answerable by multimedia means; in contrast, serious inquiries into the philosophical, literary, economic, or other elements that make the historic past relevant to contemporary understanding will still be answerable through the only means known to man, until the twentieth century: the record of document and artifact.

If the changing capacity of print has any meaning, then the most drastic change in libraries will occur, not in research libraries nor even in reference libraries, but in neighborhood community libraries, which cope with the myriad of consumer demands, ranging from the availability of the latest best seller to the need for information on moth control. Having neither monumental buildings nor retrospective collections, these community libraries will prove most responsive to societal change, a variance in their case determined by the changing capacities of print in the twentieth-century milieu.

Ironically, it is the attempts to cope with low-income readers, resulting from experiments with storefront facilities, that are now influencing metropolitan area-wide service. Just as "Sesame Street" has been adopted by middle-class as well as lower-class children, so the concept of the rented ghetto library facility is being extended to middle-class shopping centers. The factors involved are these: an increased desire on the part of local communities to govern their own institutions; the growing recognition that neighborhoods need a facility where books, toys, films, and packaged instructional materials can be circulated (I might even suggest here that the ephemeral nature of paperback books will lead to a free distribution of printed materials); and the ultimate acceptance by librarians and educators that in a populist culture such facilities need not take up the majority of their floor space with stacks housing reissues of the classics.

These facilities partake of many names: community learning centers, library-learning centers, neighborhood learning centers, etc.[5] They all have the following characteristics in common: the initiation of multi-sensory education, in which the participants can touch, manipulate, hear, watch, and respond as well as read; the involvement of the community itself in determining the education of both adults and children; and the participation of the community through employment opportunities within the centers as well as volunteer activities. What may be emerging is a new authority, based on a coalition of school and public library interests, an authority that could be conceived as an alternative to the traditional institution.

The cultural "happenings" of some innovative poverty projects, with their art shows, their children's games, their indigenous publishing programs, their sense of cultural life and identification—all these have given us a glimpse into a trend of tomorrow. These agencies reflect in part the transcendence, the impermanence, of contemporary life. Libraries will become part of the here and now, and at least some of them will bear little resemblance to those neat Carnegie branches once dedicated with marble plaques ensuring their usefulness "forever."

Because print has changing utilities, or perhaps because we are better able to articulate the varying usefulness of print, libraries will reflect these variables. Consequently, one library may indeed preserve the record of past achievement for the dedicated student and serious reader. Another may disseminate its wares to a very different group of users, who will in part determine the stock of libraries and may even help to create them.

The "library" then, and that word will have many connotations, both loses and gains from our changing concepts about print. In part, it loses its identity as physical plant and institution, for its location will be impermanent and its resources ever changing. Yet, it will gain in adaptability, since its clientele will become no longer readers but an audience (in the older meaning of that word), an audience of younger people attuned not only to reading but also to listening and watching.

There is something to be said in relation to this loss and to this gain. Buildings decorated with marble carvings honoring Dante, Shakespeare, and Homer smack only of the past; they do little to remind us that the future is yet to be explored. If the world without walls is a just notion, and I believe that it is, then those institutions that are to survive in it must partake of the flavor of that concept. A library where things do not always have to be brought back is an extremely attractive idea.

Notes

1. George Steiner, "The Future of the Book: I Classic Culture and Post-Culture," *Times Literary Supplement* (October 2, 1970): 1122.

2. Emily Dickinson, "There is no Frigate like a Book," *The Complete Poems of Emily Dickinson*, ed. Thomas H. Johnson (Boston and Toronto: Little, Brown and Company, 1960), p. 553.

3. Lowell Martin, *Library Response to Urban Change* (Chicago: American Library Association, 1969), p. 28.

4. William Manchester, *The Death of a President* (New York: Harper and Row, 1967), p. 211.

5. For descriptions of an innovative community learning center, see John Q. Benford, "The Philadelphia Project," *Library Journal* (June 15, 1971): 2041–2047; and Lynne and John Waugh, "Albuquerque's Free-Wheeling Library," *American Education* (August–September 1971): 33–35

Metropolitan Area Library Problems:
An Annotated Bibliography

Leonard Grundt

With the continuing growth of metropolitan areas, the problems affecting library service in these areas have increased—and so has the output
of literature relating to these problems and the efforts made to alleviate
them. Because many of the recently published materials are redundant,
I have made an attempt to be selective rather than comprehensive—to
include in the list of items that follows only publications that contribute
substantially to a better understanding of the problems of providing
adequate library service to all residents of metropolitan areas, including
young and old, rich and poor, white and black, urban and suburban,
laymen and specialists. (The identification of the authors in this bibliography reflects their professional appointments at the time of their
authorship.)

American Library Association. *Student Use of Libraries: An Inquiry
into the Needs of Students, Libraries, and the Educational Process*.
Chicago: American Library Association, 1964.
This volume contains the papers delivered at the American Library
Association conference-within-a-conference held in 1963 in Chicago.
Dealing with all aspects of the student use problem, the conference
consisted of the delivery of background papers and commentaries,
followed by meetings of study-discussion groups. Lowell A. Martin
summarizes the recommendations of these groups.

Beckman, Norman. "The Metropolitan Area: Coherence Versus Chaos."
Wilson Library Bulletin **43** (January 1969): 438–443.
A political scientist urges public libraries to concern themselves with the
problems of education, health, transportation, and housing in urban
areas—politically relevant issues—because elected officials hold the key
to library budgets. He states that urban planning should be a joint
activity involving librarians as well as planners and other professionals.

Bendix, Dorothy, ed. "Urban Ferment—Libraries, What Drummer?"

Pennsylvania Library Association Bulletin 24 (November 1969): 311–328, 331.

This issue of *PLA Bulletin* contains five papers discussing the urban public library today. The director of the Brooklyn Public Library describes how it serves the varying needs of Brooklyn's citizens. A social worker urges libraries to respond meaningfully to their communities or be forgotten. A black parent berates white middle-class librarians for failing to attempt to make lower-class blacks feel welcome in their neighborhood libraries. A suburban library trustee exhorts libraries to try to cause a shift in attitudes in their communities so that residents will become more receptive to social change. A social scientist concludes by pointing to the inevitability of change, the importance of education, and the need for planning.

Benford, John Q. "The Philadelphia Project." *Library Journal* 96 (June 15, 1971): 2041–2047.

Established in 1968 under the joint sponsorship of the major school and public library agencies in the city, the Philadelphia Student Library Resource Requirements Project is a multiphase research undertaking directed by the author. With funds from the U.S. Office of Education, the project staff conducted a comprehensive study of students in Philadelphia's public, parochial, and independent schools during 1969–1970 to determine their library requirements, use patterns, and attitudes toward school and public libraries; teachers, school librarians, public librarians, and parents were also surveyed. During the demonstration phase of the project, the sponsoring library agencies—on the basis of survey findings—plan to create cooperatively an experimental community library and student learning center that will be operated in the inner city "free of the traditions and constraints of existing programs." Benford expects this innovative center to be developed during the 1970s with community involvement and participation. What is happening in Philadelphia has considerable significance for other large cities.

Berelson, Bernard. *The Library's Public: A Report of the Public Library Inquiry*. New York: Columbia University Press, 1949.

A survey and evaluation of characteristics of users and patterns of use in American public libraries, this book constructs a unified pattern from individualized research studies. These studies reveal that the library was founded to serve a small minority of the population who are better educated and tend to be the community decision makers. After more than twenty years, Berelson's findings are still valid.

Blank, Blanche D., et al. *New York City Libraries: A Comparative Study of a Small Sample*. New York: Urban Research Center, Hunter College, 1968. The authors, two political scientists and an urban planner, view the library as a bureaucratic structure. On the basis of statistical analyses of data from thirteen public library branches, they conclude that there is poor allocation of library resources and services within the city system and that the clientele's appreciation of the library is more dependent upon cultural and environmental factors than upon the library's administrative organization and programs. This study illustrates the kind of multidisciplinary research that is needed.

Blasingame, Ralph. "Equalization of Opportunity." *Library Journal* **90** (May 1, 1965): 2071-2075.
A professor at the Graduate School of Library Service at Rutgers University discusses problems facing large urban public libraries, such as the low percentage of local tax funds allocated to them and the need to reexamine library objectives in the light of their failure to reach the disadvantaged. Blasingame criticizes librarians for serving primarily the middle class and for their preoccupation with the establishment of library systems based upon centralized administration; he believes systems should be founded without subordinating existing libraries and without encroaching on local sources of funds. The need for broadening the bases of support for public library service in urban areas is demonstrated.

Boaz, Martha. *Strength Through Cooperation in Southern California Libraries: A Survey*. Los Angeles, 1965.
This comprehensive study was undertaken for the purpose of assembling information and evaluating the services of the twenty public libraries that serve four counties in the Los Angeles metropolitan area. The general objective was to explore the feasibility of establishing a cooperative library system or systems for libraries of all types in Los Angeles,

Orange, Riverside, and San Bernardino counties. On the basis of data collected by means of checklists, questionnaires, and interviews, the author recommends a system providing three levels of service—through community libraries, area libraries, and research libraries—with centralized processing of materials.

Booz, Allen & Hamilton, Inc. *A Research Design for Library Cooperative Planning and Action in the Washington, D.C. Metropolitan Area.* Washington, D.C.: George Washington University Medical Center, 1970. Under the sponsorship of the Librarians' Technical Committee of the Metropolitan Washington Council of Governments, the official planning agency for the region, an overall research design consisting of nine separate projects was created for the purpose of identifying library problems, providing solutions, and developing feasible programs of library cooperation within the metropolitan area. For each project, the following are provided: a priority rating, a statement of the problems, objectives to be sought, the methodology to be employed, time schedules, staffing needs, and estimated costs. Although prepared for libraries in the Washington area, this research design is applicable to other metropolitan regions where libraries are interested in exploring opportunities for cooperative planning and action.

Bundy, Mary Lee. *Metropolitan Public Library Users: A Report of a Survey of Adult Library Use in the Maryland Baltimore-Washington Metropolitan Area.* College Park, Md.: University of Maryland, School of Library and Information Services, 1968.
This report is based upon nearly 21,500 responses—an 80 percent return —to a questionnaire distributed to a 20 percent sample of the users of 100 library units in the eight library systems of metropolitan Maryland in the spring of 1966. It was found that half of the users twelve years of age or older were students and that the libraries seemed to satisfy their traditional middle-class clienteles without attracting others. A bibliography of public library user studies is included in this volume.

Campbell, Henry C. *Metropolitan Public Library Planning throughout the World.* International Series of Monographs in Library and Information Science, vol. 5. Oxford: Pergamon Press, 1967.

The librarian of the Toronto Public Library describes in some detail library planning in nineteen metropolitan areas throughout the world with populations exceeding one million. New York, Los Angeles, San Francisco, and Detroit are the areas covered in the United States. Additional references to others, such as Boston, Minneapolis, and St. Louis, are included.

Campbell, Henry C., ed. "Metropolitan Public Library Problems around the World." *Library Trends* **14** (July 1965): 1-116.
How public libraries on four continents—North America, Europe, Asia, and Africa—are struggling to solve the problems created by the growth of metropolitan areas is described in this group of articles by librarians from Johannesburg, Warsaw, East and West Berlin, Hamburg, Vienna, Stockholm, Brussels, Liverpool, Tokyo, Detroit, Los Angeles, New York, and London.

Carnovsky, Leon, ed. "Library Networks: Promises and Performance." *Library Quarterly* **39** (January 1969): 1-110.
Included in this issue of *Library Quarterly* are papers presented at the 1968 conference of the Graduate Library School, University of Chicago. John C. Bollens, a political scientist, describes local governmental linkages in the metropolis, including councils of governments. Dan Lacy and Edward A. Wight discuss the traditional library and early public library systems. The director of the Minneapolis Public Library, Ervin J. Gaines, deals with the large municipal library as a network. Interrelations among various types of libraries are described by G. Flint Purdy and William S. Budington. The development of public library systems and of the three Rs program in New York state is related by S. Gilbert Prentiss, former state librarian. John Mackenzie Cory, the director of METRO, the three Rs system for the New York City area, characterizes his network as a "third-generation" library organization, because it is a combination of different types of libraries, including independent libraries and systems. Finally, William G. Coleman of the U.S. Advisory Commission on Intergovernmental Relations discusses federal and state financial interest in the performance and promise of library networks.

Carnovsky, Leon, ed. "The Public Library in the Urban Setting." *Library Quarterly* 38 (January 1968): 1-108.
At the 1967 conference of the Graduate Library School, University of Chicago, various aspects of library service in metropolitan areas were discussed in papers delivered by Raymond W. Mack, Kenneth E. Beasley, Paul W. Briggs, H. C. Campbell, Harold Hacker, Philip J. McNiff, Margaret A. Edwards, Ewald B. Nyquist, Lester L. Stoffel, and Lawrence L. Durisch—a mixture of social scientists, educators, and librarians. Their papers, which are published here, deal with such topics as the economic costs of urbanization, governmental and financial problems of metropolitan areas and their libraries, educational trends, materials and services in the urban libraries, suburban libraries, and planning metropolitan library service for the next twenty-five years.

Castagna, Edwin. "Involvement in Federal Programs." *Wilson Library Bulletin* 41 (January 1967): 478–483.
The director of the Enoch Pratt Free Library describes how this facility serves the entire metropolitan area around Baltimore under programs funded by the federal government. There is a reciprocal borrowing arrangement for the entire region, which embraces the city of Baltimore and seven suburban counties. The Enoch Pratt Free Library provides reference services to the entire area, supplemented by the daily delivery of interlibrary loans. In the inner city, the library is involved in community action programs, supplementary education centers, and neighborhood library centers.

Cloud, John M. "Overdue: Why Didn't They Burn the Libraries?" *Wilson Library Bulletin* 43 (April 1969): 787, 812.
A black librarian tells it like it is! Libraries were not the targets of inner-city rioters because the rioters didn't care about libraries. Librarians fail to reach ghetto residents because (1) big-city public library systems are not psychologically prepared to change their policies in some branches so that these branches may be more responsive to inner-city needs; (2) white middle-class librarians are afraid to work in the inner city; and (3) libraries as they presently exist have nothing to offer the militant, the oppressed, and the poor. To survive, big-city libraries must change and get involved with the inner city and its problems.

Coit, Coolidge, and Wight, Edward A. *Planning for Public Library Service in the San Francisco Bay Area.* Berkeley: Public Library Executives of Central California, 1963.
As one of their recommendations for solving the library problems of a metropolitan area, the authors of this report propose that the nine counties in the area be grouped into four regions, each of which would have its own system of public libraries. The unusual feature of this document is that it was one of the first to view library planning as a matter of regional concern, rather than a purely local service problem.

Conant, Ralph W. "Black Power in Urban America." *Library Journal* **93** (May 15, 1968): 1963-1967.
An expert on urban affairs predicts that black political leaders will take over the major cities in this country within the next twenty-five years. They will aggressively reorient institutions like libraries in the interest of establishing a black identity.

Conant, Ralph W. "The Future of Public Libraries: An Urban Expert's Optimism." *Wilson Library Bulletin* **44** (January 1970): 544-549.
In the context of the variety of public libraries, the author predicts that suburban libraries will continue to serve a margin of the fiction market and provide household and family reference services, limited circulation of recordings and films, preschool children's services, and group services for adults. In addition, they will be local outlets of metropolitan library systems. Central-city public libraries will continue to grow, improve in quality, and be innovative as the keystones of sophisticated metropolitan library systems supported principally by federal funds; they will serve as research institutions, and their branches will serve as neighborhood centers for the underprivileged. It is inevitable, claims Conant, that the greatest portion of public library funds will come from the federal government. The need for library research and evaluation of present services is cited.

Conant, Ralph W. "The Urban Library in Metropolitan Development." *Illinois Libraries* **51** (March 1969): 183-189.
The author foresees the emergence of a federal network of metropolitan constituencies over the next twenty years. The knowledge business will

be one of the great growth industries of the future, and workers will frequently have to retool intellectually. In ten years, Conant expects, economic poverty will have been eradicated through a system of income subsidies. Big-city libraries will develop and maintain centralized storage and retrieval systems while simultaneously creating a network of accessible outlet facilities. It is unrealistic, according to Conant, to think in terms of unique local needs, because a national community, requiring national planning, exists. Metropolitan governments will serve as the primary implementers of national development policy when the federal government forces the issue through the massive introduction of federal resources. A shift in the locus of decision-making power from the municipal to the metropolitan level is anticipated by the author.

Conference on Library Service to the Undereducated, Drexel Institute of Technology, 1965. *Library Service for the Undereducated: Report of a Conference Directed by Dorothy Bendix*. Drexel Library School Series, no. 15. Philadelphia: Drexel Press, 1966.
A conference was held in 1965 to alert public librarians to their role in the antipoverty program and to stimulate them to participate actively in their own communities' efforts in this field. Ira DeA. Reid discussed the dimensions of the problem from a sociologist's viewpoint, and Eleanor T. Smith spoke on the place of librarians in the antipoverty program. Public librarians from New Haven, Brooklyn, Baltimore, Kalamazoo, and Philadelphia presented reports on their work with the disadvantaged, all of which are included in this volume.

Cuyahoga County, Ohio, Regional Planning Commission. *Changing Patterns, a Branch Library Plan for the Cleveland Metropolitan Area: A Report to the Cleveland Public Library and the Cuyahoga County District Library*. Cleveland, 1966.
Two libraries within a metropolitan area cooperated in calling for this study. The Regional Planning Commission conducted an at-library survey of users and an at-home survey of users and nonusers and developed five library planning models that were used in the determination of the recommended branch library plan.

Dalton, Phyllis I., et al. "Reference, Research, Networks—the Here and Now." *News Notes of California Libraries* **65** (Summer 1970): 527–556.
This issue of *NNCL* contains descriptions of newly formed information, reference, and research networks in the state of California, including the Mountain-Valley Information Center, the Bay Area Reference Center, the Southern California Answering Network, the Information Center for Southern California Libraries, and a reference demonstration project of the Sierra Regional Library System. These networks serve metropolitan areas and consist of a number of libraries in these areas.

Danton, J. Perriam, ed. *The Climate of Book Selection: Social Influences on School and Public Libraries*. Berkeley: University of California School of Librarianship, 1959.
This volume consists of papers presented at a 1958 symposium held at the University of California as a direct outgrowth of a sociological study of book selection and censorship in California libraries conducted by Marjorie Fiske. Selection and retention practices in school and public libraries in metropolitan areas and elsewhere were examined. In addition to Fiske's summary of her research, articles contributed by newspaper columnist Max Lerner, sociologists John W. Albig and Talcott Parsons, political scientists Norton E. Long and Harold D. Lasswell, and educator Ralph W. Tyler are of special value to students of urban area library problems.

Drennan, Henry T. "The Inner-City Library: Strategies for Survival: The Problem of the Inner-City Library." *Southeastern Librarian* **18** (Spring 1968): 11–18.
A library official at the U.S. Office of Education argues that public libraries in the central cities of metropolitan areas must change to survive. He recommends (1) alliance with the urban coalition in attacking problems, (2) vitalizing the consultant service of state libraries, and (3) using the new research complex involving universities and research organizations.

Dubester, Henry J., ed. "Issues and Problems in Designing a National

Program of Library Automation." *Library Trends* **18** (April 1970): 425–
568.
Automation experts and librarians discuss standards, economic problems,
manpower problems, information networks, hardware, bibliographic
problems, administrative problems, and research involved in the design
of a national program of library automation. Contributors to this issue
are Ronald L. Wigington, James L. Wood, Ralph M. Shoffner, Mary Lee
Bundy, Henriette D. Avram, J. Francis Reintjes, Scott Adams, Richard
DeGennaro, and Vladimir Slamecka. Metropolitan libraries would be
included in a national library network.

Eastern and Southeastern Seminar on Problems of Library Services in
Metropolitan Areas, Drexel Institute of Technology, 1965. *Problems of
Library Services in Metropolitan Areas: Report of a Seminar Directed
by Dorothy Bendix and Co-sponsored by American Association of
State Libraries and Drexel Institute of Technology*. Drexel Library
School Series, no. 13. Philadelphia: Drexel Press, 1966.
This volume reports on one of three regional seminars held in 1965 to
explore the role of the state library agency in relation to metropolitan
library problems. Participants included librarians from state and local
public libraries and urban planners. Papers were contributed by Marshall
Stalley, Emerson Greenaway, and S. Gilbert Prentiss.

Ennis, Philip H. *Adult Book Reading in the United States: A Preliminary Report*. National Opinion Research Center Report, no. 105.
Chicago: University of Chicago, National Opinion Research Center,
1965.
This pilot study on adult reading consists of three main chapters—the
first based on in-depth interviews with eighteen persons, the second
analyzing data from a variety of opinion surveys, and the last docu-
menting the variation among 43 large American cities in terms of book
availability as measured by statistics on public libraries, academic libraries, special libraries, and bookstores. The comparative data on book
availability in the central cities of 43 metropolitan areas are especially
interesting. A proposal for a larger study of adult book reading that
embraces entire metropolitan areas and includes more measures of
book availability is included.

Evans, Charles. *Middle Class Attitudes and Public Library Use*. Research Studies in Library Science Series, no. 1. Littleton, Colo.: Libraries Unlimited, 1970.
This volume, based upon doctoral research at the University of California, Berkeley, focuses upon the relationship between library use and predetermined attitudes toward the library, revealing some reasons why people do not use public libraries. A comprehensive analysis of previous studies is provided.

Fenwick, Sara Innis. "School and Public Library Relationships." *Library Quarterly* **30** (January 1960): 63–74.
This article is a report on a study of high school and public library resources in 27 suburban communities around Chicago. Four patterns of suburban library development were detected. The author notes the wide variation in quantity and quality of resources that exists within a metropolitan area.

Frantz, John C. "Big City Libraries: Strategy and Tactics for Change." *Library Journal* **93** (May 15, 1968): 1968–1970.
The director of the Brooklyn Public Library argues that central-city libraries must be converted into institutions that are more responsive to community needs by decentralizing control of their branches so that they may provide different services especially geared to the areas in which they are located. Also, nonusers must be converted into users. The author believes that metropolitan library problems can be solved only after the federal government accepts the responsibility of setting "a floor under library support, not just for brilliant ideas, but also for sound housekeeping."

Frantz, John C., ed. "Outreach—or Oblivion?" *Wilson Library Bulletin* **43** (May 1969): 848–903.
Sixteen experts from various disciplines discuss library outreach—taking the library to the people—and describe programs for implementation. Since the urban disadvantaged do not come to the library, the library must go to them—or it will go unused into oblivion.

Gaines, Ervin J. "The Urban Library Dilemma." *Library Journal* **94** (November 1, 1969): 3966–3970.
The director of the Minneapolis Public Library points out that to the local politician, the library is expendable. Because the library's budget is a tiny fraction of a city's expenditures, budgetary cushions against loss of income can seldom be included. The only real variable is the book budget—the one item that ought to be protected against attack. Decentralization with many small service units increases the personnel budget and—assuming no great increases in total budget—decreases the book budget, thus affecting the traditional middle-class reader. Rather than providing more service outlets to reach the poor, Gaines recommends improving communications and transportation. Besides, he argues, the poor don't really care about libraries, and libraries should not become social service agencies. The urban public library spends about 25 percent of its budget on children's services. As school libraries develop, public libraries might give up children's services and concentrate on fewer, larger units for adults. A fee system for specialized reference services is proposed for consideration.

Garceau, Oliver. *The Public Library in the Political Process*. New York: Columbia University Press, 1949.
A report of the Public Library Inquiry, this volume evaluates the political world of the public library. Of special interest to persons thinking about metropolitan area problems are chapters dealing with the library's political potential and the unit of government for library service.

Garrison, Guy. "Library Education and the Public Library." *Library Journal* **95** (September 1, 1970): 2763–2767.
The dean of the Graduate School of Library Science, Drexel University, presents an excellent summary of the problems affecting public library service in metropolitan areas and then proposes that library education change drastically to prepare professionals who can cope effectively with these problems. He favors a two-year graduate program incorporating work in libraries and study in such fields as social service.

Gaunt, Rezia, ed. "Cooperative Practices Among Public Libraries." *PLD Reporter*, no. 5 (November 1956).

This publication describes the successful efforts of public librarians in metropolitan regions and elsewhere to cooperate with one another in the areas of reciprocal borrowers' privileges, interlibrary loans, centralized purchasing of books and supplies, union catalogs, centralized cataloging, rotation and exchange of materials, cooperative consultant service, planned referrals, cooperative publicity, and duplication of catalog cards. Although sixteen years old, this volume points out some of the ways in which libraries may cooperate if they are willing to do so.

Geddes, Andrew, ed. "Current Trends in Branch Libraries." *Library Trends* **14** (April 1966): 363–457.
For almost a century, the means of extending library service in metropolitan areas has been through the branch library. Librarians Milton S. Byam, John T. Eastlick, Henry G. Shearouse, Jr., John M. Carroll, Wyman H. Jones, Harold L. Hamill, Meredith Bloss, Learned T. Bulman, Walter H. Kaiser, and Emerson Greenaway discuss aspects of branch public library service.

Gocek, Matilda A. *Library Service for Commuting Students: A Preliminary Study of Problems in Four Southeastern New York Counties.* Studies in Interlibrary Relations, no. 1. Poughkeepsie: Southeastern New York Library Resources Council, 1970.
This study of public library service to commuting students from neighboring colleges was conducted by means of interviews with public library directors and selected students and questionnaires distributed to a sample of students visiting public libraries in Orange, Rockland, Sullivan, and Ulster counties; part of this area lies in the New York metropolitan area. Although the methodology employed is subject to criticism, the study is useful in pointing out (1) that public librarians often do not know whom they serve, (2) that commuting students prefer libraries near their homes because they are more accessible, and (3) that more research is needed.

Goldstein, Harold, ed. *The Changing Environment for Library Services in the Metropolitan Area: Papers Presented at an Institute Conducted by the University of Illinois Graduate School of Library Science,*

October 31–November 3, 1965. Allerton Park Institute, no. 12. Champaign, Ill.: distributed by Illini Union Bookstore, 1966.
Included in this volume are contributions by geographer Jerome D. Fellmann, sociologist Philip H. Ennis, political scientist Charles Press, educators Carl F. Hansen and E. K. Fretwell, urban planner Matthew L. Rockwell, industrial scientist George L. Royer, and librarians Ralph Blasingame, William H. Carlson, Bill M. Woods, Sara Innis Fenwick, and H. C. Campbell. Problems affecting public, school, academic, and special libraries were covered in depth by the distinguished participants.

Grundt, Leonard. *Efficient Patterns for Adequate Library Service in a Large City: A Survey of Boston.* University of Illinois Graduate School of Library Science Monograph Series, no. 6. Champaign, Ill.: University of Illinois Graduate School of Library Science, 1968.
This research study, conducted during 1962–1963, demonstrated that in Boston the only public library outlet providing adequate library service to all age groups was the central library. Adequate public library service was defined as the level of service provided by the main libraries in independent cities and towns in Massachusetts serving populations between 20,000 and 100,000 persons. A system with 8 large regional libraries and 52 small neighborhood branches was recommended in place of the 26 traditional branches found in Boston; the cost of the proposed regional library system was estimated to be far lower than the cost of an adequate traditional system.

Guthman, Judith Dommu. *Metropolitan Libraries: The Challenge and the Promise.* Public Library Reporter, No. 15. Chicago: American Library Association, 1969.
This book grew out of hearings held in 1967 by the Metropolitan Area Library Service Committee of the Public Library Association. Librarians from cities that had been the scenes of riots the previous summer made suggestions about ways in which libraries could help alleviate the conditions that spark riots. Inner-city library programs were reviewed and necessary legislative actions recommended. The section on "The Urban Ghetto Resident," which emphasizes the role of the public library as an agent of urban change, is of special interest.

Hayes, Robert M., and Becker, Joseph. *Handbook of Data Processing for Libraries*. New York: Becker and Hayes, 1970.
Because some metropolitan area libraries are already employing computers to reduce clerical burdens and accelerate service to readers—and will probably be using them more in the next decade—this guide to the principles and methods available for the application of modern data processing to library operations should be of interest to all, especially with the proposed establishment of national library-based information networks that involve a high degree of mechanization. Sponsored by the Council on Library Resources, this compendium was prepared by two of the foremost authorities in the library automation field.

Hiatt, Peter. "Urban Public Library Services for Adults of Low Education." *Library Quarterly* 35 (April 1965): 81–96.
This article summarizes a doctoral study conducted at Rutgers University in 1962. From interviews with users at two branch libraries, one in Cleveland and the other in Baltimore—plus studies of the areas served by the libraries and the libraries themselves—the author found that there was a direct relationship between interest in library use by adults of low education in big-city neighborhoods and adaptation of branch library services in these areas. Certain elements of library services were identified as encouraging library use by adults of low education; these elements included accessibility of librarians, good physical layout of the branch, and group programs.

Institute on Public Library Service to the Disadvantaged, Atlanta, Ga., 1967. *Public Library Service to the Disadvantaged: Proceedings*. Atlanta: Division of Librarianship, Emory University, 1969.
The purpose of this institute was to describe the environment of the disadvantaged, to define the role of the public library in serving the various elements within this group, and to identify feasible services to fulfill this role. Speakers were social workers Gloria S. Gross and Hugh Saussey, Jr., and librarians Meredith Bloss, Pauline Winnick, and Mildred L. Hennessy.

International Research Associates. *Access to Public Libraries: A Research Project*. Chicago: American Library Association, 1963.

This study deals with the extent to which the public has access to library resources. Segregation based upon race was found to exist not only in the Deep South but in central cities of northern metropolitan areas as well. The methodology through which segregation in branch libraries of selected cities was measured was seriously questioned by librarians; therefore, the findings of the study relative to branch library segregation were not accepted as valid by the American Library Association, for which this report was prepared. The study also called attention to restrictions on student use, inadequate foreign language materials in libraries, and an inequitable regional distribution of library resources; these findings were received with little criticism.

Joeckel, Carleton B. *The Government of the American Public Library*. Chicago: University of Chicago Press, 1935.
A classic in library literature, this volume describes, analyzes, and evaluates the position of the public library in the structure of government in the United States. The types of administrative structures and the relation of the public library to the local political unit of which it is a part are adequately dealt with. Chapters 9–11 are of special importance to students of metropolitan area problems.

Johnson, Harold G. *Detroit Metropolitan Library Research and Demonstration Project: Final Report*. Washington: U.S. Office of Education, Bureau of Research, 1969.
With the aid of a federal grant, the Detroit Metropolitan Library Research and Demonstration Project was launched in 1966 by Wayne State University in order to (1) provide area-wide research-level reference service and free borrowing to all residents of the six-county Detroit metropolitan area, (2) measure resulting nonresident use of the main public library in Detroit, (3) measure costs, and (4) create a design for the continuance of the project with a formula for financial support. This report indicates that 38 percent of the Detroit main library users during the 1967–1968 survey period were nonresidents and that 64 percent of the users were students. Nearly 26,000 users were included in the survey sample.

Jones, Milbrey. "Socio-economic Factors in Library Service to Students." *ALA Bulletin* 58 (December 1964): 1003–1006.

This article is based upon research that demonstrates that provision for library service (both school and public) to senior high school students varies according to the socioeconomic level of the neighborhood. School and public libraries in eight well-defined districts or neighborhoods in two large cities and four suburban towns were studied. The author recommends that libraries in depressed areas be strengthened.

Jordan, Robert T. *Tomorrow's Library: Direct Access and Delivery*. New York: Bowker, 1970.
The library director at Federal City College, Washington, D.C., a proponent of the home delivery of library materials, reviews past and present delivery experiments, with particular emphasis upon mail delivery, and suggests how libraries can implement a regional direct access and delivery service using book catalogs—like the Sears catalog—and the postal service. Metropolitan area libraries that wish to reach out to the community may find this idea of interest.

Josey, E. J. "Community Use of Academic Libraries." *Library Trends* 18 (July 1969): 66–74.
One problem facing metropolitan area libraries is the need to share resources. This article by an academic librarian points out that college and university libraries for the most part open their doors to outsiders, even to the point of sometimes lending materials for home use. College librarians should apprise public librarians of the needs of commuting students who may not use college libraries. Undergraduate students in metropolitan areas tend to use a variety of libraries. Even when different types of libraries enter into cooperative arrangements, each library in a sharing program has the obligation to provide basic library service to its own clientele.

"A Kaleidoscopic View of Library Research." *Wilson Library Bulletin* 41 (May 1967): 896–949.
Twenty-five librarians, employed in a variety of academic, public, and school libraries or engaged as faculty in library schools, delineate areas of the profession in which research is badly needed. Of particular interest to those concerned about metropolitan area library problems are the statements by Rose Z. Sellers, Meredith Bloss, Keith Doms, John F. Anderson, Hardy Franklin, and Johanna G. Sutton. One of the contribu-

tors, sociologist Philip H. Ennis, characterizes library research as "non-cumulative, fragmentary, generally weak, and relentlessly oriented to immediate practice."

Knight, Douglas M., and Nourse, E. Shepley, eds. *Libraries at Large: Tradition, Innovation and the National Interest*. New York: Bowker, 1969.

The National Advisory Commission on Libraries, which was established in 1966 by President Lyndon B. Johnson and which submitted its report two years later, recommended that it be declared national policy that the American people be provided with library and informational services adequate to their needs and that the federal government, in collaboration with state and local government and private agencies, should exercise leadership assuring the provision of such services. This significant report, together with a wealth of material on library services in all areas—based upon special studies ordered by the commission—is included in this volume. On July 20, 1970, President Richard M. Nixon created the National Commission on Libraries and Information Science —a body of fifteen individuals, including five librarians—to provide advice and recommendations on long-range library planning. This national body will surely have an impact on metropolitan library service.

Leigh, Robert D. *The Public Library in the United States: The General Report of the Public Library Inquiry*. New York: Columbia University Press, 1950.

This document is based primarily on the nineteen special studies conducted by the staff of the Public Library Inquiry, which the Social Science Research Council organized for the American Library Association. Chapter 4, "Library Units and Structures," is especially important to students of metropolitan problems. More centralized public library service in larger library units is recommended.

"Library Cooperation for Reference and Research." *ALA Bulletin* **60** (December 1966): 1133–1155.

Some of the problems affecting library service in metropolitan areas include insufficient use by inner-city residents and inadequate resources

for students and researchers. This issue of *ALA Bulletin* deals with the
sharing of library resources on a regional basis. There are reports on the
three Rs program in New York, the New Jersey plan, and the Hawaii
system, in which all public and school libraries are under a single state
department. Kenneth E. Beasley, a political scientist, points out that
libraries can no longer be self-sufficient and that cooperation will result
in change in the cooperators; he urges librarians to question their basic
assumptions because libraries cannot continue providing services in the
way they have up to the present.

Lyman, Helen Huguenor, ed. "Library Programs and Services to the
Disadvantaged." *Library Trends* **20** (October 1971): 185–471.
This issue of *Library Trends* contains articles by a sociologist, an anthro-
pologist, reading specialists, library consultants, library science educators, and library administrators. These authorities discuss social change,
minorities and the library, multimedia approaches, research in reading,
changing environments and the responses of library agencies, the library's
responsibility to the young and students, and education and training
for library service. The twenty-one articles present significant research
findings and recent developments relating to library service to members
of disadvantaged groups, particularly those in metropolitan areas.

MacDonald, Bernice. *Literacy Activities in Public Libraries: A Report
of a Study of Services to Adult Illiterates*. Chicago: American Library
Association, 1966.
This study was undertaken on behalf of the American Library Associa-
tion's Committee on Reading Improvement for Adults. Fifteen libraries
were identified as having literacy programs. Of the fifteen, eight—
Kalamazoo Public Library, Cleveland Public Library, Cumberland
County Public Library, Yakima Valley Regional Library, Dallas Public
Library, Brooklyn Public Library, New York Public Library, and the
Free Library of Philadelphia—were treated as case studies. Data were
obtained by means of observations and interviews with participants.
The author concludes that public librarians serving adult illiterates are
limited by the lack of appropriate easy reading materials and by the
lack of knowledge regarding the teaching of reading skills to adults.

Martin, Lowell A. *Baltimore Reaches Out: Library Service to the Disadvantaged*. Deiches Fund Studies of Public Library Service, no. 3. Baltimore: Enoch Pratt Free Library, 1967.
This is an inquiry into the reading potential of city residents of limited cultural and educational background and the role that the public library can and should play in serving these people. The primary source of information about reading and nonreading was a series of interviews with a sample of Baltimore families, including readers and nonreaders. The author strongly recommends that the Enoch Pratt Free Library serve all the people, both advantaged and disadvantaged. It is a "matter of social value more than a matter of efficiency or logic."

Martin, Lowell A., et al. *Library Response to Urban Change: A Study of the Chicago Public Library*. Chicago: American Library Association, 1969.
An intensive survey of the Chicago Public Library commissioned by the library itself, this volume stresses adaptability and the restructuring of the library in a period of change. A program of service is presented that calls for the Chicago Public Library to adjust to the people of Chicago in all their diversity, rather than expecting them to conform to a standardized institution. Of special importance to students of metropolitan area library problems is the chapter on "Metropolitan Library Relations." Another noteworthy chapter, "New Technology and the Chicago Public Library," shows how the library can use automation to improve service.

Martin, Lowell A. *Students and the Pratt Library: Challenge and Opportunity*. Deiches Fund Studies of Public Library Service, no. 1. Baltimore: Enoch Pratt Free Library, 1963.
A report dealing with student use of the library, this is the first part of a comprehensive study of central-city library services in Baltimore. This survey found that although the schools depend upon reading as a significant element in education, adequate provision has not been made for student reading materials, either in the schools or in the public libraries. Public libraries supply almost two-thirds of the library service provided to high school students, in both number of books supplied and number

of hours of use; school libraries supply only about one-third of the library needs of their students. Approximately three-fourths of the student readers surveyed were found to prefer the public library to the school library because of (1) better collections, (2) more suitable hours of service, and (3) fewer restrictions and controls.

Martin, Lowell A. "The Suburban System in Metropolitan Library Networks." *Illinois Libraries* **53** (March 1971): 197–206.
A major critic of metropolitan libraries addresses the question of what a suburban library system should be, with specific reference to the North Suburban Library System in Illinois. Martin notes particularly the need for centers of experimentation within the current public library movement. Since they do not have extensive commitments to past practice, suburban library systems could provide a base for experimental programs and patterns of service.

"The Metropolitan Public Library." *Wilson Library Bulletin* **40** (June 1966): 917–929.
Six librarians—Ervin J. Gaines of the Minneapolis Public Library, Emerson Greenaway of the Free Library of Philadelphia, Harold L. Hamill of the Los Angeles Public Library, John A. Humphry of the Brooklyn Public Library, Lewis C. Naylor of the Cuyahoga County Public Library, and Kathleen Molz of *Wilson Library Bulletin*—and George Beaton, a city planner, discuss various aspects of metropolitan library problems.

Minder, Thomas. *The Regional Library Center in the Mid 1970's: A Concept Paper*. Pittsburgh Studies in Library and Information Sciences, no. 1. Pittsburgh, Pa.: Graduate School of Library and Information Sciences, University of Pittsburgh, 1968.
The executive director of the Pittsburgh Regional Library Center, a cooperative library organization whose members include the major public and academic libraries in the Pittsburgh metropolitan area, identifies the major characteristics of the center as it might look in the mid-1970s. A computer with remote terminals is seen as the most powerful bibliographic control device for maintaining a central file of holdings of member libraries. The center would maintain a core collection of little-

used materials and would provide centralized technical processing for all items. In this paper, Minder assumes that money and personnel are available.

Molz, Kathleen. "Gradus ad Parnassum." *Illinois Libraries* **53** (March 1971): 185–191.
This article presents a brief analysis of the present state of library networking with special attention paid to the need for networks devoted to nonprint materials, which are often more expensive and more difficult to obtain than books or journals.

Molz, Kathleen. "The Public Library: The People's University?" *American Scholar* **34** (Winter 1964–1965): 95–102.
The editor of the *Wilson Library Bulletin* critically examines the current functions of the urban public library and concludes that the library tries to serve the student population while it fails to respond to the needs of the disadvantaged. It is recommended that the large-city library seek to motivate use by lower-class minority groups through the provision of materials and services that are suited to their needs and through the employment of staff members who understand their problems and who will reach out to attract them.

Monat, William R., et al. *The Public Library and Its Community: A Study of the Impact of Library Services in Five Pennsylvania Cities.* Pennsylvania State Library Monograph Series, no. 7. State College, Pa.: Institute of Public Administration, Pennsylvania State University, 1967. Political scientists from Pennsylvania State University studied the libraries of five medium-sized cities—Altoona, Erie, Pottsville, Lancaster, and Williamsport—to determine (1) the nature of library use, (2) attitudes of users and nonusers toward the library, (3) finances of the library and the attitudes of concerned individuals about the financial arrangements, (4) how well the library meets community needs, and (5) where the library fits into the overall pattern of government services within the communities. Using interviews and questionnaires, the researchers confirmed the findings of Bernard Berelson regarding use and found that the library is a nice middle-class institution.

Morse, Philip M. *Library Effectiveness: A Systems Approach*. Cambridge, Mass.: MIT Press, 1968.
A professor at the Massachusetts Institute of Technology demonstrates how the systems approach may be employed to help solve library problems. In the first part of this volume, he develops general mathematical models with which to analyze the use of library materials; in the second part, he shows how to apply the models. Librarians should be mindful of operations research as a technique in evaluation of services.

National Book Committee. *Neighborhood Library Centers and Services*. New York, 1967.
Programs for the disadvantaged offered by eleven public libraries—New Haven Public Library, Enoch Pratt Free Library, Brooklyn Public Library, New York Public Library, Queens Borough Public Library, Pioneer Library System, Charlotte and Mecklenburg Public Library, La Retama Public Library, Corpus Christi Public Library, Cleveland Public Library, and Los Angeles Public Library—are analyzed in this study. These programs were all funded under the Library Services and Construction Act.

Nelson Associates, Inc. *Library Service in the Capitol Region of Connecticut: A Study with Recommendations for Future Development*. New York, 1968.
This survey of a metropolitan area's libraries includes all types of libraries—public, academic, special, and school. An assessment of existing library resources, services, and needs was made by gathering data through (1) a questionnaire to all libraries, (2) interviews with a cross section of individuals, and (3) a review of reports and statistics. It was recommended that a Capitol Region Library Council be established to (1) coordinate library planning, especially at the reference and research level, (2) conduct further library studies on particular problems as needed, and (3) undertake experimental and demonstration projects. A program consisting of cooperative acquisitions, reciprocal borrowing, a regional reference resource center, and fast delivery of interlibrary loans was also recommended. This survey is typical of studies of metropolitan area library services conducted recently by Nelson Associates, Arthur D. Little, and similar consulting firms.

Nelson Associates, Inc. *Public Library Systems in the United States: A Survey of Multijurisdictional Systems*. Chicago: American Library Association, 1969.

As defined in this 1966–1967 survey, multijurisdictional public library systems are those that offer services in more than one village, town, city, county, or state and that existed before 1964; large-city library systems, provided they do not serve the suburbs, are excluded. This survey covers services, staffing, organization, and financing in 491 systems, of which 58 are dealt with in depth and 6 are examined in great detail as case studies. The systems studied include many that serve metropolitan areas. The volume concludes that "the most decisive factor in the success of a system appears to be the competence of its director."

Nolting, Orin F. *Mobilizing Total Library Resources for Effective Service*. Chicago: American Library Association, 1969.

The executive director emeritus of the International City Managers' Association prepared this document as a background paper for a meeting held at the 1969 American Library Association conference. He succinctly discusses (1) barriers to effective cooperation among public agencies within metropolitan areas—psychological, informational, traditional and historical, physical and geographical, and legal and administrative; (2) criteria for the allocation of local government functions; (3) alternative solutions for effective area-wide performance—informal cooperation, parallel action, creation of regional councils and planning agencies, intergovernmental agreements, annexation and consolidation, city-county consolidation, granting of extraterritorial powers, transfer of functions, creation of urban counties, regional agencies and metropolitan federation, and creation of special districts and authorities; and (4) the future of intergovernmental cooperation.

Nyren, Dorothy, ed. *Community Service: Innovations in Outreach at the Brooklyn Public Library*. Public Library Reporter, no. 16. Chicago: American Library Association, 1970.

Eight librarians at the Booklyn Public Library describe how the library has learned to respond to the variant and constantly shifting needs and desires of the people of Brooklyn. A new materials selection policy was adopted; rules were overhauled; audiovisual materials were utilized more; the community became involved; collections and the atmosphere in library units were changed; a community coordinator program was introduced; and a district library plan with specialists to serve adults, young adults, and children was initiated.

"Our Other Customers." *Wilson Library Bulletin* **45** (January 1971): 465-493.
Five librarians discuss library service to groups other than students and the disadvantaged—the aged, the affluent, ethnic groups, shut-ins, prisoners, and hospital patients, all of whom are found in metropolitan areas.

Overmyer, LaVahn. *Library Automation: A Critical Review.* Washington, D.C.: U.S. Office of Education, Bureau of Research, 1969.
This volume reports on a 1967-1968 survey of the use of automation in about fifty libraries across the country, including public library systems in the Los Angeles area, greater Cleveland, suburban Baltimore-Washington, and Nassau County, New York. While there are presently many problems associated with the use of automation, libraries will undoubtedly be using it more in the years ahead. The author concludes that the technology now exists for developing vast information networks and for making the world's knowledge accessible to every library patron; librarians have the primary responsibility for making this possible.

Parker, Edwin B., and Paisley, William J. *Patterns of Adult Information Seeking.* Stanford, Calif.: Stanford University, 1966.
Because libraries serve as sources of information, this sociological study of adult information seeking, which was conducted in various California communities, should be of interest to those concerned with problems affecting metropolitan area library service.

Peil, Margaret. "Library Use by Low-Income Chicago Families." *Library Quarterly* **33** (October 1963): 329-333.
Part of a larger study, this is a report on research conducted among 180 low-income families in the central city of a metropolitan area. One-

quarter of the mothers were found to have visited the public library during the year prior to the study. The library use of first-graders was strongly related to their mothers' use, as was the number of books each child owned. Positive relationships were found between (1) educational level and library use and (2) propinquity and library use.

Public Library Association, Committee on Services to the Functionally Illiterate. *Public Library Services for the Functionally Illiterate: A Survey of Practice*. Edited by Peter Hiatt and Henry T. Drennan. Chicago: American Library Association, 1967.
This publication lists the efforts libraries have made to reach the functionally illiterate. Many of the programs that were started in the 1960s as part of the War on Poverty have been terminated because of the decline of federal funding.

Sattley, Helen R. "Run Twice as Fast: Service to Children." *American Libraries* 2 (September 1971): 843–849.
The director of School Library Service in New York City's Board of Education eloquently argues for a continuation of dual opportunities for children in both the school library and the public library. Critical of current recommendations to discontinue juvenile service in public libraries, Sattley urges the expansion of services to children and more adequate budgeting for essential resources and programs. The problems of providing good school library service in so overcrowded a city are well delineated.

"School-Public Library Relations: Where Do We Stand?" *Library Journal* 94 (January 15, 1969): 259–268.
School library specialists Frances E. Henne and Richard L. Darling and public librarians Emerson Greenaway, John M. Cory, and Dinah Lindauer discuss the relationships between school libraries and public libraries in metropolitan areas. While the national *Standards for School Media Programs* call for the schools to meet all the library needs of students, public librarians generally feel that schools cannot possibly do the job well without public library assistance. Some examples of cooperation between school libraries and public libraries are cited.

Seminar to Study the Problems Affecting Library Service in Metropolitan Areas, Rutgers University, 1964-1965. *Research on Library Service in Metropolitan Areas: Report of a Rutgers Seminar, 1964/65.* Directed by Ralph Blasingame. New Brunswick, N.J.: Graduate School of Library Service, Rutgers-The State University, 1967.

In 1964-1965, Rutgers University conducted a federally funded seminar to identify problems affecting library service in metropolitan areas and to promote research that might contribute to the solution of these problems. Specialists in various social sciences and library service participated. While the library practitioners viewed administrative problems as most important, social scientists were more concerned about the assumptions and objectives of libraries. It was evident that public library administrators were not always prepared to confront the social and political changes that affect their institutions.

Shaffer, Kenneth R. "The Affluent Ghetto." *Library Journal* **94** (March 15, 1969): 1093-1097.

The dean of Simmons Library School claims that there will be a crisis in suburban libraries—just as there has been first in rural libraries and now in city libraries—because (1) the walls that separate the cities from the suburbs will be broken down and discriminatory zoning will be eliminated, (2) the suburban libraries are subject to censors' attacks, and (3) the school libraries will compete with the public libraries, especially if the schools "become less like prisons." Suburban library planning will have to be rethought—and this restructuring should begin now.

Sherrill, Laurence L., ed. *Library Service to the Unserved.* New York: Bowker, 1971.

This volume consists of thirteen papers presented at a conference held in 1967 at the University of Wisconsin, Milwaukee, on the subject of how the library can improve service to reach a larger proportion of the population. It includes a selective bibliography prepared at the ERIC Clearinghouse for Library and Information Sciences. Papers cover the historical development of middle-class attitudes toward library service for the disadvantaged, trends in national library programs for the disadvantaged, difficulties in training librarians for serving the disadvantaged, and ways in which librarians can give practical help to people in ghetto communities. Participants included Edwin Castagna, Ralph Conant, Eileen D. Cooke, Faith Murdoch, and Roy G. Francis.

Stone, C. Walter, ed. "Library Uses of the New Media of Communication." *Library Trends* 16 (October 1967): 177–299.
Like all other libraries, public libraries in metropolitan areas are beginning to develop services utilizing media other than books and similar printed materials. C. Walter Stone's lead article in this issue of *Library Trends* calls for a redefinition of library functions so that libraries will no longer be concerned with supplying specific media, but rather will concentrate on providing access to recorded knowledge and communication services generally. Evaluative articles on audiovisual materials and other new media were prepared by Paul Wendt, Jean E. Lowrie, Fred F. Harcleroad, William Peters, John H. Moriarty, Harold Goldstein, Charles J. McIntyre, William J. Quinly, Jay E. Daily, and Fred S. Siebert.

A Study of Library Services for the Disadvantaged in Buffalo, Rochester, and Syracuse. Directed by Virgil A. Clift. New York: Center for Field Research and School Services, School of Education, New York University, 1969.
On behalf of the Division of Library Development of the New York State Education Department, a team of researchers evaluated existing library services for the poor in the central cities of three metropolitan areas, identifying areas of weakness or omission. Characteristics of library users and nonusers are analyzed in this study. It is recommended that the poor be involved in shaping library programs and that there be community control of libraries.

Symposium on Library Functions in the Changing Metropolis, Dedham, Mass., 1963. *The Public Library and the City*. Edited by Ralph W. Conant. Cambridge, Mass.: MIT Press, 1965.
This volume includes papers read at a 1963 meeting sponsored by the Joint Center for Urban Studies of the Massachusetts Institute of Technology and Harvard University and the National Book Committee, as well as items especially prepared for the book. The significance of the

meeting was that it brought together for the first time experts from a variety of disciplines—library science, sociology, education, political science, city planning, and economics—to discuss the varied problems of metropolitan public libraries.

University of Illinois, Library Research Center. *Studies in Public Library Government, Organization, and Support.* Directed by Guy Garrison. Washington, D.C.: U.S. Office of Education, Bureau of Research, 1969. This volume consists of six individual reports prepared by staff members at the Library Research Center as part of a general examination of public libraries in Illinois. There are excellent, detailed studies of (1) three unsuccessful campaigns for financing library expansion, (2) variations among suburban libraries, (3) public opinion on library support and use, (4) library referendums, (5) library systems and the service levels of their members, and (6) membership and nonmembership in library systems.

Winsor, Charlotte B., and Burrows, Lodema. *A Study of Four Library Programs for Disadvantaged Persons: Conducted by Bank Street College of Education.* Albany: New York State Education Department, Division of Library Development, 1968.
Two staff members of the Bank Street College of Education studied in depth four programs in three New York City library systems: (1) the preschool project at the Brooklyn Public Library, (2) the community coordinator project for adults at the Brooklyn Public Library, (3) New York Public Library's North Manhattan project, and (4) Operation Head Start at the Queens Borough Public Library. The evaluation of these demonstration projects pointed out that while all of the projects accomplished much of what they sought to do, there remained a great need for (1) better planning, (2) staff indigenous to the local communities, (3) deviation from library policies developed by and for the middle class, and (4) cooperation between the libraries and the public schools. This study points up the necessity of objective evaluation of demonstration projects and other forms of research.

Index